David Batty was ~~born~~ ~~made his~~ debut for his home ~~town~~ ~~club~~ ~~Leeds~~. ~~He~~ went on to play more tha~~n~~ ~~game~~s for them, winning the league champi~~onsh~~ip in 1992, before being transferred to Blackburn Rovers in 1993, who were to win the Premiership title the following season. In 1996 he joined Kevin Keegan's Newcastle United, but moved back to Leeds at the end of 1998 for £4.4m as one of David O'Leary's first signings. Injury disrupted much of his second spell at the club, but he fought his way back to fitness and has played in nearly every game in the 2001–02 season. David Batty made his England debut in 1991 and has since won 42 caps. He lives near Leeds with his wife and twin sons.

Bill Thornton, who collaborated with David Batty in the writing of this book, has been a national newspaper sports reporter for twenty-eight years, working on the *Daily Mail*, *Daily* and *Sunday Mirror* and currently, the *Daily Star*. He lives near Manchester, with his wife Pauline and has a grown-up daughter.

David Batty
The Autobiography

David Batty

HEADLINE

First published in 2001
by HEADLINE BOOK PUBLISHING

First published in paperback in 2002
by HEADLINE BOOK PUBLISHING

10 9 8 7 6 5 4 3 2 1

ISBN 0 7472 4519 3

Typeset in Cochin by
Letterpart Limited, Reigate, Surrey

Printed and bound in Great Britain by
Mackays of Chatham plc, Chatham, Kent

HEADLINE BOOK PUBLISHING
A division of Hodder Headline
338 Euston Road
LONDON NW1 3BH

www.headline.co.uk
www.hodderheadline.com

contents

dedication

To my wife Mandy, and to Jack and George

acknowledgements

Thanks for all your help in the writing of this book to Mandy, Mum and Dad, Terry and Lynn, James Brown, Hayden Evans and Bill Thornton.

Best wishes also to William Harris, and thanks to Nicola Mafulli.

early days

I have been fortunate to play for some of the biggest names in English football management: Billy Bremner, Howard Wilkinson, Kenny Dalglish, Kevin Keegan, Ruud Gullit and David O'Leary, not to mention England coaches Graham Taylor, Terry Venables and Glenn Hoddle. Yet not one of these famous and distinguished figures has had anything like as much influence upon my career as my biggest fan – and also my biggest critic – my dad, Al.

I am the most determined, self-driven and, I admit it, downright bloody-minded person I know. But there is absolutely no doubt in my mind that I would never have got to the top in football without my dad pushing me all the way. In fact, most probably, I would never have played the game for a living at all.

From virtually the first time I kicked a ball across the living-room floor, Dad encouraged me to develop that particular skill. And, as I steadily improved during my childhood years, it was his ambition, more than mine, that swept me along the path that was to lead to fame with Leeds United, Blackburn Rovers, Newcastle United and, finally, back to hometown club Leeds, with 42 caps for England along the way.

My father was a Leeds Corporation bin-man – refuse collector is, I believe, the politically correct term these days – who worked hard to feed and clothe his close-knit family, which comprised my mum, Mary, me and my brother John, who is a year older than me. He also dedicated many years to his other labour of love, which was moulding me into a professional soccer player. His devotion to that cause is preserved for posterity in a series of red, hardback exercise books which, in his handwriting, mention every match of my footballing career, from the day I played my first game, for Horse and Groom Under-12s, on 6 September 1978 when I was just nine years and ten months old. I was to grow accustomed to playing out of my age group over the next few years.

In those treasured pages, Dad painstakingly charted my course from skinny, underdeveloped teenager to battle-hardened Premiership and international midfielder. I have relied on those books for the accuracy of much of the material used in the following pages. Dad's notes also demonstrate, quite coldly in many places, how ruthlessly objective he was about my ability and progress – or lack of it, in his opinion. There was never any question of him allowing paternal bias to cloud his judgement of my game. To this day, he remains my biggest critic. Even though, deep down, I suspect he has always fought a more natural inclination to sing my praises.

During my formative years, the frequent upbeat references to my man-of-the-match displays are tempered by many a carping comment: my heading and shooting weren't strong enough; my running off the ball was ineffective. But not once did Dad accuse me of not trying. And I can say, hand on heart, that from being a boy to a full-blown international footballer, the one thing I have always given in every game is 100 per cent effort. I would defy anybody to say different. I do admit there have been one or two isolated incidents of which I'm not exactly proud, but more of those later.

That try-your-damnedest trait was partly etched into my psyche by my dad's never-diminishing efforts to aid my physical and footballing development. But, also, it is something, and I can't really explain why, that has been a dynamic force within me for as long as I can remember. When I used to storm to my room and slam the door behind me after losing in the final of our often-staged snooker tournaments on the table we had in the double garage, or hurl my tennis racket to the ground in disgust after being beaten on the court, it wasn't because I had lost. It was because I was uncontrollably frustrated with myself for not having played that much better. My dad used to come to my bedroom and insist I rejoin my friends downstairs, including the much older boy, of about 16, called Wickham who was usually my conqueror in the 'Grand Final' of those snooker tournaments. Now I can look back on such acts of temper and petulance with embarrassment, and I would be horrified if either of my twin sons, Jack and George, behaved in such a way. Nevertheless, I can only conclude that had I not been so passionate about my own performance at such a tender age, I wouldn't have grown into the competitor I eventually became, battling for supremacy, week in, week out, with the toughest midfielders in top-class football.

The first sign that I was blessed with some natural

talent came when I was four years old and my father returned home with one of the many 'prizes' he collected in the course of his daily refuse-collecting rounds. It was a three-wheeler bike, which a lady had suggested might be put to further use rather than discarded on the council tip. I took to riding this machine like a duck to water – but the daredevil little Batty rode it on two wheels, always at a ridiculously perilous angle. Clearly, I had balance, which is one of the essential ingredients in the footballer's – indeed, any sportsman's – make-up.

I use the word daredevil deliberately, because that is just what I was as a kid. Whereas my brother John was a cautious, think-before-you-act type, I was out of the reckless, repent-at-leisure mould. And that all too often landed me in trouble – and the casualty department of St James's Hospital, since made famous by the TV series *Jimmy's*, which was conveniently situated just round the corner from our first house in the Harehills district of Leeds. My long-suffering parents made many a mad dash to Jimmy's to get emergency treatment for their boy. I can't recall brother John once needing hospital attention, yet I was a veteran of the Accident and Emergency unit long before footballing injuries made me all too familiar with hospital wards.

My first need of urgent medical attention was when I was three years old and I fell backwards while straining to look out of a window at home, cutting open my head. Apparently, I made such a racket down at the hospital that a blood- and sweat-stained nurse left the treatment room to tell my anxious mum and dad: 'We're having a bloody nightmare with him in there.' A few years later, while playing 'war' in the grounds of the local church, I slammed a heavy iron gate on my hand and took the ends off two of my fingers. After getting my hand patched up at St James's I insisted on taking home the lost bits as a trophy and put them into a little cardboard box. They remained there for some years, virtually forgotten, until the day my teacher at Scott Hall Middle School told the class to bring in unusual items the following day, which was the last day of term.

What to take? I couldn't think of anything better than my finger tips, which by now had been rotting away for about four years at the back of the wardrobe. As my classmates unveiled their typical collectors' items – stamps, books, football programmes, even an old sewing-machine – I proudly produced the remains of the grisly accident, but I was cute enough not to reveal the identity of the strange, blackened little objects. Just about every kid in the class tried and failed to guess what they were, many going for birds' eggs. Finally, the form mistress delicately held the mystery objects aloft and said: 'Okay, David, you've got us all baffled. What are they?' When I told her, the poor woman let out an ear-piercing shriek and promptly hurled them to the floor like they were red-hot coals. But when she had recovered her composure, she was big enough to award me a Mars bar!

It wasn't too long after that that I was back in Jimmy's again, this time after a cycling accident. John and I had graduated to two-wheelers and, typically, there was only ever going to be one kid leading the way, however many in the pack. We were pedalling down Stainbeck Lane in Chapel Allerton, where we'd moved to in 1980, when I was 12, and I was storming out in front. I lost control on a bend, shot over the handlebars and slid down the road on my back, shredding my shirt – and my back. A local resident did her best for me before delivering me to my long-suffering parents.

My impatience and need to be the Action Man also left me embarrassingly entangled with the chain of that same bike. Again, a neighbour had to send for my folks, who found me with my hand trapped in the chain, which I had foolishly attempted to wind back on after it had come off. It was yet another example of me acting without thinking through the problem. The fact is, I was – and still am – hopelessly impractical. To this day, I can't hammer a nail into a piece of wood. Yet John, now an accomplished antique restorer, has always been exactly the opposite.

The fact is I wasn't much good at anything apart from sport – and football in particular – though I did have a good voice as a kid. I used to love singing and was one of the few boys in the Shakespeare Middle School choir. One of my proudest moments was when I was chosen to represent the school in the annual Christmas carol concert at Leeds Civic Hall when I was 11. But I'm not outgoing enough to have ever attempted to serenade any of my professional team-mates in the dressing-room or on the bus. That's just not my style. In any case, I was never going to be a second Elvis Presley once my voice broke.

Instead, and increasingly, from the age of 10, I dedicated myself to physical fitness and to football. And, when I clinched an apprenticeship at Leeds, at 16, I abdicated all responsibility for my academic needs – and didn't pass a single O-level. It's a good job I made the grade at kicking a ball for a living! By the time I was honing my skills on the two-wheeler I was three years into organised, team football and starting to make a name for myself on the school soccer circuit. Not least of the reasons for that was my willingness to get stuck in on the pitch, invariably against bigger, stronger lads. That was simply because I was so small for my age, a problem that dogged me until I was 19 and had broken into the first team at Leeds.

Being at such a physical disadvantage – on the first day of my Elland Road apprenticeship, when I was 16, I stood five foot four and weighed in at just over eight stone – served as an incentive and helped me to develop a never-say-die attitude which, I like to think, has remained an integral part of my game throughout my career. From as far back as I can remember I have been driven by a fierce will to win and an equally strong dislike of defeat. But those traits have been complemented by a passionate aversion to cheats and a tendency not to dwell on defeat. I can't explain why, but I have never dwelt on a bad result, being blessed – if it is a blessing – with the ability to focus on the job in hand and then switch off before logging on again for the next match. I can even switch on and off at half-time and I've never felt the need, like so many players, to psyche myself up by having a warm-up. As soon as the whistle blows I switch on. When the final whistle blows I switch off.

I am the same after victory or defeat, though I fear this aspect of my character is sometimes interpreted as a form of apathy by those who don't know me personally. I want to win and I enjoy winning as much as any player.

But I can truthfully say that I get no pleasure from winning unless it is fair and square. Play it hard. Hell, yes, I do that all right. And I may have been a bit reckless over the years, but never deliberately dirty. And I have NEVER been a cheat.

I recall playing cricket when I was seven or eight years old with another lad in the local cemetery. I must have bowled at him for half an hour, repeatedly imploring him to do the decent thing and 'be out'. Stubbornly and, in my opinion, outrageously, since I had 'dismissed' him several times, he repeatedly refused to hand over the bat. It was time to act. I walked down the 'wicket' and gave him a sharp dig, bursting his nose. That was out! But I hadn't bargained for him running home for his older brother, of whom I lived in fear for the next few days.

The David Batty method of meting out instant justice was seen again during a school cross-country race when I was 13. Now, I loved cross-country. I have always been strong on stamina, especially during my teens and twenties. But I was never blasé about the effort you have to put in – and I was appalled by anyone who sought to win by devious means. On this occasion, pounding over the uneven terrain, I was furious to see one of my competitors cut through the cones placed to mark our route and take a massive short-cut, avoiding a long section of the run. Even though I could hardly spare the extra energy, I took off in pursuit of this lad, obviously driven by my loathing of cheating, caught him at the top of a steep grassy bank – and pushed him down it!

For me, there is no finer feeling than winning – but by fair means rather than foul. At 11, while at my second school, Shakespeare Middle, I confided to my father on the eve of the annual sports day that I was fed up with always losing out in the mile race to a lanky, long-legged lad called Hartley. Dad told me that the way to beat Hartley was to tuck in right behind him from the start and let him 'hear your feet pounding and feel your breath on the back of his neck'. I did what he told me, breathing down Hartley's neck until the final bend when the pressure got to him and I licked him down the home straight. It was a wonderful feeling and seemed like a big achievement at the time. For a couple of years by then, I had already been straining every sinew – under the ever-watchful eye of my father – to become a stronger athlete and a better footballer. It all began when Dad used to take me, and many of the local kids who knocked on our door, to the park where we would play most evenings until dark. I still vividly recall getting back to the brightly lit house and realising how much our eyes must have adjusted to the fading light in the park.

A lot of us used to play in the playground of our primary school in the evenings, where I was dedicated to practising my ball skills. After the neighbours complained about the noise and the occasional broken window, the headmaster put a stop to it by locking the gates. But he made one, secret, exception. Unknown to all the other kids and their parents, he telephoned my dad and, in a hush-hush, nod's-as-good-as-a-wink conversation, suggested that he would never know if young David scaled the gates at the far side of the playground and continued his ball work in isolation. Apparently, the head acknowledged that he had recognised in me a rare talent and that it would be a shame to curb my enthusiasm.

Soon after I first played organised football for Horse and Groom, I joined Tingley Athletic. My mum had seen Tingley's advert in the *Yorkshire Post*, appealing for recruits. I started as centre-forward, but my now legendary lack of goals was already evident early in my career and it was quickly decided that midfield was the role for me. From the age of 10 I used to play on both Saturday and Sunday. At least one of the matches would be in the under-12s age group, so I quickly became accustomed to playing against bigger lads. I also relished getting stuck into them, something that has stayed with me until this day!

Money was always tight in the Batty household. Dad worked hard, but the pay on the bin rounds wasn't the best in the world; Mum used to take various jobs, such as cleaning, to eke out the family budget. One of the perks of Dad's job was that he would often come home with cast-off shirts and shorts for me to wear. The one item he insisted on always buying new was my boots, even if they did have to be worn until they were worn out. He and I once sat in the car, in filthy weather, before a training session with Tingley. My first pair of boots – they were the old moulded style – were in my bag. I had worn them right down until the soles were no more effective than a pair of trainers. Dad looked at the weather and said: 'You'll be slipping all over the place, David.' Producing his Stanley knife from the car boot, he proceeded to carve grooves into the soles of my boots.

It was for Tingley that I suffered the misery of my first missed penalty – never, of course, imagining that, on a fateful night nearly 20 years later, I would miss from the spot in the World Cup. On this particular October day in 1978, Tingley were being hammered 8–0 by all-conquering Garforth League side Batley Crusaders when we were awarded a penalty. I volunteered to take it and proceeded to miss the target completely. I was very upset: not for myself, but because I'd let the side down. My dad wrote in his book: 'David never stopped running in this game and was by far Tingley's best player. He missed a penalty 10 minutes from the end and was very upset.'

But that was nothing to the pain I used to feel when I'd had a poor game and could sense my dad's disapproval and disappointment. The atmosphere in the house would be sombre on such occasions, a feeling that lives with me to this day. I was confused and unhappy with the idea that I had let Dad down and I know I could never put my own kids through it. Dad was fiercely critical of every aspect of my game. Looking back, I'm sure that helped me to become stronger, mentally, and drove me to endless effort. I know he now feels some regret for being so demanding; at the same time, I readily acknowledge the huge input he had into my development. In fact I often instigated an increased workload by asking him to devise more demanding training schedules.

He certainly wasn't as harsh as some fathers. One kid, Mark Russell, who went on to play for Halifax Town and Sheffield United, would be kept back on the pitch and put through his paces by his dad after a game had been lost, with all the other kids and their parents looking on. Even Dad thought he was a hard taskmaster – yet the end result was that we both became professionals. Mark clattered into me and broke one of my ribs a few years later when I was a Leeds apprentice. Burdened by the pain, I missed a penalty in that match, too! Not that I held it against him: we remained the best of pals and he and his wife are two of our best friends to this day. He and I were so close that when I was a first-team player at Leeds and Mark had left the game, I used to help him in my spare time with his potato delivery round, dropping off sacks of spuds at chip shops.

My first two games ended in defeats, by 4–0 and 6–1. I was centre-forward both times. They say you learn more from defeat than victory and I believe I did. Setbacks drove me on, increasing my determination to do better next time. But always I was troubled by my size, or the lack of it. Dad and I were constantly seeking ways of building me up. We would visit the library to read up on fitness, body-building and training methods. Dad devised a circuit of push-ups, squat thrusts and pull-ups for me to do at home in the garage. I used to be so embarrassed in the showers when I was about 13. The other lads were developing hairy legs, chests – and other parts. But not me. Mum and Dad became so concerned that they took me off to my second home, St James's Hospital, where the problem was looked at seriously. It was a humiliating experience for me. I was photographed in the nude from all angles and felt like the object of a strange medical experiment. In the end, after agreeing that I was physically underdeveloped, the doctor wanted to put me on a course of tablets. But my parents decided against it. I was left to continue my long fight for physical parity with my peers by natural means – which meant a lot of bloody hard work.

In schools football, size, of course, is everything. Yet I managed, through sheer bloody-minded determination, to keep competing with lads both bigger and older than myself. One method Dad employed to ensure I stayed battle-hardened was to take me to the parks. He would seek out higher-age matches and tell me to go over and ask if I could have a game. I hated doing that, but I'm sure it paid off. I broke into the Leeds City Under-15s side when I was in the Under-14s. Our striker Brian Deane, who went on to play for Sheffield United, Leeds and Middlesbrough, was as big then as he is now, and he's six foot three! I was barely five foot in those days.

Four years earlier, I had already had my first accolade from someone other than Dad. An entry in the little red book, dated 11 March 1979, when I was 10, reads: 'Staincliffe 1, Tingley 3. This game should never have been played as the ground was up to the ankles in mud. The little blond lad played well again and some supporters were asking me what I feed him on. Colin Broadhead calls him Billy Bremner.' Yet only one month later, after Horse and Groom had lost 4–2 to Yorkshire Arms, Dad wrote: 'The more I see of these young Hammers the more I realise how hard it's going to be for David to make the grade in soccer. These 10-year-olds can really play. David did well enough, but he'll have to get more strength into his kicking.' After the next match, this time for Tingley, he wrote: 'David's worst performance of the season by far. Missed his second penalty of the season.' It's a good job Glenn Hoddle never got his hands on the Batty Files. If he had, would he have let me step up for that shoot-out spot-kick 19 years later?

Another feature of those formative years that has stayed with me until today – and, presumably, always will – was my tendency to get homesick when I started to travel as a teenage player. I have always been a home bird. Even during my years with Blackburn and, farther afield, at Newcastle I have always lived in the Leeds area. My wife Mandy and I are dyed-in-the-wool locals. The bright lights of London have never held any appeal for me and a move to a club in the capital has never entered my thoughts – not that I'm suggesting Arsenal, Spurs, Chelsea or West Ham would have wanted me in the first place.

I found a two-day trip to Durham for the North of England schoolboy trials an ordeal. Coming as they did just after a trip to Denmark with Pudsey Juniors, those 48 hours in the North-East seemed like a fortnight. I was so unhappy that I phoned home on the first evening to say I was fed up. Mum and Dad came up the following day to offer comfort. Mind you, my mood wasn't helped when I didn't get through the trials. At the next training session with Leeds City Boys my dad told coach Graham Thornton he thought I'd done enough in Durham to be selected. Mr Thornton answered: 'Can you imagine David playing at Wembley, the size of him? He just wouldn't be able to cope.' I was 14 and probably wouldn't have passed for more than 12 years of age!

It was yet another example of how small I was – and how well I must have been doing even to be competing. But just to hold my own with the older, bigger lads was never enough for me. My quest for higher and higher levels of fitness and stamina knew no bounds. When I was only 12 I asked Dad to chart a long-distance run for me to do once a week. He went around the city ring-road and clocked up a seven-mile route on his speedometer. I would set off, leaving Dad, stopwatch in hand, to await my return. Every time I did that run I bettered my previous time. So keen was I that I even insisted on doing it the night before we set off on our annual camping holiday, a highlight of the year for me and John. But I lived to regret my enthusiasm for fitness on that occasion. We were going to Weston-super-Mare the next morning and I remember Dad telling me to give it all I'd got as it would be my last run for a couple of weeks. I did just that, pounding the tarmac like a young man possessed in a lung-bursting effort that knocked several seconds off my personal best. But I ran over the 'line' telling Dad: 'My Achilles is hurting.' By next day, the pain was so bad I couldn't walk, let alone run, for the whole of the holiday.

I have fond memories of those trips around the country sleeping under canvas. One occasion my mum doesn't like to recall is the time we finished a tour of Scotland with a visit to Ben Nevis, the highest mountain in Britain. On arrival the four of us gazed up at the mist-shrouded peak and Dad announced: 'We're going up. All the way.' Mum said: 'No, we're not,' but it was too late. Batty Junior had already made a start on the ascent, disappearing into the distance, and she felt obliged to follow, if only for fear that she might never set eyes on me again. John stuck close to Mum and Dad but that was the last I saw of them until we rendezvoused at the summit. When the three emerged through a last layer of clouds to reach the top of the mountain, there was I, standing on a huge outcrop of rock with my arms open to the heavens, welcoming them like an Everest-conquering hero. Mum told me later that, had there not been a few other people around, she would have brought me down to earth with a bang!

I was 11 then and more of a motorbike-racing fan than a football fanatic. The family gained its fascination for bikes from Dad, who owned one and loved to watch the daredevils who rode them for a living. Again, we used to go all over the country, sleeping under canvas, to the big race meetings. My happiest memory was of the time I went to the public toilets for a pee at Silverstone and found myself standing alongside the great Ron Haslam, the hot-head racer of that period. He lost two brothers on the track, one killed at Scarborough and one in Holland. When Haslam had buttoned up his leathers I got him to give me his autograph. Guys like him remain my sporting heroes. Outside football, bike racing is my sporting passion. I know it always will be, long after I have severed all connections with soccer. You never fall out of love with bikes.

Back on the soccer scene, perhaps the most significant step along the road to joining Leeds as a 16-year-old was my spell with Pudsey Juniors, who became Ashley Road. The team comprised the cream of the kids from West Yorkshire and we were coached by a guy called Dave Camm, who I reckon was the best coach I have ever had. Dave had been the youngest player ever to turn out for Scunthorpe United, at 15, and went on to Leeds United, where he didn't make it. After playing non-League football for a spell he put this team of youngsters together.

It was while with Pudsey, on that trip to Denmark I

mentioned earlier, that the David Batty story might well have ended before it had begun. Sleepwalking and sleep talking dogged me in my childhood days; in fact, I'm still affected by them. Anyone who suffers from this mysterious syndrome will, I'm sure, sympathise with some of the predicaments in which sleepwalking has landed me. On that particular occasion, aboard the ferry carrying the cream of West Yorkshire's early-teenage talent, I came to, walking through the ship's corridors in my pyjamas. As I regained my waking senses and beat a hasty retreat to my cabin, I was intensely relieved that no one was around to witness my embarrassment – and even more pleased that I hadn't made my way on deck and potentially to my death.

One of the scariest aspects of sleepwalking is that you can be discovered, or wake up, as I did on that ferry, in the most unusual and unexpected locations. I once stayed at the home of a Leeds City Boys team-mate, Rob Moverley, a keeper who was later taken on by Bradford City. It is amusing to recall the story his dad told my parents when he brought me home the following morning. He told how, long after retiring to bed with his wife, he awoke with the unnerving feeling that someone was in the room. When Mr Moverley's eyes adjusted to the gloom he was confronted by the spectre of me, standing at the foot of their bed, staring straight ahead and tapping my front teeth, another curious childhood habit of mine. It must have scared him and his wife half to death. Apparently, he kept calm and asked coolly: 'What are you doing, David?' Without a word, I turned and calmly walked back to bed.

I was always wandering the family home in the dead

of night, something my folks got used to. They would lie in their bed listening to me rambling out loud in my sleep. One night, when I was 13 or 14, Dad was alerted when my sleepy mutterings suddenly ceased to be replaced by a noise he couldn't identify. His curiosity aroused, he came into my bedroom, peered at the crumpled duvet on my bed and, assuming I was underneath it, returned to bed. Then he heard my voice again. Returning to my room he noticed something out of the corner of his eye. It was my feet, dangling out of the loft. I had slid back the panel in the ceiling and climbed through. Heaven knows why, or how, because it was quite a way to climb up there. I was helped down and back to the safety of my mattress. Next morning Mum and Dad decided not to mention the incident in case it embarrassed or even frightened me. But, unconcerned, I brought the subject up over breakfast, even though I had no explanation for my nocturnal adventure.

No doubt Aston Villa's England squad goalkeeper David James has been in similar situations. I roomed with David on an England trip. It proved to be an alarming experience, for I discovered, in the dead of night, that he is plagued by the same problem. David is a very big lad and his tendency was to become agitated and lash out in his sleep. That can be not only disturbing to witness, but also potentially dangerous. I weathered the storm, but quickly and diplomatically asked to be moved to a 'safe' room. To my knowledge, David has the privilege of rooming alone these days.

There was nothing dream-like about my progress through the ranks of junior school football. The reality was several years of hard graft. Within 12 months of my first matches for Horse and Groom and Tingley I had my first training session with Leeds City Boys, at Pudsey Grammar School. I was to represent them for the next five years. It was while playing for the city teams, Pudsey Juniors and West Yorkshire, that League clubs' scouts started to notice the skinny little blond kid who was scared of no one. Billy Bremner, the Leeds legend who was later to be my manager, told me how he had noticed me, too, during a victory over Doncaster Boys when he was manager of Doncaster Rovers. Bremner's impression of me that November day, in an English Schoolboys Trophy tie, sowed the seeds of a very special relationship between the two of us.

Still, there were setbacks along the way to clinching that first schoolboy forms signature. I was one of 70 boys invited to the English Schoolboys (North) trials in Durham. As I have already mentioned, I wasn't selected as one of the 25 to go through to the next stage, at Lilleshall. They thought I was too small. Yet, within three months, I signed schoolboy forms with Leeds. Manchester City and Middlesbrough had wanted me to go for trials; Bradford and West Brom, too. But I had set my horizons no further than Elland Road. I still had a lot of effort to put in over the next two years before securing my apprenticeship contract. Now, I can reflect on what an unpredictable business football talent-spotting is.

For example, I used to play with a lad called Ian Scott in the Leeds City Boys side. What a player he was. You would have backed Ian to go all the way to the top – especially when he went off to have trials with Manchester United. Though I was a hometown lad through and through, I can't deny I felt a tinge of envy – perhaps admiration – when Ian would return after a training stint at United. I could barely contain my jealousy when he once told us he had spent a week in the same digs as Norman Whiteside – and had come home with the budding superstar's pyjamas as a memento!

Dad tells me I outplayed Ian in a Leeds v Manchester United Juniors match. I don't recall that. But I do know that Ian's Old Trafford adventure must have ended in heartache – and that he never made it as a professional. United offered him a two-year apprenticeship to be followed by a one-year pro contract; but, when the time came, they told him he wasn't going to make it and didn't offer him the 12-month deal. He must have been devastated. He went on to Stockport County and he didn't even make it there. Maybe he burnt himself out, as so many youngsters do in their mid to late teens. Maybe he simply never got over the crushing disappointment of coming so near and yet being so far from making it as a Manchester United player.

Happily, there was to be no such setback for me. While I was at high school, the Elland Road staff gave me special training schedules designed to build up my physique. They were obviously pretty sure that my potential was worth investing their time and effort in. I became a member of the Leeds United Under-16s team that finished third in an end-of-season international youth tournament in France in 1985. Just before going to France, Ashley Road had won the league championship and beaten Whitkirk in the League Cup final. Then, after I'd helped Ashley Road sweep the board with a 5–0 Minor Cup final triumph against Carlton

United, at Elland Road, Dad wrote: 'If David keeps this up and tries to improve his pace and finishing, he has an outside chance of becoming a good pro footballer.'

By now, the die was cast. I was totally committed to a career in the game and thrilled to bits at the prospect of starting my apprenticeship. On 15 July 1985, I reported to Elland Road to take the first major step along the road that was to lead to fame, fun, pleasure and pain as a professional at some of the biggest clubs in the land.

CHAPTER 2

apprentice days

Some of the staff at Elland Road must have wondered what had arrived in their midst when this skinny little youth, barely eight stone wet through, checked in at 9 a.m. on that July day in 1985. But I soon showed that I meant business and that a big heart pumped inside my small frame. The determination that had characterised my schoolboy years was very much in evidence as I set about proving myself on the first day. When the club doctor had completed the new boys' medicals, we were given our first test, a five-and-a-half-mile run through Roundhay Park. The record time was 31 minutes and I wasn't at all disappointed to clock 35 minutes. On day two we did long runs around the streets outside Elland Road. And, on the Wednesday, when the professionals reported for pre-season duty, I made my first real impact, finishing second to Roundhay Park record holder Terry Phelan, who was 19 then and one of the fittest players I have ever known.

Phelan, who went on to play for Wimbledon, Manchester City and Everton, was the top man for stamina and general physical fitness. I was pretty good – damned good, in fact – but I could never catch Terry. Trying to beat him became a personal but unfulfilled crusade for me in those early days. Every time I closed on him, he upped a gear and surged ahead. But it didn't stop me trying harder and harder. In fact, my near-obsessive running became a source of irritation to some of my less enthusiastic colleagues, especially when Billy Bremner became manager. He would watch us through his binoculars as we pounded the pathways of the park. Knowing the boss was watching from afar put the lads under increased pressure. I can remember Ian Baird, the striker, pleading with me to slow down to give him and the others a break. I wouldn't oblige, though. They must have hated me!

What the others didn't know was that Dad had already taken me into the park before pre-season training began. He had me running the circuit to prepare me for the tough tests to come. On one occasion, I was so knackered I just couldn't finish the course; but it stood me in good stead when it came to doing it for real. That first week was gruelling for me, so I dread to think how much it must have taken out of some of the other boys. I went home with blisters on my feet after a two-touch football session on the Friday. The next day, our sixth in succession, we were hauled off to the park once more. I was second again to Phelan – but in a tremendous time of 31 minutes 17 seconds, not far off his record run mark. I think I slept all day Sunday before getting back on to the treadmill on Monday morning.

Another of the city's parks, Wortley, was the scene of yet more legalised torture, the murderous uphill runs that were designed to really sort the men from the boys. How well I can remember seeing some of the older lads being physically sick in Wortley; presumably they hadn't looked after themselves during the summer break, no doubt over-indulging in the booze once the pressure of playing was off. It was quite common to see people throwing up during those first couple of weeks of exhausting stamina work. It came as no surprise – indeed, I think it was accepted as the norm – but I'm convinced players couldn't survive with that attitude nowadays.

Though the work was hard and we apprentices quickly had to cotton on to our lowly place in the pecking order, I have mostly happy memories of my two-year stint as a starry-eyed wannabe. We were a bunch of naïve boys, straight from school, who were thrilled to be embarking on such a great adventure. The only pressure I felt came from within and I thoroughly enjoyed the whole experience. Mind you, I recall receiving an early blow to my pride: not from anything or anyone at the club, but from a woman on the bus. Though 16, I probably looked about 12 or 13. I climbed aboard the bus, along with some of my fellow apprentices, one morning and the woman said: 'Have the schools broken up?' The other lads found it very funny, but I wasn't laughing. 'No,' I indignantly replied. 'I'm going to work!'

I used to catch the bus into Leeds city centre from a stop in Chapel Allerton. It was from the centre that a lot of the teenage players used to congregate for the start of the journey to Elland Road. The banter was good and I always looked forward to that journey. The professionals were usually at the ground when we trooped in and we soon accepted our role as gofers and general dogsbodies for the guys whose exalted role in life we all dreamed of emulating. Times have changed so much in the years since that the modern teenager would have no conception of what life was like for an apprentice in the mid-eighties. We were scared even to talk to the pros unless they spoke first and we accepted, without question, that we were put on this planet to serve them. Often, the first thing you would do after arriving at the ground would be to leg it straight back outside to the little café across the road with an order for bacon-and-egg and sausage sand-wiches for our seniors. We were simply lackeys. I didn't mind; it was an honour to fetch that sublime midfield playmaker John Sheridan a bacon butty! But can you imagine the lads nowadays eating that sort of grub – and before going training?

Sheridan was one of the few senior pros who was genuinely interested in us kids. I developed a real friend-ship with him, which we maintained through to our time together as first-team midfield partners. 'Shez', a Republic of Ireland international, was a top man during my early days at the club. His status as a key player in the first team was endorsed by his sponsored XR3 car, a seriously trendy set of wheels. He also loved trendy clothes. But he wasn't bigheaded; in fact, on more than one occasion he detailed one of us to drive his XR3 into town to pick up a new pair of trousers or a suit that had been altered. You felt you'd really arrived if you were the chosen one. I got so cocky that I would ask him if I could use his car when he was away overnight on first-team duty, and he used to let me. Such a thing would be unthinkable now. Looking back, I like to think Shez appreciated what I went on to do for him when I broke into the team – namely, his running. That was one of my main functions in my younger days and the team-mates who benefited from my energy were usually openly grateful.

These days, the kids at Leeds's plush Thorp Arch training ground at Wetherby aren't going to get the opportunity to nip down the motorway in a million-pound-a-year superstar's £60,000 BMW. But there are pluses as well as minuses when you compare their learning-curve career time to that of my age group. For instance, the modern teenage footballer won't have to stand 'trial' like I did. The infamous Elland Road 'court cases' were a feature of apprentice life for the fledgling Batty and his mates. We were the ones in the dock; the pros sat as judge and jury. One would be the prosecutor, another the defence counsel. But there was never a verdict of 'innocent'. The defendants who were brought before those kangaroo courts were all pronounced 'guilty' after a sham trial, and the punishment was terrible to behold. The standard sentence for a heinous crime, such as failing to polish a pro's boots to his satisfaction, or not putting enough sauce on a sausage sarnie, amounted to total humiliation.

Just as a guilty verdict was inevitable, so was the form of punishment meted out. With only slight, but sadistic, variations on the theme, the guilty party would be stripped naked in the dressing-room, tied to a treatment table, plastered from head to toe in boot polish – with maybe a more painful substance for the private parts – and probably doused in water. But the misery didn't end there. The final, fiendish act would see the poor soul – and that was me on more than one occasion – taken down to Fullerton Park, tied to a goalpost as naked as nature intended – and left there. The 'court' was in session about once a week, and I have to admit I found it great fun as long as I wasn't the poor bugger in the dock. If you were the wretched accused it sent shivers down your spine. A lad from Huddersfield, Peter McGuire, was so scared he ran out of the ground, through the huge car park, up the embankment and over the railway bridge. We gave chase but his fear must have driven him to superhuman speed and we couldn't catch him. He was so terrified that he wasn't seen for three days. God knows what he told them when he returned, for I don't remember the staff ever giving the slightest impression that they were aware of the professionals' court-case capers.

Like so much that went on in those days, such a thing couldn't happen now. But, at the time, we accepted it as just another feature of our daily lives, an obligatory part of our toughening-up process. It was so funny to see one of your mates squirming through the ordeal; it was cold fear if you were the 'accused'. I went on to play first-team football with many of the perpetrators of that Spanish Inquisition-style justice. I bore none of them any grudges. It might make harsh reading, but it was all part and parcel of a fun- if sometimes fear-filled apprentice-ship.

I made my first appearance in the Leeds Juniors side on 29 July 1985, a 4–1 away win against York City, coming on at left-back 10 minutes into the second half. There were some real characters among my teenage team-mates, and those made my apprentice days some of the happiest of my life. One of them was Lee Warren, a Geordie boy whose parents followed his career with a passion, just as my folks did mine. Lee's dad, Jack, always had us in stitches – I'm sure he was never aware that he gave so many so much pleasure! Jack Warren was seriously poor-sighted and used to wear bizarre, thick-rimmed spectacles with lenses that looked about two inches thick. One afternoon, while waiting for the bus at the stop outside Elland Road, a group of us fell about laughing at the amazing scenes Jack was enacting in a petrol station opposite. He drove a Marina – if drove is the right word – and had just filled up the tank. What followed was like a scene from a Carry On film. I can't recall if he was facing the wrong direction, or whatever, but he proceeded to attempt a three-point turn. He was banging into pumps, walls, buckets – everything that was there to be hit, Jack hit it. Pieces of tail-light and wing mirror were falling off, indicators were blinking and hazard warning lights flashing. It was chaos. By the time Jack extricated himself from the courtyard, the scene resembled a battleground. But to our astonishment he simply drove off down the road without a backward glance.

I can only assume that Darren Sheridan, younger brother of John, didn't witness that scene. If he had, he would never have put himself through the ordeal of terror he suffered a few months later on the M1 motorway. It followed a Juniors match at Doncaster when Jack's wife offered Darren a lift home in the family car. By then, the Warrens had moved from Newcastle to Leeds in order to give Lee the benefits of home comforts and their day-to-day support. They had bought a house in Beeston, just a stone's throw from Elland Road. Darren also lived in Beeston, so he accepted the invitation and gratefully jumped into the back seat. It wasn't long before he was wishing he was anywhere but in that Marina. He later described how he sat, terrified, as Mrs Warren manoeuvred driver Jack into the middle lane of the motorway and then, with a non-stop monologue of 'Left a bit, love, right a bit, love, left again, now right again, love, keep it steady, keep it steady,' endeavoured to ensure that he stayed in the same lane until they reached their turn-off, whereupon she had to lead him through the devilishly difficult step of switching lanes and leaving the motorway! We were all killing ourselves when Darren told the story. But he assured us it was no laughing matter at the time.

Mrs Warren started taking in apprentices once they'd moved to Beeston. Many hilarious stories about Jack found their way back to the club. One that sticks in my mind is of the time the TV set broke. Jack got another set which, for some reason, he stood on top of the one that was kaput. The lads were in stitches one evening as Jack went up to the telly and spent minutes fiddling with the buttons, becoming increasingly exasperated trying to change the channel – on the set that was broken! Then there was the day that Mark Fella, who was given his first-team debut by Billy Bremner before I made mine, arrived at the ground one morning to see Jack Warren stealing a couple of bottles of milk from outside the players' entrance, where the milkman left a crateful every day, putting them under his coat and getting in his car. Little did the lads in digs at the Warren house realise they were pouring Leeds United's milk on their cornflakes every morning. Mark, as you can imagine, was much amused by the sight of Lee's dad furtively driving away with the milk. He told us what had happened but not a word was said to Lee. Later that morning, Mark put a ladder against the dressing-room wall and proceeded to hide several bottles of milk in Lee Warren's high-altitude pigeonhole, where he kept his boots. Mark was in the middle of his prank when Lee walked in. Mark nearly fell off his ladder as, covered in confusion, he blurted: 'It wasn't me!' I don't think anyone ever told Lee the truth.

At the Juniors and Reserves games you could always hear Jack, in his distinctive Geordie accent, voicing the endlessly repetitive cry of: 'Come on, Leeds. Come on, Leeds.' He would keep it up from first whistle to last in every match. On one occasion, after Lee had been transferred to Rochdale and the two teams were playing each other, sure enough Jack was droning: 'Come on, Rochdale. Come on, Rochdale.' But then, to everyone's amusement, he began to call out: 'Come on, Leeds. Come on, Leeds.' He had slipped back into his former mode, not realising why so many of the Leeds parents were laughing so much. My dad tells the story of the day when he was watching me in a Juniors match at Fullerton Park. Billy Bremner had also come along. It seems that, for some time, Jack had been slagging Bremner off to the other parents, accusing him of not giving young Lee a fair crack of the whip. Spectators were standing four deep, with Bremner on the front row and Dad and Jack alongside each other four rows back. Bremner got a cigar out and put it to his lips. Before he could even reach for his box of matches, Jack sprang forward through the ranks, lighter in hand. He couldn't get to his son's tormentor quickly enough. My dad said that what surprised him most about the incident was that Jack could even recognise Bremner from four paces.

Two of my best mates were Dave Bentley, a big strong left-sided midfielder who made his first-team debut at 16 in a West Yorkshire Cup match, and Vinnie Brockie, a tough boy from Scotland who was as dedicated as I was; maybe even more so, if that were possible.

Dave was a really promising player whose career was cut short by the dreaded cruciate knee ligament injury. It is bad enough to fall foul of that injury during a match, much worse to suffer it in the bizarre fashion that poor Dave did. He had started to make an impact at Leeds and I, for one, fancied his chances of going all the way. But it all went horribly wrong one winter's afternoon at the bus stop outside the Elland Road souvenir shop. A gang of us were standing in the snow having our usual *craic*. Bentley was rolling a big snowball and he had his eye on his target. As he hurled the missile, his foot went from under him in the slush. He went down and was soon writhing in agony. He had 'done' his knee. We had to carry Dave back into the club. It was the beginning of the end of his career, at barely 17. He played one more match, against Huddersfield Juniors, and the knee went on him. There was no way back after that.

Vinnie, with whom I became really good friends, didn't make it either. Yet every minute of every day, Vinnie would practise, practise and practise. When we were having lunch, he would disappear after grabbing a quick sandwich and you would soon hear him outside, kicking a ball against the wall. He lived for it, just as I did. He was a right-back or midfielder, an aggressive redhead who used to have some real ding-dongs with me during training. In a game at Newcastle Vinnie 'did' Paul Gascoigne's younger brother. There was all hell on: Vinnie went up for a header and stuck his elbow in Gazza Junior's face. As their physio came on, young Gazza leapt to his feet and ran off the pitch, with the physio in pursuit. The physio yelled at him to stop, but he kept on running. He must have been concussed.

Billy Bremner gave Vinnie his debut and he played three of four games towards the end of the 1987–88 season. But I felt he never got the chance he deserved from Howard Wilkinson, who became manager in October 1988. Wilko obviously didn't rate him and he shipped him out to Doncaster the following season. There, poor Vinnie received a nasty knee injury. He went to non-League Guiseley after being advised by the doctor that he couldn't sustain a pro career with his knee condition. I felt genuinely sad for him when he was sold by Leeds. Of all the youngsters I shared those formative days with, I felt Vinnie was the one who deserved to make it. He had ability and endless enthusiasm; nobody put in more effort than he did. I often pondered how much it would have hurt me if they had let me go and how hard it must be to come back from such a disappointment. Thankfully, I never had to deal with that trauma.

Not many of that group went into the first-team or professional ranks anywhere, for that matter. One of the problems is that there are so many distractions when you are young and fit and you've got a few bob in your pocket, like girls, drinking beer and going out on the town. But I was lucky, because I was so immature at 16 and 17. I was only interested in football, in getting bigger and stronger and becoming a better player. I never thought about girls and going out. I was happy to work hard at my game and go home to my mum and dad and brother John in the evening. I didn't get sidetracked – as so many of my contemporaries did – from the tough task of putting in consistently good performances on the pitch. I realised at an early age, maybe helped by the fact that I'd always had to fight that bit harder to compete with the bigger lads, that you had to be seen to be the best on a regular basis to have a chance of making it. There aren't many players, even at that age, who can achieve such a high level of consistency if they are socialising every night.

There are other reasons, too, for not progressing in a profession that demands dedication. One lad was potentially one of the best of that bunch. He had a brilliant left foot – that most sought-after of commodities in soccer. But, frankly, he didn't have a lot of bottle. I've never forgotten how, on a sleeting, cold day at Ashley Road Juniors, coach Dave Camm, presumably knowing him all too well, asked him: 'Do you want to play today?' He replied: 'No. I won't bother.' It wasn't very pleasant out there, but the rest of us were champing at the bit nevertheless. On another nasty, wintry afternoon he was wearing an anorak-type garment under his shirt. Now, what kind of message does that send out to the opposition? He had loads of ability, but I always felt his heart wasn't really in it.

Another reason I didn't go out much was that my mum and dad used to take my £35 a week digs money off me. That was more than our pay. Other lads who weren't in digs but who nevertheless kept their money were always boasting about being quids in and I must say I felt a bit miffed that my parents didn't let me keep mine. Unknown to me, they were putting it all in a savings account, which held the princely sum of £900 by the time I passed my driving test. It was enough to buy my first car. When the other lads had been going out buying clothes, shoes and other things, I had been envious and a bit resentful because I had to hand my digs money to my mum. But my indignation gave way to undiluted gratitude when Mum and Dad revealed what they'd been doing with the money. I bought a silver Morris Marina coupé with a vinyl roof, definitely more up-market than the Marina Jack Warren drove so erratically to and from the football grounds of the North of England! I was dead proud of that car. I drove it for the next two years, beyond the time when I made my first-team debut. The irony was, for someone like me who wasn't prone to extravagance, that I put a radio in that car that was valued at £1,000 – £100 more than the car itself!

bremner and me

Billy Bremner was still the boss when I got my driving licence, and he had already given me a licence to kill on the football field. I don't mean that literally, of course. But I have to say that, after my dad, I rank the Elland Road icon as my biggest fan and driving force. Unlike his successor, Howard Wilkinson, Bremner never once said or did anything to try to curb my natural aggression on the pitch. He was totally supportive of my all-action style. I do, however, recall him having a cautionary word with me before a Zenith Data Systems Cup tie at Millwall very early in my first-team life. He told me in the dressing-room that if I wanted to avoid having the notoriously nasty Den crowd on my back I should think twice about steaming in early in the game. The trouble was, even at 19 and when confronted with advice from my hero, my stubborn streak still came to the fore. What did I do in response to the manager's words of wisdom? I went straight in, in the first minute, on Terry Hurlock, one of the hardest midfielders who ever played the game.

Bremner, I learned later, was cringing in the dugout. But I was unrepentant. I never had any respect for reputations as a young lad. I would always get stuck in, regardless of how famous – or infamous – the opponent. Come to think of it, I never changed much. I'm not sure if that is fearlessness or foolhardiness; perhaps it's a bit of both. Whatever it was, Bremner, himself one of the toughest players who ever kicked a ball for a living, was an open admirer of my aggressive style. I, of course, loved him for that as well as revering his memory as one of the key players in Don Revie's all-conquering team of the seventies.

Eddie Gray, a Scottish compatriot of Bremner and a devastatingly effective winger in the Revie era at Leeds, was team boss when I started my apprenticeship. Eddie is a nice bloke and I'm delighted that he went on to coach at the club under David O'Leary, but he insisted on playing me at full-back when I first went to Elland Road and that brassed me off. I didn't consider myself quick enough to be a full-back and I always felt exposed in the position. When he parted company with the club early in October 1985, most people were really upset. But I confess I remember thinking it might be good for me because the new man might give me a new lease of life in midfield. That new man was Bremner, and he certainly gave me the lift I was looking for. I was only sorry he wasn't around long enough for me to repay his faith by playing for him in a successful Leeds side.

Bremner came in from Doncaster Rovers and quickly let me know that he had remembered me from the previous season, when I had played for Leeds Schoolboys at Belle Vue. In fact I had come off that day with stomach ache, brought on by eating treacle sandwiches before kick-off, but Billy told me he had recognised my fierce will to win. He switched me to the midfield role I had occupied on that day the previous season – and made me captain of the Juniors. After my first match under Bremner's management, a 1–0 Northern Intermediate League win over Grimsby Town, he came over to me after the final whistle, put his arm around me and told me I had been 'different class'. I grew about two feet at that moment. It was my proudest moment to date in the Leeds United shirt.

Mind you, I remember being booked for the second time that season and, with hindsight, perhaps Billy was inadvertently encouraging an over-aggressive side to my game. A few weeks later, after a 4–0 defeat at Sheffield United, my dad wrote in his book: 'David worked hard and was one of Leeds's best players. I just think he should concentrate more on his football and cut out the rough stuff. The ref told him after the game he came close to being booked.' I only wish more refs had done the same in the next two or three years, instead of brandishing the cards first!

After I skippered the team for the first time in a Youth Cup tie at Elland Road – when we were hammered 5–0 by Chester – Dad wrote: 'David was second best and the question is whether he is good enough. He was down on strength, pace and alertness.' Those were pretty harsh words he penned that day in December 1985. Fortunately for me, Bremner wasn't so disillusioned, and by the end of the season, Dad had seen enough positive signs to deliver this summing-up: 'David has improved his game but he has a long, long way to go. Next season he has to establish himself in the reserves. He has to be able to run at players more and score more goals. Billy Bremner is probably his biggest fan, apart from his mum and myself, that is.'

I don't think Dad was far wrong; Bremner really did seem to think the sun shone out of my backside. My parents jokingly labelled him my second dad. He was brilliant with me. He never told me so himself, but he told others that he saw in me a clone of himself in his youth: a cocky little so-and-so who wasn't going to lie down for anyone, a kid with a bit of a swagger whose attitude was 'the bigger they are, the harder they fall'. I was an all-over-the-pitch operator, just as he had been, and he never once tried to knock any of that out of me. Ironically, I now say to Lee Bowyer, Leeds's all-action midfielder: 'I used to be just like you at your age: covering every blade of grass, up and down, non-stop.' You forget so easily how fit you must have been!

But back to Bremner and those exciting days when he took the Elland Road hot seat. Every apprentice was given a mundane job to do and mine was to clean the coaches' room. One of my tasks was to put out the gaffer's kit every morning. Every afternoon, after training, Bremner would shout: 'Batty, go get me twenty cigs.' I would run over the road to the shop and dutifully bring him his fags. It was a privilege to be Billy Bremner's gofer. The other lads used to take the piss and call me his blue-eyed boy, but how could I complain about that? It was true. I remember him putting his arm around my shoulders after a pre-season game at Ossett and keeping it there as we walked across the adjoining cricket pitch to the dressing-room, all the while giving me words of encouragement.

As far as I was concerned, Bremner was the greatest. How many other managers, and former superstars, would you find playing with the apprentices at 4.30 in the afternoon, long after the rest of the staff and players had gone home? Billy used to do that with us – and often in his suit and shoes! Our daily jobs were normally finished by around 2.30 p.m. when we would frequently have a circle of keep-ball or some other form of ball-skill practice. Billy would see us from his office, or from the car park when he was about to leave for home, and come over and join in. He would be there, in the cold and the mud of midwinter, bending free kicks in his patent leather shoes. And he enjoyed regaling us with stories of his marvellous playing days, tales of how George Best never had a good game for Manchester United against Leeds. He loved the game and he loved giving us his time. It earned him a lot of respect, especially from me.

I was a bit of a bugger on the training pitch, just as I was during matches, and I showed as little regard for my Leeds seniors as I did for opponents from other teams. Occasionally, you would be called over to join in with the first teamers. I loved it when I got the nod to mix in with those guys, but I think it got to the point where they weren't so chuffed as I was to have me in their midst. Certainly Gary Hamson, the full-back, wasn't best pleased with my presence. He collared me after one training session at Fullerton Park and gave me a slap. Dad told me not to worry and that I mustn't let it affect me. More importantly, Bremner called me in the follow-ing day to tell me Hamson had been complaining about my over-physical approach. I suppose Bremner was worried that I might injure one of the first-team boys. But, to be fair, he didn't order me to cut it out. I don't think he expected – or even wanted – me to change my approach.

At the end of the 1986–87 season I had to attend an FA disciplinary hearing after being booked 14 times and totting up 48 disciplinary points. I was fined £50. But I had played in 65 Juniors and Reserves matches that long, hard season and I was quietly pleased that I was making progress and continuing to impress Billy Bremner, the man who mattered. In fact, I was on the verge of my first-team breakthrough. However, there was a disappointment to swallow that summer when I received details of my first professional contract. Bremner had told me I would be offered a two-year deal with the wages negotiable. In the event, it was what I believe you call a *fait accompli*. They made a firm offer of £100 per week – and for only one year.

That really upset me. I spent two weeks chewing it all over before deciding that I wasn't going to accept without a fight. The gritty streak that characterised my football was also very much in evidence when it came to standing up for myself in other ways. We started pre-season training on 13 July; the following day, I went in to see Bremner to voice my unhappiness with the terms I had been offered. I was even more unhappy when he told me I had no chance of an increase on the £100 a week and that he wouldn't extend the one-year term to two years. He said I was perfectly entitled to turn down the contract but that I would have to put my refusal in writing. On 15 July that is precisely what I did. I took the letter in to Elland Road and also wrote to the FA, informing them of my action.

A nervous nine-day wait followed, during which time

I found it hard to concentrate on my training. Though I had no regrets about taking my stance, I was nevertheless nervous about the outcome. What would I do if the club refused to budge and gave me a 'take it or leave it' ultimatum? I had never wanted to be anywhere other than Leeds. I had enjoyed my two-year apprenticeship and I loved playing for Bremner. The thought of starting afresh somewhere else held no appeal for me. Then, on 24 July, Bremner told me the club had decided to make me an improved offer. They would increase my pay to £120 a week and give me a two-year contract. I accepted, hopefully without giving the impression I was biting their hand off! Now I could concentrate all my efforts on the big push for first-team recognition.

That was, in fact, just around the corner. After a 2–2 friendly draw at Denaby United I was held up by the boss as an example of someone who exuded a real will to win. I went home that night feeling quite chuffed. The very next day, 28 July, I had my first experience of first-team football when I came on as a sub for the injured Micky Adams in a 3–0 win at Goole Town. I even scored, and as if that wasn't enough of a rarity, I managed it with a header! The start of the League season was only three weeks away and I was beginning to experience a sense of destiny. The annual curtain-raiser, the West Riding Senior Cup, was the competition in which I played my first full match for the senior team. We beat Halifax Town 1–0 at Elland Road and I played the whole 90 minutes. I was 18 years and eight months old. It was a big thrill for me to be lining up in midfield alongside my mate and mentor John Sheridan. Bremner picked me for the next two Senior Cup matches, a win against Huddersfield and a draw with Bradford, and I had one match for the Reserves before the big kick-off on 22 August.

Leeds had a home fixture against Reading and everyone in the family held their breath, wondering if this was to be my biggest day yet. It wasn't, but I could claim further progress by being named on the substitutes' bench. In those days, there were only two subs so I had a real sense of an impending breakthrough. But a niggling injury problem was threatening my progress, and it struck me down early that September. I had struggled through pre-season with pain in my left ankle, the legacy of ligament damage I had sustained during an end-of-season international youth tournament in Augsburg, Germany. Back in the mid to late 1980s there wasn't the same intensive treatment for injuries, nor the attention to detail that youngsters are privileged to enjoy nowadays. By and large, unless you had broken your leg, you got on with it. I had had the ankle strapped up during the tournament in Augsburg, when I had been in a lot of pain. But, at that age, my thoughts weren't of possible long-term damage, only of playing on and not missing out on the opportunity to make that breakthrough into the first team. That is just what I did that summer, but it caught up with me on 8 September at Maine Road. I went over on my ankle five minutes into the Central League match against Manchester City and was carried off. I'll never forget how annoyed my dad was. He and Mum had rushed across the Pennines to watch me play, as soon as he had finished work. They didn't make the kick-off, but were just in time to watch their son making an early, painful exit.

With hindsight – especially after suffering so many serious setbacks in my later career – I realise what a risk I took and how lucky I was to get away with it. I had, in fact, broken a bone in my foot and it was in plaster for three weeks. I had a frustrating stop–start training period of nearly four weeks before making my comeback in a Central League defeat to Liverpool. A few more reserve-team outings followed as my foot got stronger, before Bremner again put me on the first-team bench when we beat Shrewsbury 2–1 at Elland Road. I didn't get on the pitch but I received an £80 win bonus on top of £100 appearance money; £300 in all, taking my basic wage of £120 into account.

Though my next match was in the 3–1 home Central League defeat by Huddersfield, Dad wrote: 'I think he could be ready for the first team.' Bremner clearly thought so, too. I was again unused sub for the Second Division match at Millwall on 14 November. One week later – 21 November 1987 – I proudly walked out in front of 15,457 supporters at Elland Road to start my first senior match for the club. We weren't getting huge crowds in those days when the team was struggling along in the old Division Two, but it seemed to me as if the world began and ended in the famous stadium that day. I didn't have any nerves. My overriding emotion was one of anticipation and excitement at finally achieving the recognition I had craved during eight years of unstinting effort and devotion to my fitness and my football.

The opponents were Swindon Town. We beat them 4–2 and I had a good game in my favourite central midfield position. The national newspapers were generous in their praise of 'the new Billy Bremner'. Another debut-maker for Leeds was striker Bobby Davison, a £350,000 signing from Derby County, who scored the first goal. It was a dream debut for Bobby, too, but I was the *Yorkshire Evening Post*'s Man of the Match. I started that landmark match as I meant to go on for the remainder of my career, having a real battle with the biggest lad on the pitch, Swindon's centre-forward Dave Bamber. He must have been six foot four to my five foot seven. I was into his ribs from the off. I caught him once too often and we were soon toe to toe; the referee had a very stern word with me. The crowd loved it. Big Dave had long, shaggy hair, like a gypsy, and the fans were chanting: 'Where's your caravan?' Apparently, they were laughing on the bench too, watching me square up to a guy who could have eaten me for breakfast.

The stubbornness and individuality that run through my character came out in that very first flirtation with big-time football. At half-time, Bremner came in to give us his pep talk. Yet, even then, 11 days short of my 19th birthday and with just 45 minutes' first-team action to my name, I switched off suddenly as soon as the whistle stopped play. There I was, half a game into my career, when I was jolted by Bremner bawling: 'Batty, what the hell are you doing?' Startled, I looked up from reading the match programme to see all the other lads respectfully hanging on his every word as he outlined his strategy for the second half. I hadn't intentionally been insubordinate, but that is the way I was and it's the way I've remained. In some people's eyes I'm not a model professional because I can't focus unless I'm actually playing. But my conscience has always been clear because I know I have never given less than my all on the pitch.

I certainly gave everything I had that day and it all turned out right. 'There will never be a bigger day in soccer for David – or for us,' Dad wrote in his book. 'All the hard work he has put into improving his game has finally paid off. If he keeps working on his game, he could go right to the top of his profession.' They were heart-warming words from my No. 1 fan. But I was quickly to learn that this game can kick you in the teeth just as readily as it can lift you to the clouds. A midweek Simod Trophy success followed that debut-day victory and I travelled to Crystal Palace on the Saturday full of the joys of being a regular in a winning team. What happened? We got hammered 3–0. Ian Wright and Mark Bright were Palace's talented strikers, a pair of sharp-tongued blokes who delighted in winding up the raw lad from up North all afternoon. It was a sobering experience and a timely reminder to me that I must never forget the basic principle that had driven me since I first started playing as an enthusiastic nine-year-old; namely, that you need to be totally focused in every match so as to give yourself and your team-mates the best possible chance of coming out on top. Bremner kept me in his team that season, and the first sign that the club appreciated my progress came less than four weeks after my debut. On 15 December 1987, I signed a new contract, which added a year to the two-year deal I had agreed in July. My basic pay more than doubled to £250 per week. I got another £100 every time I appeared in the team, with £80 for a win and £50 for a draw. It all added up to a possible £430 for a winning outing. I had just turned 19 and I felt like a millionaire.

As if to repay the club for their generosity, I scored the first League goal of my career two weeks later, the winner in our 2–1 success at Manchester City on Boxing Day. Mum and Dad were sitting with my team-mate Peter Swan's parents, right in the middle of the City punters. When I struck the winner past keeper Perry Suckling, from the edge of the area on a wet surface after Swanny had let the ball go through his legs, all four parents leapt to their feet in excitement and celebration. They quickly shrank back in their seats when they realised they were inviting an unpleasant reaction from the hundreds of Blues surrounding them. Unfortunately, those people – my father included – who hoped this goal would be the first of many were to be disappointed. If I'd known then that it would be so long before I would strike again, I might have made more of it at the time. But scoring was never an issue for me and I have to say that some of the biggest-name managers in the game obviously didn't have a problem with that, either. Dad had written that my lack of goals would stop me from getting into the England team, yet I won 42 caps for my country. Not bad for a man who only did half a job!

We went on to beat Middlesbrough in front of 33,000 fans at home two days later, and on New Year's Day 1988, 36,004 were at Elland Road to see us record our fifth successive League-match success with a 2–0 win over Bradford City, when I recall getting the better of Bradford's emerging midfielder Stuart McCall. Stuart, of course, went on to have a marvellous career with Everton, Rangers and Bradford again. Later that month I was awarded a silver salver and named the Barclays League Yorkshire Region Young Player of the Month for December.

That personal accolade was followed by another major landmark. On 18 February I took delivery of my first sponsored car, a Ford Escort 1300L, valued at £6,500. It seemed to me that the Batty bandwagon was on a roll, an impression reinforced when, towards the end of the season, I was invited to join emerging players like Matt Le Tissier, Andy Hinchcliffe, Dalian Atkinson, Neil Ruddock and Tim Sherwood in an England Under-20s trial at Lilleshall. In May, I was selected for the Under-21 squad to go to Lausanne for a match against Switzerland. Dave Sexton, the Under-21s' manager, had watched me play at Oldham in April. He must have liked what he saw, even though I was booked for a late tackle! I was also selected for the Under-20s tour to Brazil in June.

The last home match of that season, against Crystal Palace, was also memorable for all the right reasons. Before the game – a 1–0 win for Leeds in which my pal Vinnie Brockie made his debut at right-back – I was presented with £150 worth of vouchers by club sponsors Burtons the tailors for being their Player of the Month. Afterwards, I was given a bottle of champagne and two tickets for a four-day cruise by match sponsors Yorkshire Ryder, the bus company, after being named Man of the Match. And still the accolades rolled in! The Galway branch of Leeds United Supporters' Club presented me with a crystal bowl after naming me their Young Player of the Season. And yet, following the final match, a goalless draw at Birmingham, which left us in seventh place in Division Two, Dad was still hammering away at my shortage of goals.

It was while in Switzerland three weeks later that I first came across a certain Paul Gascoigne, with whom I shared a room in Lausanne. What a character. What a smashing lad. Okay, in the words of England manager Bobby Robson, Gazza was 'daft as a brush'. But he was also the most loveable rogue you could wish to meet. I can understand how he must have driven coaches and managers mad with his non-stop clowning around and mickey-taking, but there is no denying he was great fun to be around. I remember him walking into the hotel room one day while I was on the phone talking to my mum. He grabbed the handset from me and proceeded to baffle my poor mother with a stream of heavily Geordie-accented babble. He was always on the phone to people back home. We used to get a daily allowance for phone calls, which was to be shared between the two occupants of the room. I reckon Gazza spent at least 75 per cent of ours, keeping up a stream of calls to various friends and family on Tyneside. In those days he really liked his chocolate and, of all the places to be situated, here we were in Switzerland, the home of the stuff. I don't think he once walked past the hotel reception without plunging his hand into the huge glass jars full of fabulous, but fattening, Swiss-made mini chocolate bars.

Lads like Teddy Sheringham, Julian Dicks, Chris Fairclough – who became a team-mate at Leeds in the Championship-winning side – and Stuart Ripley, who I was to play with at Blackburn, were in that squad. I came on for the last 25 minutes as we played out a 1–1 draw in a prelude to the senior international teams' meeting on the same pitch. I went on to finish my season as a member of the Under-20s squad which toured Brazil, under the management of Graham Taylor, from 2 to 6 June. The whole trip was a culture shock; I'd never seen anything like it. There were prostitutes on the street flashing their arses at us on the coach. And when we went to one of the livelier bars, these guys came along and pulled guns on us all, just as we were about to leave, demanding that we pay them more money.

It had been a personally satisfying eight months, from the moment I had made my League debut. Leeds had enjoyed a reasonable season, finishing in seventh place, though eight points adrift of a play-off spot, and I was full of optimism for the next campaign and life under Billy Bremner. But, as is so often the case in this game, the story didn't unfold as expected.

CHAPTER 4

wilko's revolution

I went into the 1988–89 season full of enthusiasm, even though I had to sit out the first two matches because of a suspension carried forward from the previous campaign. Nevertheless, I was champing at the bit, eager to resume my first-team career as a key player in Billy Bremner's team and, from what I could tell, someone who figured large in the manager's plans for the future. The games I missed were a 1–1 home draw with Oxford and a 4–0 battering at Portsmouth: not the most auspicious start, I must admit. Still, I finished my suspension and went straight into the side for the Elland Road clash with Manchester City, playing on the right side of a midfield three. We were held 1–1 by City and, a week later, battled out a 0–0 draw at Bournemouth. I was booked, proving I hadn't learned from my experiences.

The Yorkshire derby clash at home to Barnsley, our fifth League match, brought us our first win, 2–0, and I won the Man of the Match champagne. That helped to take some of the pressure off the team and the manager and the public responded three days later when we had a 26,000 crowd – 9,000 up on the Barnsley gate – for the visit of Chelsea. Sadly, it proved to be the last League match of Bremner's reign as team manager. We were beaten 2–0, leaving the team with just one victory from the first six matches of the season. It obviously wasn't good enough for the board of directors. Though we won our next game, a Littlewoods Cup tie at Peterborough, Bremner was sacked the following day, Wednesday, 28 September 1988. I was stunned. We hadn't had the best of starts but Bremner was a Leeds legend. To me he typified everything that was good about the club. And I was only 19, a rookie first teamer and by no means hardened to the harsh realities of life at that level, where players – and even more so, managers – live and die by results.

Bremner's departure was made all the more poignant for me by the fact that, after that defeat to Chelsea – when I got booked again, by the way – he singled me out for special praise. The atmosphere in the dressing-room wasn't good, as you can imagine, and I was completely unprepared for the moment when, during a half-hour inquest into our performance, Bremner called out my name and held me up as an example to the rest of what he expected from his players. It was with embarrassment, and not a little pride, that I sat there as he told much more experienced players how outrageous it was that he had to point to a 19-year-old as his shining example of a motivating force on the pitch. Little did I realise that Bremner would sing my praises no longer.

The team stumbled to three successive defeats, at Brighton, Sunderland and home to League leaders Watford before, on 10 October, Howard Wilkinson was unveiled as Bremner's successor. On hearing the news, a shudder of apprehension ran through the first-team squad. Wilko was boss at nearby Sheffield Wednesday, where his direct style of football and Commando-style training routines had earned him a reputation as a hard taskmaster and a man of inflexible routine. We weren't excited at the prospect of his arrival. I certainly wasn't looking forward to the new regime. Although I have always been a physical player, someone who is prepared to mix it with the best of them in the midfield, it isn't widely recognised that I am a fan of good football, played on the floor. I love nothing more than being a part of a passing team. I hate long-ball stuff. So, already gutted at Bremner's sacking, I was even more depressed at the prospect of Wilko's succession to the hot seat. My misgivings were well founded.

The basis of his philosophy at Hillsborough seemed to have been that as long as his players were fitter than any others, it would compensate them for not being as good, a sort of 'we'll outrun, outfight and outlast them in the end' credo. It soon became clear that, at Leeds, we weren't matching up to Wilko's demands. So, under the watchful eye of Mick Hennigan, Wilko's 'sergeant-major', we had to endure 12-minute runs flat out around the pitch – as warm-ups! With Wilko and Hennigan doggedly clocking every individual's performance, you had to complete a minimum eight, maybe nine, laps of the pitch in those 12 minutes. In Bremner's day a 12-minute run, once or sometimes twice a week, was the only running we would do in training. Now, we were doing it as a warm-up every day. Hennigan, Howard's Mr Motivator, had previously worked as a pylon erector. There was many an occasion when I – and others – would have willingly pushed him off one if given the chance.

It was the start of a strange, often strained relationship between Wilko and me. Though I now realise that his attitude towards me was designed to make me a better player, it would be hypocritical to claim that I enjoyed working for him or that I admired his methods and the way he had us play. The truth is that I never came to terms with Wilko's management style and I constantly railed against an outlook which I can only describe as schoolmasterly. As I've already admitted, I wasn't the world's No. 1 pupil.

I stayed in the team when Wilko arrived, but he dropped me six weeks later, for the 0–0 draw with Birmingham. I didn't even make the subs' bench. Dad wrote the cryptic message: 'The manager told David he was dropping him from the first team. It is an awful feeling.' Dead right, there, Dad! I had already told Wilko I preferred a central midfield role and a deepening feeling of dissatisfaction was developing within me. There is no doubt I was entering the most unhappy period of my career to date. The harsh and, in my opinion, unimaginative training system had come as a shock to me, although I was a lad who prided himself on being in good shape and never shirked the physical grind of the training pitch or the running track. I was also quickly growing disillusioned with the way we were being told to play, a style very much in the mould of the Sheffield Wednesday side Wilko had left to join us.

Within a few months, I felt that Wilko was trying to knock a lot of the natural aggression and arrogance out of my game. It became a battle of wills between us. I'm sure he was determined to show who was boss, and the obstinacy in me came to the fore. Howard had, in fact, once been a schoolteacher and that, in my opinion, constantly shone through in his dealings not only with me, but with all the players. Maybe from the early days he recognised in me something of a free spirit, a youngster who didn't readily take to being told to toe the line.

Billy Bremner would tell me to go out there, impose myself, be a bit arrogant and let the opposition know who was boss. That's exactly how I saw myself: never bigheaded or cocky off the field, but certainly full of myself once the whistle blew. I grew more and more convinced that Wilko's mission in life was to try to take me down a peg or two, to knock a bit of the stuffing out of me and make me bend to his will, which was based around the total teamwork ethic. He was frustrated with me for constantly getting booked and I admit I was going through a period where I was making too many reckless challenges and starting to rack up suspensions. Quite rightly, he would tell me that players missed enough games through injury without compounding the problem by getting banned. I had no argument with Wilko's basic logic; it was his manner I never came to terms with. He was the authoritarian, do-it-my-way-or-not-at-all type and I just couldn't respond to that.

It got to the stage where Hennigan would call me every single morning to see the manager. I trooped from the dressing-room to Wilko's office feeling like a schoolboy heading for his daily lecture. I have come to accept that, in his own way, he was doing what he thought was best for me and, ultimately, the team, but at the time I felt he was crushing my spirit. It was as if he was attempting to clone me, to fit me, robot-like, into his vision of the well-oiled machine. I could never understand quite what he was driving at. I would sit there in his office, pretending to listen while he droned on, responding with the odd 'Yes,' 'Okay, then,' 'Okay, gaffer,' but I hardly heard a word he said.

I was getting more and more brassed off with it all. Bremner never once told me to calm down. Being the type of player he was, he would never try to knock anything out of a player, especially if that man had the sort of aggression and competitive spirit that I was blessed with. Bremner seemed to believe you are what you are and he certainly encouraged me to be what I was. He may have winced a few times when I flew in to a tackle a bit too wholeheartedly, but he reckoned that I would learn through harsh experience when to cool it. Wilko got straight into my ribs from day one and I deeply resented it. He would tell me that Billy Bremner might have been a great player but he wasn't such a good manager. I was really indignant at that because Bremner was everything to me, though I can now see that my hero-worship for Bremner might have clouded my judgement of Wilko, who was such a completely different character. I saw myself being swept from the heady enjoyment of playing for a man who had done it all, won it all himself and who openly appreciated my talents to a sort of classroom, clipboard revolution masterminded by a guy who was never any great shakes as a player himself.

Howard would address the first-team squad surrounded by bizarre paraphernalia that gave him an air of authority more suited to the lecture room than the dressing-room. He would come in and plonk clipboards and sheaves of paper on the table. And, of course, there was the famous whiteboard – as opposed to blackboard – on which he would write a cryptic daily message for us to digest. It was always something simple like 'Be professional', or 'When the going gets tough, the tough get going'. Presumably, it was meant to be quietly inspirational. Frankly, we thought it was a joke. One day, when we were waiting for Howard to come in, I erased every other letter from his daily slogan. I can't remember what the words said, but I do recall how visibly upset he was that they had been violated. 'Who's done that?' he demanded to know. Nobody said a word and he continued his team talk in a bad mood. What I found particularly irritating was that Hennigan approached us on the training ground afterwards and told us it was a disgrace that we had done such a thing. It was an insult to Wilko, he insisted. All right, it was a schoolboyish thing for me to have done. But I would have had much more respect for Hennigan and Howard if they had laughed it off and dismissed it as just that. It was their slightly overbearing, officious attitude to us and to our football that made me – and others in the team – play up from time to time.

As the mood grew increasingly sombre that season, Vince Hilaire, who had joined us from Portsmouth, did his bit to lighten the leaden atmosphere one day. Vince was a fun-loving lad who enjoyed pulling the odd prank, and that was a necessary means of light relief as Wilko and Hennigan battled to impose their will upon us. One of Vince's most memorable capers came when we had all been assembled to receive the wrath of sergeant-major Mick, who was occasionally wheeled out by Wilko to give us a collective rollicking, though these blasts, designed to bring us to heel, did not necessarily succeed. It was at the time those noise-activated dancing flowers were all the rage. Remember them, the flowerpots that started to dance when activated by sound? Vince brought half a dozen of the things into the dressing-room at the training ground and placed them on a high shelf above where Mick always took up position to deliver his blistering words.

Mick walked in, puffed out his considerable chest, planted his feet firmly apart and proceeded to berate the assembled senior squad. As soon as he started to rant and rage it wasn't the players who danced to his tune but the flowerpots lined a metre above his head. Six of them swayed, rocked and rolled along the entire length of the shelf. The more amused we looked the more puzzled, frustrated and angry Mick grew, and the louder he shouted. And the louder he yelled the more frantically those plants gyrated. It was hilarious. How we didn't give the game away I'll never know, but Mick finished raving, red-faced with fury, turned and stormed out without seeing the dancing flowers above his head. To the best of my knowledge no one let him in on the secret of why his lecture was received with such mirth and lack of respect, and if he reads this, it will be the first he's known of it.

I suppose our subsequent success shows that the Wilko–Hennigan approach had its merits. Howard did, after all, go on to become one of the most powerful men in English football, as FA Technical Director. But, for the life of me, I didn't understand what he was talking about. His team talks were so boring! They went on for so long that, by the end, I had forgotten how they had started and had certainly missed the point. Before matches, he would play hell with me, accusing me of not concentrating on what he was saying. He was right. A battle of wills developed between us. It eventually tapered off into a kind of uneasy, unwritten stalemate, with Howard reluctantly accepting that he was never going to tame me. But that wasn't before we'd had a fair few run-ins and my attitude had driven him to distraction on several occasions.

One of those was during a match at Oldham towards the end of the 1989–90 promotion season when Howard substituted me in the second half. Now, as I've already stated, once I'm not involved on the pitch I'm simply not interested; it doesn't matter if it is an A-team outing or an England international. On this April day at Boundary Park, I was brought off the pitch – and, true to type, I switched off. I slumped into the back row of the dugout and, frankly, paid little attention to what was going on in front of me. In the dressing-room afterwards, Wilko made a point of telling the rest of the team how indifferent I'd been to their labours after he had replaced me with Chris Kamara. Obviously, he was determined to belittle me in front of my team-mates, presumably in the belief that it would shame me into a new enlightened attitude. But that was a mistaken belief. If the other lads thought any the worse of me, then they certainly didn't say so, and I wouldn't have worried if they had. I can understand how my attitude must have been like a red rag to a bull to the dictatorial Wilko. There is no denying he expended a lot of his time and energy trying to tame me and, to be fair, to improve my game. In the end, though, I think he recognised that the stubborn streak within me is far stronger than it is in the majority of players and that the more I am pushed the more I resist. And I readily concede that I must have pushed his patience to the limits on many an occasion.

At Christmas 1988, I had been out of the team for six weeks after being axed and there were reports in the newspapers that QPR and Leicester were following my situation. By now, the teenage teetotaller had become a fully paid-up member of the first teamers' lager-swilling club and I was hell-bent on drowning my sorrows over my relegation to the reserves by giving the players' fancy dress Christmas party my best shot. I went as a Russian Cossack wearing high boots that were much too tight. As the lager flowed, I became less and less aware of the discomfort, but when I got home late that night, I wrenched off the boots to discover a nasty gash down my big toe, which later became infected. I didn't dare admit my irresponsibility, so I made up some cock-and-bull story as to how I'd got the cut, and went into games having pain-killing injections.

It was so bad I had to wear size eight-and-a-half boots instead of my normal sevens; I still have a calcified lump on the side of my foot. But I played through the pain, something which I have always been prepared to do. My doggedness paid dividends when Wilko restored me to first-team duty at the end of January 1989 – after I had served a three-match suspension for a sending-off at Huddersfield in a Central League match. My troubled times continued until the end of the season, my frequent bookings increasing Wilko's exasperation. For my part, I was struggling to come to terms with the team's direct style and the nagging feeling that my way of playing wasn't to the manager's liking.

One of the strict rules was that you didn't go out in the 48 hours before a match. Early in April, we had a Sunday trip to Plymouth so a few of the lads decided to got out on the Thursday, figuring that it was okay as we had three days before the game. Unfortunately, one of the lads got involved in a massive with a copper in the city centre. He was arrested. There was trouble at Elland Road and the club went mad. Wilko had several of us in to his office and he told me he was fining me. I was at a low ebb; I'd been back in the Central League side for a few weeks and I was starting to wonder where it had all gone wrong. I simply wasn't prepared to accept a fine. Wilko was adamant that the punishment stood, so I took him on. I went to the Professional Footballers' Association, the players' union. My case was heard at an appeals board and the fine was overturned, which couldn't have pleased him. For me, it was a point of principle: I wasn't the guy who had been arrested! But my refusal to toe the line led to a period of even more seriously strained relations between us.

I had already had a lot of the stuffing knocked out of me that season. I had immense faith in my ability but I was beginning to doubt that Wilko shared that feeling. I was fed up with the football we were playing – when I was a part of it – and the battle over the fine. My spirits were lifted by my selection for the squad to contest the annual Under-21s international tournament in Toulon, but not sufficiently to eradicate my unease at the way things seemed to be going at Leeds. So I asked for a transfer.

promotion year

I went into the summer of 1989 in troubled mood. Most of the optimism and excitement that had consumed me 12 months earlier, after making my breakthrough into the senior side, had given way to a growing feeling of disenchantment. Instead of the surge I had anticipated for myself the previous season, there had been only frustration and I was concerned that Howard Wilkinson didn't rate me. I had never wanted to be anywhere other than Leeds United: to pull on the white shirt had been my ambition from the moment I started playing for Horse and Groom 10 years before. But now I had misgivings gnawing away at me. After turning the situation over and over in my mind I decided that, whatever your job, you need to enjoy your work to produce your best or you might as well move on. At that point, all I could think was that I must get to a club where I could play decent football for a man who would appreciate what I had to offer. So, two days after my last game of the season – another Central League outing – I went to see the manager and asked for a transfer.

Wilko talked to the board and it was rejected. So my dad advised me to put the transfer request in writing, which I did. Then Dad made an anonymous phone call to the *Yorkshire Evening Post*, saying I had asked for a move. That put the cat among the pigeons. The newspaper reported the story and the club had to respond, admitting they had turned down my request. The report included references to how highly Howard Wilkinson rated me and how he didn't want me to leave. It also claimed that I had a valuation of £850,000! I couldn't believe it.

I feel I owe it to myself to claim that though I have always been blessed with bucket-loads of self-confidence on a football pitch, that isn't the same thing as having a big ego. If anybody I've played with or against said different, I'd say he'd got the wrong man. So when I read that Leeds and Wilko had put such a valuation on me – and £850,000 was a lot of money in 1989 – I was surprised and flattered. Bradford, QPR, West Brom, Hull City and Chelsea were said to be interested in me and there was talk of mighty Liverpool having had a £500,000 bid turned down. But after Wilko, in not quite so many words, told me he really valued my presence in the team, I shook the muddled thinking from my brain and refocused on the job of becoming a Leeds regular.

Just before I had asked for the move, Dad had written his postscript to my season. It didn't make good reading. 'Judging by the way David shot to prominence last season, this season has been a bit of a let-down.' I wasn't in any position to disagree with his assessment, but I had no regrets about putting in the transfer request. If nothing else, it had cleared the air a little between me and the manager. I went on to Toulon with the Under-21s in a much better frame of mind, which was reflected in my personal success in the tournament. Though England disappointingly lost a third/fourth place play-off to the United States, I went home delighted to have been voted third-best player in the whole event.

It was an eventful close season at Elland Road. Wilko had begun putting into action the team-building strategy that was to prove so triumphant by the following May, when he led Leeds out of the Second Division wilderness where the club had wallowed for eight years. That summer, my mate and midfield partner John Sheridan was transferred to Nottingham Forest. First teamers Mark Aizlewood and David Rennie followed him out of the door. Wilkinson, who had pulled one masterstroke the previous season when he signed Gordon Strachan from Manchester United, now produced another rabbit out of his hat. He signed six players: John Hendrie, John McLelland, Mel Sterland, Mickey Thomas, Jim Beglin – and Vinnie Jones, the hard man of Wimbledon's Crazy Gang. The press and public threw up their hands in horror. What on earth was Wilkinson thinking off? How could he risk blackening the name of a famous club by bringing in a player of such notoriety? Vinnie's arrival, the media claimed, was an admission that Leeds intended to muscle their way back into the First Division. I admit that I had my doubts, too. I think it's safe for me to claim I had proved by then that I was no shrinking violet on a soccer pitch. But Vinnie Jones! Was this really necessary?

The answer proved to be a resounding yes. Vinnie's stay at the club was a brief one of 14 months, but in that period he played a vital part in the promotion push that saw us crowned Second Division champions. And he and I became the best of mates, as well as midfield workhorses, in the most direct-style side I have played in. Vinnie really got stuck in that season and did everything Wilko could possibly have wanted of him, but I'm sure he would readily agree with me when I say we were both desperately relieved to hear the final whistle blow on the last match of that season. Throughout the campaign, he and I spent the majority of our time watching the ball sail over our heads and ploughing from box to box to pick up knock-downs from our front men. Vinnie and I had to keep up a relentless pace week in, week out and I don't mind admitting I was knackered by the end of the season. It probably wasn't so hard on Vinnie because he had been doing the same sort of thing with Wimbledon for years. If you play in that style, the opposition get lured into doing the same and it comes down to the survival of the fittest.

Though I had been reassured by Wilko that my presence was required, there was no getting away from the fact that I wasn't on his wavelength. Training became more and more boring, with I felt too much concentration on practising free kicks. Howard constantly told us that dead-ball situations led to goals. It struck me as route one mentality and it did my head in. Around that time, having been one of the most dedicated trainers I knew I became one of the worst, and it has stayed that way ever since. I can appreciate working hard on particular areas if you get the benefit, but we used to put in countless hours defending against free kicks and corners, presumably because we were conceding more goals from them in matches than at any time in my career. It all seemed pointless to me and, typically, I didn't disguise the feeling. I was never involved in taking free kicks, anyway, so being forced to participate in the mind-numbing exercises on the training ground was just a bind as far as I was concerned, though it may have been more useful for the others.

It got to the stage where, in open displays of frustration and disapproval, I would aimlessly blast balls all over the pitch, often hitting players – and Mick Hennigan, for good measure. Finally, Wilko brought the situation to an end when he walked up to me one day and presented me with a ball, on which he had written 'Batty's Ball'.

'Go to a quiet part of the ground and amuse yourself until we've finished,' he told me. 'I'll call you over when I'm ready.' So there I was, with my very own private training ball, on a separate pitch at the Fullerton Park training ground, doing what I wanted for up to 90 minutes at a time. By then, I think Wilko had mellowed a little towards me, though probably more out of a sense of resignation than respect. I'd like to say I had been inspired by Wilko's endless efforts to get through to me and, indeed, by the example set by Gordon Strachan, whose enthusiasm in training was unbelievable, but I wasn't. As always, I did it my way.

Strach, who was 30 when he joined us, was the star during that promotion campaign. Vinnie and I were the muscle men, the non-stop runners whose ceaseless grafting was a motivating force in itself. But Strach, in our eyes, was the big-name player in our midst, the man who had already done everything in his glory years under Alex Ferguson at Aberdeen and Manchester United.

Strach was the one man who had a go at me for my attitude on the training pitch. And, with unfailing consistency, I'm afraid my response was to tell him where to get off, even though I did have the greatest respect for him. Strangely, I don't recall any of the coaching staff getting on my back once I had begun to rebel at training. Perhaps, by then, everyone, from Wilko down, realised that they were banging their heads against a brick wall trying to make Batty toe the line. I developed an attitude that if I trained too hard on a Friday, I wasn't going to have enough in the tank on Saturday. It got to the point where it was pointless my turning up on Fridays, an attitude that still prevailed when I was at Blackburn and Newcastle. Even worse, I started coasting all week before coming almost to a dead stop on Friday, when all I did was wander aimlessly around the training ground while everyone else ran their socks off. After all my intensive effort as a teenager I had reached a stage where I switched off from the endless grind of the training ground. But my saving grace was an innate belief that I was naturally fitter than all the rest. Come match day, I buzzed around the pitch. Nobody could ever point the finger at me when the chips were down.

The rebellious streak was always a feature of my make-up. It is a form of stubborn resistance to authority that once manifested itself in a manner which, to this day, I have never revealed to a living soul, let alone my dad who, unwittingly, was the cause of the outrageous act I'm about to describe. Dad sat, of course, in the same seat in the stand at Elland Road week in, week out, season in, season out. During that promotion season he was, as ever, my fiercest critic. Throughout a match, I would constantly look in his direction as if hypnotised by his presence. After all, he had been there for me, walking the touchline, throughout my childhood and my teenage years. Now that I was a fully integrated member of the Leeds first team, he was just as much a presence at matches as he had always been. He had a habit of catching my eye and making one of two gestures to indicate his opinion of my performance, either a two-thumbs-up sign to show I was doing okay, or an exaggerated pumping of the air with both hands to urge me to greater effort.

On this fateful occasion, against Stoke City in January 1990, I glanced his way and got the 'step it up, you can do better' signal. For some inexplicable reason I flipped. I remember thinking: 'Right, I'll bloody well show you.' There had been many an occasion when I'd gone home after being named Man of the Match and Dad had said he thought I'd been rubbish. It was as if he daren't praise me to my face for fear of displaying some sort of paternal weakness. I don't know if the years of toil and a perceived lack of appreciation had created some sort of pressure point within my head, but I decided to give him something to get really worked up about. I deliberately gave away a penalty!

I can recall staring at Dad, his arms waving frantically, and muttering: 'Sit down, you silly sod. I'll show how fed up with you I am.' Then, fully aware of the consequences, I deliberately upended one of the Stoke players inside the penalty area. Something inside me just snapped. I dumped this lad on his backside, the ref pointed to the spot and I turned to my dad and made a gesture of defiance at him. I knew exactly what I was doing. It was a scandalous act of bloody-minded anger. Luckily for me, our goalkeeper Mervyn Day saved the spot-kick and we won 2–0.

It was a moment of madness, a red-mist thing that I was unable to resist. I don't know how many players suffer from similar momentary acts of insanity, or whether they would ever admit it if they do, but I will describe the one other incident for which I am truly sorry. It happened the same season, an indicator, perhaps, of the mixed-up state I had got myself into in that period of my career. We were playing Oldham Athletic and I was being shadowed by their midfielder, Nick Henry, who was obviously under instructions from manager Joe Royle not to let me out of his sight for a split second. Henry, a good, honest player, stuck to me like glue and, heaven alone knows why, I took violent retribution. It isn't as if I can claim he was kicking me or giving me verbals. All I know is that he was getting on my nerves and I committed an act for which I am genuinely ashamed.

Oldham were awarded a penalty and I was standing on the 18-yard line as their player prepared to take the kick. Inevitably, Henry was breathing down my ear. Just as with the conceded-penalty incident against Stoke, I snapped – and smashed my elbow into the defenceless Henry's face. Again, though a spur-of-the-moment reaction to my mood, it was a coldly premeditated offence for I can remember thinking, as Roger Palmer ran up to take the penalty, that the referee's attention would be focused on him and I wouldn't be seen carrying out my unprovoked assault on Henry. For the remainder of the match,

Henry, obviously outraged and with a bloodied nose, was hell-bent on revenge. I managed to keep him at bay but I deserved nothing less than a good kicking in return. It was the type of offence of which I am fiercely critical in others.

It is of no consolation to Nick Henry that I had never done anything like that before, nor have I since. Don't get me wrong, I'm no saint on the pitch. You can't play where I do, where the ball has to be won, and not be prepared to mix it with the best of them. But there is a huge difference between two guys having a tit-for-tat tussle and what I did that day. I never apologised to Nick Henry. From that day to this, probably out of guilt, I have followed his career, noting that he moved on to play for Sheffield United and Tranmere.

It really is amazing what can happen, undetected, on a football pitch, in front of many thousands of people. The most uncomfortable experience – literally – that I ever had was in a match at Wolves at the end of March, a few weeks before we clinched the Second Division champion-ship. Everything was normal as kick-off approached. After a few minutes' warm-up we were leaving the dressing-room. I had no inkling of the discomfort that was about to strike and that would lead to the most desperate 20 minutes I have ever experienced on the pitch. As we started the walk down the tunnel at Molineux I was suddenly gripped by tell-tale griping pains in my stomach. The timing was unbelievable: two minutes earlier and I would have been okay. It would have been a bit of a rush, but I could have sought instant relief and rejoined my team-mates for the walk on to the pitch. But here I was, walking out in front of 22,500 fans, knowing that if I relaxed for a moment I would be in big trouble!

Common sense told me I should turn round, mutter my excuses and rush back to the dressing-room. As so often happens in such delicate situations, you don't do the right thing. I walked on to the pitch and the match kicked off. From the first moment I knew with absolute certainty that if I let my muscles relax I wouldn't be able to control the consequences. My mind was split between my desperate need to get to the toilet and trying to prevent a disaster in front of all those people. I was running around in torment, going for headers and tackles and tensing myself every time, not against the shudder of a collision but in an increasingly frantic attempt to stave off the inevitable. Then, I delivered a weak back pass from which Wolves' centre-forward Andy Mutch scored what was to be the only goal of the match. I was in a right old state by this time. My condition was playing havoc with my concentration on what was going on around me and I remember thinking: 'I can't carry on like this. I'm simply going to have to relax.' I did, with fatal results. The bottom fell out of my game – literally.

The instant relief I felt at having been released from my torment was more than superseded by the excrucia-tion of sheer embarrassment. I didn't say a word to anyone, not to any of my team-mates nor to the referee. I just ran off the pitch, pathetically trying to ignore the distressing state of my undergarments and give the appearance of a man with any other problem than the wretched one I was stuck with. I started to rub my eye as if to indicate that I might be having difficulty with a contact lens, even though I don't wear them.

Picture the scene. I suddenly turned away from the action and, with 21 players, a ref, two linesmen and more than 22,000 people watching, ran – as best I could – towards the tunnel. All I could think was: 'I'm not letting any of these people know I've shit myself!'

Confusion reigned, of course, on our bench where manager Howard Wilkinson, his coaching staff and the substitutes were as nonplussed as everybody else in the stadium. Only I knew the grim truth as I beat a lonely path for the sanctuary of the tunnel. Wilko screamed at the physio, Alan Sutton: 'Where the hell's he going? Get after him.' Sutty caught up with me as I stumbled up the tunnel, the whole of Molineux looking on. 'What's up? What's up?' he hissed at me. 'I've shit myself' was my stark reply. Even as I reached the welcome anonymity of the changing-room my torment wasn't over. The door was locked. I was stunned and, at this point, in despair. I located the elderly groundsman, who began to fumble through his massive bunch of keys. There must have been a key for every door in the stadium. I was in an increasing state of desperation, as he tried one after another in an unsuccessful attempt to open the changing room. Finally, he let me into the referee's room and there I made the best of a bad job. I cleaned myself up as best I could and got back out on the pitch, where the fans and the players remained unaware of my plight.

I'm not sure how many minutes I was away from the action, but I vividly recall sitting on the toilet contemplating what on earth everybody out there must have been thinking had gone wrong. I also remember trainer Mick Hennigan hammering on the door and yelling,

'Come on! How long are you going to be? We need you on the pitch.'

I returned to the action – and a lot of puzzled expressions from my team-mates – and played out the rest of the half in some discomfort, but nothing like the distress I'd been in before making my hasty exit. Sadly, neither I nor anybody else could do anything to redress the balance of that one-goal deficit and we lost the match.

That wasn't the only embarrassing situation I found myself in that season. An accident of a different sort left me red-faced again. As the campaign was hotting up, team-mate Brendan Ormsby and I decided to have a night out and have a few beers. We had left a city-centre pub and bought a kebab and were in high spirits as we made our way towards a nightclub. Unfortunately, we never made it. We were walking over a section in the pavement covered by reinforced glass panels of the type that usually indicate a shop cellar beneath. In the dark, I didn't notice that one of them was missing – and I stepped into the hole and got stuck.

Talk about wishing you were somewhere else, preferably safe at home tucked up in your own bed! There I was, the new boy in the Leeds team and, by now, a well-known face in the city, stuck up to my knee and the object of much amusement from passers-by and my mate Brendan. The more I struggled and squirmed to free my leg, the more I realised it wasn't going to budge. So, too, did Brendan, who took the dramatic, but unavoidable, step of calling the fire brigade. By the time they arrived, I definitely wasn't seeing the funny side. Not least of my concerns was what the gaffer would say when this hit the local papers. Quite a sizeable crowd gathered, under the flashing lights of the fire engine, to watch the firemen expertly stretch the frame of the square, the only way they could extricate my leg. Word quickly spread through the dressing-room that I had been legless. Of course, literally, I had been. And it did, inevitably, hit the papers. As far as I recall, though, it was one incident for which Wilko never did call me in.

vinnie and me

The 1989–90 season was certainly eventful. Though it ended in triumph, with us booking our return to the big time of the First Division, my elation was tempered by a frustrating feeling of weariness that consumed me towards the end of the campaign. It was, I'm sure, a result of physical tiredness following the relentless demands placed upon me, coupled with a niggling sense that – however successful Howard Wilkinson's approach proved to be – this wasn't the type of football I was happy to be playing. I know that one of the game's most-quoted sayings is: 'It's all about results.' And I know that it's hard to argue with the record-books. But it remains the case that the record-books don't tell the whole story behind the statistics.

Still, apart from the title success, there were other compensations. One of the greatest blokes I had the pleasure of playing with was Vinnie Jones. We got on so well that he used to go round to Mum and Dad's house for his tea even when I wasn't in. Another was the negotiation of my first major contract at the club. For that, I have to thank both my dad – once again – and also Vinnie, who selflessly divulged details of his own pay deal, even though it probably left him ruefully reflecting that, sometimes, you can take friendship too far! I must also admit, again with the benefit of hindsight, that Wilko obviously would never have sanctioned the deal I struck with the club if he didn't truly believe I was worth every penny.

The build-up to those contract talks, in October 1989, was fascinating. I had never fancied the idea of having an agent. In fact, I never have had one. I much prefer to refer to Hayden Evans, the man who eventually took charge of my financial interests, as my adviser, and I also regard him as a friend. Hayden, who heads a Leeds-based financial-advisory company, HN Sports, is a lifelong Leeds fan. He and his partner, Drew Tiffany, follow the team home and away, including every trip into Europe. I first got to know him during Leeds's first season back in the First Division and slowly came to accept that he was a straight dealer who commanded the trust of many people in power at Elland Road, including Howard Wilkinson. Hayden gave me a lot of financial advice, though he didn't act for me in contract talks until my move from Blackburn to Newcastle six years later.

What I like about Hayden is that he doesn't demand a percentage of the deal he strikes on your behalf, preferring to charge a rate for the time he spends on your case. It is the 'Mr Ten Per Cent' image of the modern football agent that always filled me with suspicion and even disgust. Probably my attitude was nurtured in my solid, working-class background, where straight talking was the order of the day and the values of a strong, loving family unit were so important. As a young footballer, I could think of agents only as sharp-suited, smooth-tongued characters who were definitely not to be trusted to act in my best interests. Come to think of it, my view of them hasn't changed. So I put my faith in my dad. The bottom line is I trusted Dad more than anyone, even if he did continue to drive me to distraction by endlessly finding fault with my game.

Previously, as I've said, whenever I had received a pay increase it had more or less been a *fait accompli*. The club told me what I would be getting and I could like it or lump it. Now, though, as a first-team player for nearly 12 months, it was time to get down to the nitty-gritty and try to achieve something like parity with the seniors in the squad. The build-up to the negotiations couldn't have been smoother, with Leeds making a solidly impressive start to the campaign, albeit after a 5–2 walloping at Newcastle on the opening day of the season, during which I got booked. That setback was immediately followed by a home win over Middlesbrough, when I got the Man of the Match award and an accolade from Wilko. With a winning bonus of £275 and £100 appearance money, on top of my basic pay of £254, I raked in £629 and was well pleased with that.

To be fair, in view of some of the things I've written about life under Wilko, team spirit was excellent in those early weeks of the season; back, I suppose, to the 'results mean everything' cliché. We shook off the effect of that first-day defeat at St James' Park to go on a run which had carried Leeds into second place in the table by the time my dad and I went to see Wilko about a new deal. I had also played alongside the likes of Paul Merson and Steve Bull in the Under-21s side which whipped Poland 3–1, away, early in October. That can't have done my negotiating position any harm. Mind you, if Wilko had read what my dad wrote about my performance in my last appearance before going in for those preliminary talks, I probably wouldn't have got another penny. It was the perfect example of Dad's relentless insistence on improvement and must be the biggest savaging I've ever had in print. This is what he wrote after Leeds's 1–0 home win against Wolves on 21 October 1989: 'David was a disappointment against a poor Wolves midfield. He wasn't involved enough. He doesn't think enough of himself to be the centre of most of the Leeds football. He wasn't sharp enough off the mark, which is down to concentration, plus speed of mind and body. When he did get to the ball first, he didn't take it cleanly. Most midfield players score goals. David doesn't and he doesn't look as though he ever will, the reason being he has never got down to the task and worked at it 100 per cent. David is expecting a big wage rise before the end of his current contract but, if he lets the manager take the play away from him as he allows his team-mates to, then he is in for a big disappointment. Another thing David should get to grips with is opponents running with the ball. Billy Bremner used to tell David to be arrogant during a game. On odd occasions he is. But, mostly, not. It is time he started thinking he is God's gift to football – and acting accordingly.' And he added the postscript: 'David could quite easily have been substituted, in my mind.'

Phew! What a panning. With friends like you, Dad, who needs enemies? It's probably a good job I didn't read that at the time. If I had, I would most probably have told Dad where to get off, knowing what a self-willed little sod I was, and gone right ahead and conducted my wage talks on my own. But what a mistake that would have turned out to be. Dad went in to bat for me and, though I realise now he must have been pretty nervous, he did a great job, especially when you consider he was confronted by the formidable duo of the schoolmasterly Wilko and the big, imposing figure of Leeds's former general manager Bill Fotherby.

The first meeting was between Dad, Wilko and me. I don't recall much about it, because it was mainly a getting-to-know-you exercise for Wilko. He had been asking me about my father and what he did for a living. I remember telling Dad this one evening and him saying: 'You'll have told him I'm a dustman. But I'll show him I can negotiate a contract when I go in there.' That's the spirit! With Dad on my team, how could I go wrong? Dad and I did our homework. I asked Vinnie Jones, by now a solid mate and a frequent dinner guest at our house, if he was willing to tell me what he earned. Good as gold, he gave me the details. Armed with that valuable information, Dad went in to cross swords with the team manager and the man who pulled the purse strings at Elland Road. I drove Dad to the ground two days after our initial meeting with Wilko, dropping him off in the car park outside the main entrance. We had decided it was best to let Dad confront the Big Two on his own. What Dad didn't know was that I had a secret plan, which would ensure I wasn't entirely absent from the proceedings.

Work was in progress to alter all of the offices at the club. I was familiar with the layout and knew that partitions were in place while the refurbishments went on. So, once Dad was through the door and ensconced with Wilko and Fotherby, I nipped in and positioned myself outside the temporary partition guarding Fotherby's office, ear pressed to the flimsy wall. I heard everything.

'Have a whisky, Mr Batty,' I heard Fotherby say as the buttering-up process began. Dad accepted, but he was nobody's patsy. I stood there, straining to catch every word and feeling proud of Dad for having the balls to take on these big-timers. He was, after all, a corporation bin-man and not remotely trained for this type of challenge. Nevertheless, Dad was magnificent: talk about staying cool under fire. Fotherby was saying: 'What we'd like to do, Mr Batty, is put some money in a pension fund for David.' Dad replied: 'I don't want a pension fund for him. I want a bloody good wage deal!' Nice one, Dad, I was thinking.

It reminded me of a good-guy, bad-guy routine; the two of them sounded as if they were at odds over what was the best thing to do. Fotherby was saying something like: 'Now, Howard, you're on about paying David a certain amount, but next week you might be England manager. Then you're out of the equation and we have to pick up the pieces of the deal here at the club.' Dad sat tight for a while, then – armed, of course, with the details of the contract Leeds had given my fellow midfielder Vinnie a few months earlier – restated our demands. If I remember rightly, he politely declined another Scotch before standing up and saying: 'Well, seeing as how you are arguing among yourselves, I'll leave you to sort things out. As soon as you have, please let me know and we can talk again.' But he didn't leave the room before telling them: 'My lad is the best player you've got.' Dad may have continued to knock me in the pages of his books, but he wasn't going to let private criticism interfere with his paternal loyalty.

I had to move as smartly as I did on the pitch to nip back to the car and sit, innocently, waiting for Dad to return and tell me all about it. Eventually, I let him in on my eavesdropping secret. I think he was more amused at my cheek than annoyed by it; he certainly knew me well enough not to be surprised by what I'd done.

That meeting took place on 27 October. Four days later, on 31 October, Dad was summoned once more into the presence of Wilko and Fotherby where he agreed a contract on my behalf – which was slightly better than the one Vinnie had been given. Poor Vinnie was a bit miffed, to say the least, when I told him the outcome of the talks. He thought he was on top wages at the club. If he was right, I had become the biggest earner at Elland Road, six weeks short of my 21st birthday. I guess Wilko really must have rated me!

The new contract was a big boost to my ego and that reflected in my performances in the weeks following the signing of the deal. That November, I was named Young Eagle of the Month, a national award, and received glowing tributes from then England manager Bobby Robson. But if Wilko had got to know about the capers Vinnie Jones and I got involved in, he would have clipped my wings so fast I'd have been cut down from Eagle to pigeon in double-quick time.

To be fair to Vinnie, he never held my new-found wealth against me. In fact, after I bought my first house on the strength of my financial independence, in the Shadwell area of the city, Vinnie bought one a few hundred yards away. Not a good idea! His proximity to me brought us even closer socially. The two of us had hit it off from the start and, looking back, I must say I was probably fortunate not to land myself in more trouble than I actually did because of my friendship with Vinnie. He came to us with a reputation for being one of the hardest, wildest men in English football. And when he left to join his former Wimbledon manager Dave Bassett at Sheffield United, he hadn't done anything to dilute that image!

One of the occasions that Wilko must have wondered if he'd done the right thing in bringing in Vinnie was when the Jones boy decided to take over the running of the bar in a Leeds nightclub. There were a few of us in the place in the early hours. For some reason, the barman disappeared for several minutes, probably simply to go to the toilet or make a phone call. Vinnie quickly became impatient. He wasn't prepared to wait – so he vaulted over the bar and started pulling pints of lager for the lads. When the barman returned to find his briefly vacated job had been filled, there was a helluva fuss. The manager was brought in and he politely, but firmly, asked us to leave the premises. He also got in touch with Howard Wilkinson the next day. Wilko took the matter very seriously indeed. He had Vinnie into his office and told him in no uncertain terms that he would be out of the club if there was a repetition of such behaviour.

It's a miracle Vinnie survived for the rest of the season, judging by some of the capers he got up to. He telephoned me late one night to tell me, with obvious pride, how he'd returned home from the chip shop that evening to find a gang of young hoodlums trying to break into his sponsored BMW. He told me that he'd got hold of one of these tearaways and given him a good hiding. The rest, as you can imagine, had fled into the night. Somehow Vinnie managed to keep the incident quiet from the manager, but he was happy to let me know he had upheld the Englishman's right to protect his property.

Subsequently I had good reason to feel every sympathy for the kid, who presumably would never have gone near that BMW had he known it belonged to Vinnie Jones. In one of the zaniest – and, at the time, most terrifying – stunts I've been the victim of, Vinnie left me scared stiff, shaken, amused and flabbergasted all at once. It was the summer of 1990 and I was living in my house in Shadwell. My mate John Sheridan, by then a Nottingham Forest player, and I had been for a night out and had returned to my place for some kip. In those early days of home ownership, I didn't bother locking my front door. The events of that night taught me a harsh lesson in domestic security.

Shez and I got back after quite a few lagers and collapsed into bed, John flat out in the spare room and me sleeping peacefully in mine. But my sleep was suddenly and rudely interrupted when something hit me. I sprang up in the dark, and as my weary eyes slowly adjusted, I saw the offending object on my bed. I stared again through the gloom, disbelievingly. It was a dustbin lid! I switched my attention to the open bedroom door where, to my growing concern, I made out the shape of a man, dressed, it seemed, in a tracksuit, and peeping around the door. My fear gave way to confusion once I realised that John had been wearing a tracksuit that evening. 'Bloody hell,' I was thinking to myself. 'The man's a sleepwalker' – just like I had been throughout my childhood and teenage years – 'and nobody's ever mentioned it.' Then I thought: 'Hell, he's got dressed, gone outside and got the bloody dustbin lid to boot! What on earth is he doing?'

These thoughts raced through my addled mind in the space of a few seconds, during which time I started to panic and wonder what was my best course of action. I remember thinking it might be best to turn on the light and wake him from his sleepwalk when suddenly, frighteningly, the figure emerged from behind the door, dashed across the room and leapt on top of me. I was imprisoned under the bedclothes and he pinned me with his knees before starting to yell wildly like some pumped-up SAS soldier while raining blows down on me. I was terrified. This was a big, strong man. Immediately I realised it wasn't John. At the same time, I figured I might never see John again. At best I was going to be robbed and battered; at worst I might be murdered in my own bed. Just as I was preparing for the very worst, the big, shadowy figure jumped off me and switched on the light. Standing there, shaking with laughter, was Vinnie Jones! I was both relieved and furious. But Vinnie wasn't content with terrorising me; he stalked into the spare room, where John's lager-induced sleep hadn't been disturbed by the mayhem, and proceeded to give him the same treatment. I must admit that, by then, I had got over my shock and took mischievous delight in poor Shez's panic and confusion.

Then, like the Scarlet Pimpernel, Vinnie was off into

the night. But he wasn't content to go quietly. From his point of view – and ours, to be honest – the 'entertainment' was only just beginning. Vinnie was in his Mini that night. We learned later that he'd been visiting a girl he was seeing at the time who lived not far from my place. Shez and I, still dazed from our experience, had gone to the bedroom window to watch him leave. We weren't expecting any more bizarre scenes, but we certainly got them. It was about 2 a.m. and there was enough moonlight to see across my open-plan garden, unprotected by fences or even hedges. The house was situated in a quiet cul-de-sac. Only it wasn't quiet that night! Having launched his lightning raid on his mates, Vinnie jumped into the Mini and wheel-skidded it across the lawn. Then he fairly screamed off down the road and we could hear him really giving it some stick around the estate. Next, we heard another handbrake skid. We looked at each other and, though we didn't say a word, our expressions must have told each other what we were both thinking: 'Bloody hell – he's coming back!' And he was. We shot back to the window in time to see the Mini roaring down the road again, as if it were being driven by a kamikaze pilot. He rocketed back across my garden, taking out my little conifer tree, did another handbrake skid and was off into the night for the final time – but not before detouring across a few of the neighbours' gardens and flattening a chain-link fence guarding someone's drive.

Although the whole stunt lasted only a few minutes, it seemed like a never-ending nightmare. One of the weirdest aspects of it is that I don't recall seeing lights going on in the surrounding houses, so presumably no one knew anything about it until they got up the next morning. Perhaps they thought we'd been hit by a whirlwind. We had, and it went by the name of Vinnie Jones. Shez and I stood there for a while, staring at each other in a mutual state of shock. I rubbed my eyes and looked again. My conifer was bent and Vinnie's car number plate was on the grass. Yes, it really had all happened! And I got a further shock the following day when Vinne told me we'd got off lightly. He had tried to lift the whole dustbin, but was unable to do so because I had got into the habit of putting a big rock in it to prevent it from blowing over in high winds. He admitted his plan had been to tip the binful of rubbish over my bed!

Still, I wasn't surprised at anything Vinnie got up to by then. After all, I was the man he entrusted to take a razor to his head. Remember when Vinnie started sporting his famous haircut, shaved to the bone at the sides and with a V at the back? Well, I started it. Vinnie and I roomed together on away trips and nothing should have amazed me, but I was taken aback when he called to me from the bathroom of our London hotel, where he was soaking in the bathtub: 'Come in here, Batts. I want you to shave my head.' It was October 1989, a Friday evening before our match at Upton Park against West Ham. I went in and looked around for a razor. 'Just use that plastic Bic,' said Vinnie casually. So, after giving Vinnie every opportunity to change his mind, I shaved all his hair off, right down to the scalp. Now, I'm no Nicky Clarke or Vidal Sassoon: in fact, if you'd seen the state of Vinnie's head by the time I'd finished my handiwork, you would have thought he'd been savaged

Aged 18 months at the beach.

My brother John has his hand on the car, but bikes were to be our main interest.

Aged 10 I'm wearing a West Ham shirt but Leeds was always going to be the team I wanted to play for.

With my Player of the Year award from Tingley Athletic, aged 11. Dad was already charting my progress in his diary and was to remain my biggest critic.

The short skinny one second from the right in the team was me, aged 16. I was a late developer, but always highly competitive.

In my early days I was an enthusiastic trainer, but later this was to change.

Straight after promotion to the top division, I was faced with a tough personal battle against Manchester United's Paul Ince. It was the sort of challenge I relished.

Vinnie Jones and I go in hard for the ball in a game against Luton. His presence had helped inspire us to promotion, as well as livening up things around Leeds.

The Batty Golden Goal Collection

Mirror Syndication

Boxing Day 1987, I score my first league goal against Manchester City.

Manchester City are on the receiving end again in September 1991 as I double my goal tally.

Andrew Varley

Possibly my best goal, in February 1992, against Notts County. When you score as few as I do, you might as well make them something special!

Celebrating with Les Ferdinand after scoring a goal in April 1996 against my old club Blackburn.

Empics

Celebrating again, this time after scoring the winning goal against Aston Villa in February 1998 – my last league goal to date.

Leeds are champions in 1992, thanks in part to the late arrival of Eric Cantona, probably the best player I have ever worked with.

The battle of Britain. Leeds and Rangers take on each other in the second round of the European Cup in 1992, but sadly we were to progress no further.

Club action for Blackburn against Charlton in 1994. Things got even more lively off the pitch.

Popperfoto

Empics

Tim Sherwood steps in to separate me and Graeme Le Saux after our notorious confrontation by the touchline in our Champions League game against Spartak Moscow in November 1995.

My debut for Newcastle in March 1996 came in a crucial Championship crunch tie against Manchester United. The game and the Championship went to the Reds.

I needed to have stitches in my eye after a clash with Metz's Brazilian player Isaias during our UEFA Cup tie in November 1996.

by Sweeney Todd. There was blood everywhere. Not that Vinnie was complaining; in fact, he was most grateful for my efforts. He looked a heck of a sight when, patched up as best he could, he accompanied me downstairs to join the squad for the evening meal. All the lads were giving him stick and the looks on the faces of Howard Wilkinson and the staff were something to behold. Heaven alone knows what Wilko must have been thinking, but he kept his thoughts to himself and said nothing to Vinnie.

Perhaps it was as well, for, next day, we beat West Ham 1–0 – and Vinnie scored the goal that took us to third place in the Second Division table. Mind you, we were hammered by the London press, and I can't say I blame them. In those days a goalkeeper was allowed to pick up back passes, and boy, did we use that to our advantage. As soon as the goal went in, the instruction came from the bench to shut up shop and protect the lead. To make the ensuing spectacle even worse, the goal had come early in the game so we condemned the crowd to a long, tortuous afternoon. We did exactly what Wilko ordered. It was the most negative performance I think I've ever been involved in. It certainly wasn't in any way enjoyable for me. The tactics were outrageous, really. Now, of course, the game is much faster and more open because they have scrapped the rule which allowed you to pass back to the keeper and him to pick up the ball, and not before time.

Vinnie continued to be a controversial figure within the dressing-room – as well as in the press – right up to our moment of triumph that season. During the run-in to the title success, my form had slumped and I was in and out of the team. Having been axed after defeat at Oldham early in April, I had to watch from the subs' bench as we hammered Sheffield United 4–0 in a top-of-the-table clash at Elland Road. I remained a sub for the last three matches, making it a personal anticlimax when we clinched the championship. But I got on the pitch in all three matches, replacing Chris Kamara against Brighton and substituting for Vinnie against Leicester and Bournemouth. It was as we trooped into the dressing-room after the 2–1 win over Leicester in the second-last match of the season that Vinnie told the lads: 'We've done it! The other results have gone for us. It's all over.' As you can imagine, everyone was ecstatic. People were crying tears of joy. After years in the Second Division wilderness, once-mighty Leeds United were back where they belonged, in Division One. But hold on. Just as the celebrations were reaching fever pitch, Alan Sutton, the physiotherapist, came in to say that promotion contenders Newcastle had got a draw with a late goal and that meant we still had to go to Bournemouth to clinch the big step up. Everyone was furious with Vinnie, but I swear he had a twinkle in his eye. It wasn't only opponents whom he liked to wind up.

One week later, we travelled to the south coast and beat Bournemouth 1–0. There were no arguments then about the outcome of the title race. We were champions and Vinnie Jones and I had done more than our share of sheer hard graft. There is no denying that Howard Wilkinson had produced a tactical coup that season. Vinnie was sold to Sheffield United for £700,000 a few weeks into the following season so he didn't get the chance to savour our return to the top flight. He went with my sincere best wishes. Without a shadow of doubt, Vinnie is one of the most likeable characters I have met in the game. We were often partners in crime but he deflected some of Wilkinson's attention from me during his one full season at Elland Road.

As the reader will realise, I had many a skirmish with Wilko. But one escapade of mine he was unaware of – and which I'm sure he would have been horrified by – was my close-season stint working on the dustbins, after we won promotion. Mind you, Leeds City Corporation would have been as appalled as Wilko had they found out that the rising star of Leeds United was humping refuse in the summer of 1990. I co-opted my mates from my apprentice days, Vinnie Brockie and Dave Bentley, as additional unpaid volunteers for the task of emptying the Leeds public's dustbins. Those early days of summer were happy ones for us all: Vinnie and Dave had come to stay at my house, both of them in the throes of making the enforced transition from being professional footballers to having to rejoin the 'real' world. They were genuinely pleased for me and the three of us set out to have a few drinks and a lot of laughs. But I'm not sure Vinnie and Dave were expecting to spend part of their summer break as Dad's secret refuse-collecting army.

It was my idea, not my dad's. I remembered that he had once remarked that it would do all footballers good to have a go on the bins and find out just how hard working life is. On the spur of the moment I decided to take up his suggestion. I reasoned it would be a laugh, as well as a way of keeping fit, to help out Dad on his rounds. I also knew just how hard Dad worked and figured that he would be grateful for some help. Typically, I didn't stop to consider the implications if I was rumbled. Clearly, Leeds United wouldn't be best pleased if I was ruled out of action because I'd dropped a dustbin on my foot, nor would Leeds Corporation's legal department have taken a lenient view if some maverick footballer had been involved in an accident while working unofficially for their refuse collection department. So, sublimely uncluttered by such thoughts, Vinnie, Dave and I turned up one day to lend a hand.

The one concession I made to the illegality of my new-found role was to wear a baseball cap, tugged down well over my eyes, while collecting people's bins. Nevertheless, one bloke came out of his house and said to my dad: 'That young fella's the spitting image of David Batty.' But my identity was never revealed over several days of back-breaking work. Actually, Dave Bentley was a bit of a lazy type and used to jack it in early. But Vinnie had a great work ethic and got stuck in, along with me. Dad would implore me to take care when crossing a road with a bin on my back. He said: 'For God's sake, don't get knocked down. If you do, there will be hell on.' I don't think he was so much concerned for my safety as terrified at the prospect of one of the corporation inspectors arriving at the scene to find three complete strangers working the round.

So there was I, probably the first – and last – top-class professional footballer to combine his sporting role with that of corporation bin-man. I loved every minute of it, particularly that blissful hour at the end of the working day when we would accompany Dad and his work-mates to the pub for a couple of pints. I thoroughly enjoyed sitting there, one of the lads, sipping my pint and enjoying the *craic* after a hard day's graft. Maybe it was just the novelty value that got us through it, but I got a genuine sense of satisfaction out of the experience. As a working-class lad it wasn't hard to get into the swing of the work and to really appreciate the camaraderie of that end-of-the-day wind-down hour in the boozer. I have always been aware of the potential frailty of a football career and certainly of its brevity. Though I'm only too grateful for the good living soccer has brought me and my family, I've never had my head turned by the glamour side of the business.

A lot of my fellow players have never understood why I don't drive expensive, top-of-the-range cars and wear flashy clothes. If you've got it, why not spend it, why not flaunt it seems to be the common philosophy in my game. But it has never been my philosophy. To me, the trappings of being a top player are merely things on which to feed an ego. I remember that the car park at Blackburn's training ground – my second club, of course – was full of hugely expensive Range Rovers, Land Cruisers, Mercs, BMWs and Jaguars. To the amusement of my team-mates, I used to roll up every day in my Escort. It wasn't a problem: a car is a means of getting you from A to B as far as I'm concerned.

I believe you have to have an ego if you are to go into coaching or, most certainly, management. I think most managers and some coaches get a kick out of being called 'boss' and 'gaffer'. That could never be me. People have often told me my attitude will change as I get older, but it hasn't and it won't. I have worked hard at becoming a successful footballer and I understand how much effort you have to put in to get to the top. The same obviously applies to becoming a good manager. Not least of the drawbacks, for me, is the fact that you need to spend so much time on the job. If you are going to succeed in management you are going to be away from home and your family an awful lot. That isn't for me. My wife Mandy and my twin sons Jack and George are my life. I know they like me being around and I love being there for them. I couldn't spend several nights a week watching games – which any serious manager must do – knowing Mandy was raising the boys in my absence. I always had my dad around when I was a lad and I intend always to be there for my sons.

meeting mandy

The close season of 1990 turned out to be one of the happiest summers of my life. I was 21 years old and on top of the world after winning my first major honour, the Second Division championship, getting my first big contract and buying my first house. I had been linked with a move to Liverpool – with Peter Beardsley rumoured to be coming to Elland Road – but never heard anything first-hand, so I was more than happy to treat the rumours as such and concentrate on savouring the prospect of being a First Division footballer. Howard Wilkinson made three significant summer signings, bringing in goalkeeper John Lukic, from Arsenal, for £1 million, midfielder Gary McAllister, from Leicester, also for £1 million, and central defender Chris Whyte, from West Brom, for £350,000. Those sums may not sound impressive in an age when transfer fees of £10 million and more have become commonplace, but 11 years ago, an outlay of nearly £2.5 million on three players was more than enough to prove to fans – and players – that Leeds meant business. I was revelling in my status as emerging local celebrity, bachelor boy with his own pad, and top-flight player. Yet, though I didn't realise it, there was something extremely important missing from what seemed to be the perfect existence.

I made the discovery one warm, pleasant evening when I arrived at the family home of Terry and Lynn Beeton, in Rothwell, Leeds. I knew Terry and Lynn through their eldest son Mark, with whom I had played in the Leeds City Boys teams for two or three years. Mark and I had got on well and his mum and dad became friendly with my folks through their mutual support for their sons, often sharing transport to follow us to away games. However, from around the Under-14s age group, Mark didn't get picked again and we inevitably lost touch. But – thank goodness – Terry and Lynn followed my career. They had another son, Lee, who was also a wannabe footballer and a pretty good one, too. Lee was only about 10 years old and was just setting out on the road that I had trodden what seemed an age ago. His mum and dad had been following events at Elland Road that season and, in particular, the exploits of David Batty, whom she and Terry had watched so many times playing alongside their lad Mark on wind- and rain-swept playing fields around the district. So, with the intention of giving young Lee a shot of enthusiasm, his mum phoned mine to ask whether I might be willing to call round at their house and talk to Lee and one or two of his footballing friends. I was only too happy to oblige. What a good decision it proved to be.

When I got to the Beeton home – already a winner because I'd been invited for dinner – there, in the front room, were Lee and a couple of his pals. One of them was Alan Smith, the striker who, of course, went on to follow in my footsteps and become a star at Leeds United and with England. I remember how I was instantly struck by the friendly atmosphere in the house, where Terry and Lynn made me feel like one of the family; I had no idea that I was, indeed, destined to become a member of the family. One person I was completely unprepared to meet was Lee's sister Mandy, who was there when I arrived. I didn't even know that my old team-mate Mark had a sister but I quickly decided that I wanted to make up for lost time. Mandy wasn't only a lovely-looking lass, she also had such a pleasant personality; a bit shy and totally unassuming. She and I hit it off straight away. I know Lee won't mind me saying so but, though I took a genuine interest in his football and was happy to encourage him as much as possible, I was drawn back to their house by my increasing desire to see Mandy. I suggested I should pop in to see Lee every other week, and the more I visited, the more I wanted to return. My path was smoothed by the fact that Terry and Lynn were always pleased to see me, too. There was always a can of lager for me and usually a good hot meal as well.

Eventually I knew that I only had to say the words, 'Well, I must be off,' and Mandy and I would be alone together within seconds. About two months after we first met, I asked Mandy for a date; I wasn't exactly the fastest worker in the business, I suppose. Anyway, she accepted and we went to the cinema. I can't remember what the film was – I probably wasn't interested in what was on the screen – but I do remember how nervous Mandy was and that her sweaty palms melted her Maltesers. I also recall thinking, though I didn't say so then, that I was with the girl with whom I wanted to spend the rest of my life.

During my teenage years, I had had little experience of girls or, indeed, of socialising. So preoccupied had I been with playing football that the lure of lager and the opposite sex had been relegated below the passion for playing soccer. As I've already indicated, I was also such a late developer that when my contemporaries at 16 and 17 – even 18 – were enjoying nights at the pub I was struggling to get through the door because I looked under-age. I got so fed up with the indignity of it all that I just couldn't be bothered trying. But I certainly never look back and wonder what I missed out on as a youngster. I was doing what I wanted to do – play football – and my slow progress in the growing-up game was probably a blessing in disguise. Let's face it, the booze-and-birds syndrome has seen many a promising career crash before reaching the first corner. I am a strong advocate of marriage for footballers; the more stable your domestic situation, the more chance you have of focusing on your football.

By the time I met Mandy I had, nevertheless, been inducted into the world of wine, women and song. First-team League football was an automatic entry to lagerland and nightclubs. I embraced them both with enthusiasm – though not with a passion – but, in the couple of years since becoming one of the lads and hitting the clubs of Leeds, I had never met a girl who made anything remotely like the impression upon me that Mandy did. However corny it may seem, from the moment I first laid eyes on her, Mandy was the only one for me. Without wishing to sound smug, everything about us was right: Mandy and I clicked from day one. We weren't only physically attracted to each other, we were like the best of mates, as we still are. A few months into our relationship I asked her if she would move in with me in Shadwell. She agreed. I think our parents were happy to see us together and they had no problem with us living together before marriage. I'm sure everybody in the two families knew, as we did, that we were right for each other and that this was a committed, long-term relationship.

Terry and Lynn are more like pals of mine than my in-laws. Terry started watching me play for Leeds, though he drifted away from the game after injury problems put me out of action for such long periods after I returned to the club in 1999. I will always be glad that I did the honourable thing and asked Terry for permission to marry his daughter. Mind you, if he'd refused I would have gone ahead and married her anyway! Young Lee went on to sign schoolboy forms for Leeds, moving on to Bradford and Rotherham before falling out of love with the game after a series of knockbacks of the type that hurt so many of my contemporaries as an apprentice at Elland Road. But I'm getting ahead of myself. Back to that summer of 1990 and Mandy's entry into my life. The house in Shadwell was okay, but it was a typical bachelor's home, containing just the essentials, like beds and a sofa, a fridge and a massively under-used cooker. It didn't take Mandy long to start adding her personal touch to the place and generally making it a more comfortable, homely house. The problem for her was that it was always 'my' house rather than 'ours'. Mandy is a shy girl and I think it always sat a little uneasily with her that the Shadwell house was very much a bachelor pad, often populated by my mates when she returned from work. She had moved from a job at a security depot in Rothwell to the Homebase office soon after we moved in together. At Homebase, the female staff all had to wear green outfits and I remember how she would come home and rush upstairs to change out of her 'uniform' if any of my mates were in the house. She didn't want my friends to see her in that gear, although she looked pretty cute in it to me.

Shadwell had always been just a base in which to sleep, watch a video and return to after training. So, to be fair to Mandy, we agreed that we should buy a house that would be truly ours, rather than mine. The following January we moved into the home we have been in ever since, a few minutes outside Wetherby and a short drive from the Leeds training ground at Thorp Arch. I like to think that the house is typical of us as a couple and a family. It is a four-bedroomed place with more than enough space for the four of us. It might not be modest compared to the average family home, but it is compared to a lot of football stars' places. It certainly isn't a mansion. We have all the mod cons you would expect of people who are fortunate enough to be able to afford, within reason, the luxuries of life. But neither Mandy nor I are flash types. We have no desire or need to impress people and I'm sure we will always feel that way. Not the least of the reasons for our readiness to remain in the house we bought 10 years ago is the stability it has brought to the lives of Jack and George. I always appreciated my solid home life and I like to think that the boys will benefit from a fixed base. Disruption so often blights the lives of footballers' wives and children; they have to move around the country – even the world – following transfers to other clubs. It was no accident that when I moved to Blackburn, then Newcastle, I chose to commute rather than uproot from the area which will always be home to me and Mandy. Having said that, after much soul-searching, we actually sold this house when I was at Newcastle and were set to move into a place in Morpeth. But the surveyor's report revealed problems with that property and we pulled out of the deal. Talk about a lucky break! About six months later, I was on my way back to Leeds United. Imagine how I – not to mention Mandy and the kids – would have felt had we been settling into a new house in the North-East, where the boys would have been about to start school, and I had started the same daily trek in reverse. Mandy's mum always says things happen for a reason. I think she's right.

The more I reflect on meeting Mandy, the more I can't help but think that fate played a part in bringing us together. I have to admit that she came into my life at the right time, just when I probably needed the steadying influence of a loving relationship. After all, there was I, a 21-year-old footballer with money in his pocket, a home of his own – and Vinnie Jones as a mate! I had celebrated my 21st the December before meeting Mandy with a 1–0 home win over Newcastle followed by a party for all my mates in the 100 Club at Elland Road. The events of that night indicated how close I was to needing a new sense of purpose in my life. Things got a bit out of hand at my 'do' and I went in on the Monday morning to see that several doors had been damaged, along with other assorted minor acts of vandalism to the club's property. Some of the lads had been staging door-punching contests, seeing who could penetrate the panelling. A few of them succeeded and I got a bill for several hundred quid. I don't know if word of that got back to Howard Wilkinson. No doubt it did; I don't imagine much concerning the stupid behaviour of his players escaped his attention eventually. The more I think about it, the more I realise that Mandy must have been sent to me from on high! Wilko had tried his damnedest to bring me to heel – and failed. But once I met Mandy, I started to look at life more seriously.

Mandy and I didn't go out burning the candle at both ends very often even when we were courting. I was already into nightclub life by then, like most of the young, single players, but Mandy and I would invariably end up looking at each other and asking: 'What are we doing here?' We soon discovered that we preferred our own company and that of each other's families to going clubbing. That is even more the case since we became proud parents. We go out socialising very rarely these days.

Mandy and I didn't rush into tying the knot. We were engaged in October 1992, more than two years after we met, and we married in April the following year. I went along to Mandy's dad's works to ask for his daughter's hand in marriage. I know Mandy's parents never questioned our relationship and I'm sure they never had the slightest objection to the two of us marrying, but, all the same, I decided to do the traditional, time-honoured thing and I know Terry was chuffed that I had done so. Having said that, I can't claim to have maintained the romantic theme when it came to proposing to Mandy. There was no bunch of red roses or bended-knee begging speech. I simply turned up at their house one day, having decided to pop the question, and tucked the ring down by the cushion on the settee. I didn't even demand privacy for my proposal; all of her family were present when I proposed. But it was a lovely moment, nevertheless.

We maintained a low-key approach right up to our wedding, on 29 April 1993. From the descriptions I have given of myself and Mandy as two fairly quiet types, you won't be surprised that the big day was one of the most anonymous affairs the Leeds registrar must ever have witnessed. We had both decided we didn't want all the glitz and glitter that surrounds big, white weddings. In particular, we agreed there was no sense in inflicting the cost of a wedding on Mandy's parents. So we privately agreed upon the date and went ahead without telling anyone – not even our mums and dads. I was recovering from a knee injury at the time and had played 45 minutes for the reserves against Blackburn the previous day. I trained on the morning of our wedding day, changed into my suit, met Mandy and drove off to the registry office. There, we were married with only a mate of mine and his wife to witness the event. Mandy had arranged for flowers to be sent to our mums that morning, so they weren't totally in the dark.

People were soon gossiping, jumping to the conclusion that there must have been a rift in the family. Nothing could have been further from the truth. It might seem odd to some folk that we should go ahead and do it the way we did, but it was right for us. After the ceremony, Mandy and I drove down to the Fullerton

Park training ground where her brother Lee was playing as a Leeds United Schoolboys starlet. When we stepped out of the car in our finery, Lee knew immediately what had taken place. The following Saturday, we drew 1–1 with QPR at Elland Road and I skippered the team in the absence of Gordon Strachan and Gary McAllister. That evening, I took about a dozen members of our two families for a meal and on to the Holiday Inn for drinks. It was an extremely pleasant, albeit unassuming celebration of our marriage, and everyone thoroughly enjoyed themselves. We didn't have time for a honeymoon because I was straight into England World Cup-qualifying duty after the first Premier League season ended the following week, but we did grab a week in Lanzarote later that summer, which we spent freezing under towels on the wind-swept beach. I vowed I'd never go there again.

At the risk of labouring the point, I must say that Mandy and I really were made for each other. We are happy to live a quiet life, in the company of our two boys, with frequent visits to and from our respective families and to friends like Chris and Andrea Douglass. Though I've always considered myself easy to get along with when with my team-mates, it is also true that I am content to shut out the football world once I drive through the gates of my home. I am so at ease with Mandy and the kids that I have no yearnings whatsoever for the company of pals, past or present. In fact, I suppose it's a fault of mine that I don't bother keeping in touch with pals and former team-mates. I never think to pick up the phone and have a chat with lads who I've got along with well in the teams I've played in over the past

10 years. Many of them probably think of me as a bit of a weirdo – in the nicest sort of way, I trust, and I suppose I do live a bit like a hermit in my family retreat.

There is no denying that I've always done things my way. You could say I'm a bit of a modern-world misfit. For example, I have never owned a chequebook – let alone a credit card – in my life, and I never will. I must be the only England and Premier League player who can't write out a cheque or produce a piece of plastic to pay for a meal, a new suit or a car. People, especially fellow players, just can't believe that a guy earning good money deals only in cash or has to rush to the building society to get a cheque for substantial payments, but that is exactly what I do. I go to the Post Office regularly to pay my household bills, the gas, electricity and tele- phone. Like people of my grandparents' generation, I prefer to know exactly where I'm up to with money. It's very much a working-class, down-to-earth mentality. I suppose it's a bit like having your money under the mattress. Not that I keep mine there: my money is in a savings account at the Leeds and Holbeck Building Society. The account was opened for me by my mum with a £1 deposit when I was 13 and I've been quite content to keep my money there ever since. I'm happy to pop down the Leeds and Holbeck every now and then to draw out some cash. I don't even have a wallet! More often than not, I don't have more than a couple of quid in my pocket and I frequently have to rely on Mandy to bail me out if I need some cash. I'm not a complete financial dinosaur, though. I have taken a lot of advice and I do have money invested both here and overseas to ensure that we have a secure future. I am a keen investor and regularly follow my portfolio of stocks and shares on the market.

But there have been occasions when this approach to money matters has proved inconvenient, like the time we booked a holiday flatlet in Jersey, when the twins were toddlers. Having drawn a building society cheque to pay for the accommodation, we set off for Birmingham Airport in my sponsored club car. That was only the start of our problems. I pointed out to Mandy that the car was running badly and it was juddering and stuttering by the time we got to the airport. I went to pick up our tickets, leaving Mandy and the kids in the car. When I returned it wouldn't start. After a few minutes it dawned on me: it was a diesel engine and I had put forty quid's worth of petrol in the tank. We had to abandon it right there, on the road, get the luggage and leg it to the terminal building. On arrival at our holiday destination, Mandy and I were appalled by the state of the flat. No way on earth were we going to stay there. So, having demanded a better place, we stormed off to the nearest hotel to book in for the night. That was fine – until it came to paying for the rooms. I had no chequebook, no credit cards. An awkward and embarrassing stand-off ensued. In desperation, I rang Hayden Evans, back in Leeds, and my financial guru came to our rescue. I presume he picked up the tab on his credit card! Long-suffering Hayden also had to sort out the problem of the aban-doned club car back at Birmingham Airport. There was a happy ending, though: next morning, we moved into a delightful holiday home at the other end of the island. You might think incidents like that would spur me to end the habit of a lifetime and get myself some plastic or, at least, a chequebook. Well, it didn't.

Apart from one trip to Portugal, to a first-class hotel where there was nothing for the kids to do, we have always holidayed in England in caravans. People might think that isn't what you'd expect from a Premier League footballer but I have never been one to worry about my image. What Mandy and I do care about, more passionately than anything else, is the well-being of Jack and George, and it is for that reason that we have taken them on down-to-earth fun-filled holidays. You can spend as much money as you want staying in the best hotels all over the world, but you'll find that the classier the hotel the less likely it is to cater for kids. So, after the Portugal experience, when Jack and George were bored rigid, we decided that English companies like Haven Holiday Homes could give us all we needed. Everything there is geared to the family unit, with the emphasis on entertainment for children. Jack and George love it and as a result so do we. Admittedly, I do get recognised by fellow holiday-makers, many of whom look at me with a 'what are *you* doing here?' expression on their faces. The answer is simple: if the kids are happy so are we.

back in the big time

Meeting Mandy coincided with my new status as a top-flight footballer – to be precise, a soon-to-be-top-flight footballer. When she and I started seeing each other, I was preparing for my first match in the former First Division, which was to be against Everton at Goodison Park. When the fixture list was printed, I remember thinking that it was an appropriately impressive venue for my introduction to the 'big league'. The occasion lived up to all of my expectations, but I had a nervous build-up to that 25 August kick-off date, troubled as I was by a thigh strain during pre-season training. I played for an hour in each of two Yorkshire and Humberside Cup matches and then spent the final week before the big kick-off redoubling my determination not to miss out. I made it, and what a fantastic experience. It was well worth the effort I had put in to make sure I ran out at Goodison in front of 34,412 fans for Leeds's long overdue return to the elite company of English football. It was everything I could have wished for: a gloriously sunny day, a tremendous start-of-season atmosphere – and a 3–2 away win for Leeds. Gary Speed, by then a big mate of mine, probably had an even better day than I did, for he scored twice against the club he had supported as a boy. We went in at half-time 2–0 up and scored another shortly after the resumption. Even though Everton staged a fighting comeback, my memories of the occasion are only good ones.

Three days later, we were meeting Manchester United at Elland Road. Though I had spent the previous three and a half months thinking of little else, suddenly I was pinching myself, trying to come to terms with the fantastic reality of it all. Everton, then Manchester United. Yes, it really was happening. I was at last able to pit my wits and abilities against the biggest teams and the best players in the land. My only previous experience of these famous teams had been playing against them for the reserves a couple of years earlier, but this was the real thing and I was loving it.

If I had any doubts about my ability to live with the best the First Division could offer – and, I admit, even a self-confident lad like me did have a few minor misgivings – they were dispelled in those early days of Division One life. And no single match helped me to cement my self-belief more than that encounter with Manchester United, then starting their fifth season under the management of Alex Ferguson. Exciting as it was simply to be meeting one of the most famous clubs on earth in only our second fixture, I had particular reason to regard it as a personal triumph. We drew the match 0–0 but it seemed like a victory to me, for one specific reason. Not only had I acquitted myself well over the 90 minutes, but also I saw off my opposing midfielder Paul Ince, the recent recruit from West Ham who had been ever-present in the headlines since coming north from London. When the United bench signalled for Ince to be substituted I got a surge of satisfaction. I remember looking up into the stand and motioning to my dad with a gesture that said: 'Yes. I've seen him off!' If you are serious about making it all the way to the top, I believe you have to set yourself standards and not shirk from privately imposed tests of character and ability. To me, meeting Paul Ince head on was just such an examination of my credentials, mental as well as physical. Okay, I was there, in the First Division. But had I got the bottle for it? Any lingering concerns I had were banished on that Tuesday evening at Elland Road, as I watched Ince trudging towards the away team dugout. I took his substitution as a personal compliment. 'Yes,' I thought. 'You've arrived.'

Ten years later, after Alex Ferguson's former assistant Brian Kidd had joined Leeds as director of our youth development programme, he told me that he and Ferguson had discussed the possibility of taking me to Old Trafford and that he thought I would have been a smash hit at the Theatre of Dreams. Back then, though, I was happy to be playing against Manchester United for the club I had been linked with since I was in my early teens. We beat Norwich City 3–0 at Elland Road to complete a sensational first seven days in the big league. 'Can David keep this up?' wrote my dad. 'He and Gordon Strachan were the best players on the pitch. It made me feel proud to hear the Leeds fans chanting, "Batty for England." He can do it if he keeps his fitness uppermost in his mind and looks after himself.'

A few weeks after the Manchester United match,

Tottenham were the visitors to Elland Road: Tottenham and Paul Gascoigne, who had given me so many laughs when he and I roomed together a few years earlier on that Under-19s trip to Switzerland. By now, Gazza had been to the World Cup that summer and become a household name. Apart from Eric Cantona, who arrived at Leeds 18 months later, I have never competed with or against a better player than Gazza. Like the clash with Paul Ince only two and a half weeks earlier, I knew this was a major test for me and for the team as a whole. In fact, it was my biggest personal challenge. Again, I'm pleased to say, I came through with my pride intact and my reputation enhanced – even though Spurs did beat us 2–0. One of the toughest aspects about facing Gazza is that you have to be careful not only that he doesn't 'do' you for sheer skill and audacity but also that you don't lose your concentration on the job in hand. By that, I mean that it would be easy to get distracted by Gazza's antics. He is the most amazing character in terms of hamming it up and enjoying a laugh on the pitch. On that day, I well remember him telling his team-mates to 'piss off' when they asked him to pass the ball. 'You didn't give it me when I wanted it,' Gazza snapped with that cheeky grin spreading across his face. And after I had hit him with a trademark, crunching David Batty tackle, Gazza picked himself up, shook himself down and asked me to help him put his shirt back together. As I say, we lost the match, but I was content in the knowledge that I had more than matched Paul in midfield. Some time later, I was told that Alex Ferguson and his assistant of the time, Archie Knox, were in the crowd. Gazza, of course, had already passed up the chance to join Manchester United, choosing Spurs. Perhaps, as Brian Kidd told me years later, Ferguson was already taking an interest in me?

I will probably never know the answer to that question. But what I did know, after those confrontations with Paul Ince and Paul Gascoigne, was that I was made for this cream-of-the-crop stuff. Playing away from home is surely the ultimate test of a player's character, but I had a deep-rooted sense of certainty about my right to be in such exalted company after the Elland Road meetings with Spurs and Manchester United. That impression can't have been purely my own, either, for, on 4 November, I was put on standby for the European Championship qualifier against the Republic of Ireland in Dublin later that month. Also on the standby list was goalkeeper Nigel Martyn, of Crystal Palace, who went on to join Leeds and become a full England international. I was called into the squad a few days later, following injuries to John Barnes and Trevor Steven.

It had been a marvellous first two and a half months for me and for Leeds. Yet, even when my form brought me to the brink of my first full England cap, my dad's obsession with my goal-scoring – or rather, the lack of it – again came to the fore. After the 3–2 home defeat by QPR in October, Dad concluded that match report by declaring: 'From now on, there will be no reports on the games in this book until David scores another goal.' Sadly, Dad had a long wait before picking up his pen again.

There was one occasion that December when I cursed my growing reputation. Over the previous two or three years, I had come to relish the prospect of the lads'

Christmas parties, and we had already started making our plans for the festivities when I was summoned into the England B squad for a match in Algeria. I wasn't exactly excited by the prospect of going, and by the time it was all over, my worst fears had been realised about tenfold. We gained a highly creditable 1–1 draw against Manchester United at Old Trafford on 8 December. Dad had agreed to drive me to Luton Airport the next day to join the B squad players. But we never made it past East Midlands Airport because the weather was so appalling. Our journey coincided with one of the worst December snowfalls in years. We had arranged to pick up John Lukic, the Leeds keeper, who lived in the Chesterfield area, and John couldn't even get from home to the meeting point. By now, the snow was so bad that the M1 motorway was closed. We took the detour and, just when we were thinking things couldn't get much worse, there was an almighty bang, the car lurched forward and sparks and wires burst from the dashboard. We were in the outside lane of the motorway slip road and another motorist had skidded into the back of us. His Cavalier was a write-off and poor Dad wasn't too thrilled about the condition of his Rover, although at least it was still drivable. But we made the decision that we simply weren't going to make it to Luton and we turned around and limped back to Leeds.

I must confess that the prospect of missing out on a B match in Algeria wasn't exactly filling me with tears. There was also the counter-attraction of the impending Christmas party. We couldn't hold our celebrations too near Christmas because, of course, we were always heavily involved in matches over the festive period. So I decided I wasn't going to Algeria. My conscience was clear; after all, my dad and I had literally risked life and limb to try to overcome the elements and do our duty for Queen and country. Imagine my gloom when I telephoned Lawrie McMenemy, England manager Graham Taylor's No. 2, and he told me in no uncertain terms that I simply had to be there. Hayden Evans hastily got to work and sorted me out a ticket from Leeds–Bradford Airport. Mandy's dad drove me to the airport and I duly joined the rest of the lads at Luton. My only consolation at this point was the thought that I would get a bit of sun on my back and warmth in my frozen bones, but I was in for another disappointment. Don't ever consider a midwinter break in Algiers – not that any sane person would, I suppose. The match, a 0–0 draw, was played in a howling gale and I sat with the other substitutes, muffled against the cold in moon-suits, in a dugout that had no material covering its framework! I missed the Christmas bash, and I didn't even get on the pitch. All that for nowt. It was my worst trip ever. My dad had got his car smashed up into the bargain, and the FA didn't pay for that. Years later, when striker Chris Sutton, then at Blackburn, incurred the wrath of Glenn Hoddle and the scorn of the nation for refusing, for whatever reason, to join a B squad, I couldn't help but feel sympathetic.

The next match I played was a live, televised clash with Everton, over whom we did the double with a 2–0 Elland Road victory. Successive wins against Sunderland, Chelsea and Wimbledon followed and we started to think that maybe we could live in this company. We lost big games at Liverpool and at Arsenal, but we also notched impressive wins along the way, such as a 4–1 League Cup win at Aston Villa, whom we went on to thrash 5–2 in the third-last match of the campaign, and a 5–0 walloping of Sunderland. We certainly surprised a lot of teams – including ourselves. But of all the games in that first season back at the top, the one that will forever be lodged in my memory was the end-of-season clash with Liverpool, on 13 April at Elland Road. Liverpool were the reigning champions and had been the dominant force in English football for the best part of 20 years. They were the club everyone else aspired to emulate and, though none of us – least of all Liverpool – realised that they had won their last championship title for the foreseeable future, they were the benchmark by which every ambitious player and manager measured himself. They travelled to Leeds that spring day sporting all of their big guns, players like John Barnes, Peter Beardsley and Jan Molby, and they – and we – put on a show fit for a Wembley final. The score was 5–4 in Liverpool's favour. Yet not even the taste of defeat could sour the flavour of a fabulous football feast. We were actually 3–0 down at half-time; we walked off the pitch in shock with the Kop singing: 'What the fucking hell is going on?' We slumped on to our seats in the dressing-room thinking: 'Christ, we've got to go out there and face another 45 minutes of this.' But what a comeback. Lee Chapman scored a hat-trick for us, I had a blinder, and we gave Liverpool the fright of their lives. We got it back to 3–2 before Barnes popped another goal in for Liverpool to effectively kill the game, yet still we fought so well that the final margin was just one goal. Our fans, who had been so vociferously sarcastic at half-time, were cheering us at the final whistle. For our part, it was that rare occasion when we could take pride from a defeat.

A few weeks later, we had completed our return to the First Division with a fourth-place finish, behind Arsenal, Liverpool and Crystal Palace. Though our 64-point total was 19 fewer than champions Arsenal amassed, we had nevertheless done ourselves proud. From a personal point of view, it was a marvellous season. I took to the top flight like a duck to water and my contribution was recognised by the fans. I won the Supporters' Player of the Year award, the majority of the supporters' branch awards and the *Yorkshire Evening Post*'s Player of the Year accolade. It was without doubt my best season as a professional footballer – even if I didn't score a goal! And there was even better to come.

CHAPTER 9

the title

Ten days after our last match of the 1990–91 season I won my first full England cap. The immense pride I felt was shared by the family. Ever since I broke into the Leeds team, Dad had nurtured the prospect of his lad wearing the three lions on his chest, even though he had remained convinced that I would have to start scoring goals to realise the ambition. The material bonus for that substitute's appearance against the USSR at Wembley was a £5,000 payout from Leeds United. It was written into my contract that I would receive £5,000 a cap for my first five appearances. By the time I got a mid-summer holiday, I had earned an extra £25,000. My international career was well and truly launched.

When I returned for pre-season training that July, a fully fledged England player, Howard Wilkinson had strengthened his squad once again. Twins Rod and Ray Wallace came from Southampton, Tony Dorigo arrived from Chelsea, and midfielder Steve Hodge was brought in from Nottingham Forest. The stage was set for what proved to be an historic title triumph, with Leeds winning the last First Division championship before the Premier League was formed in 1992–93. Our fourth-place finish the previous season had banished our inferiority complex and I sensed a collective feeling of confidence and enthusiasm for the year ahead. I was full of anticipation for the challenge.

My growing belief that I was part of something special at Elland Road was strengthened when the club arranged a prestigious pre-season friendly against Brazilian club Botafogo. It was to be a two-legged affair with the first meeting in Tokyo, where the Japanese were developing a passion for soccer which has led them to staging, along with South Korea, the 2002 World Cup. To be flying to the Land of the Rising Sun in the first week of August to play a famous Brazilian club side seemed to me to be evidence that Leeds really were back in the big time.

It was a marvellous trip, a tremendous venue – the Tokyo Dome – and an enjoyable experience playing the Brazilians, though they beat us 1–0. On our arrival in Tokyo, Howard Wilkinson decreed that we would stick to Greenwich Mean Time, presumably having decided it would minimise disruption to our body clocks, with the kick-off to the new season looming. Tokyo time is nine hours ahead of England. We found ourselves doing the strangest things, like training at one o'clock in the morning and popping into the Hard Rock Café at 4 a.m., coming back to the hotel at breakfast time. We weren't actually staying out late, of course, because of the time we were operating to. Wilko, always a strict disciplinarian, gave the lads free rein during those few days and we all appreciated it. There was something novel about going about your daily business in the small hours of the morning and we all got a kick out of it, a little like schoolboys who had been given extra licence.

As ever, though, there was a price to pay for this freedom, at least for one of our most fanatical supporters. Martin Goldman is a wealthy Leeds businessman and a committed follower of the team; so committed that he had forked out what must have been a small fortune to come on the trip, even though it was only a showpiece match. Martin is a good lad and we were happy to have him along when we went for a drink or to do some sightseeing. For his part, Martin was thrilled to bits to be in the company of the players. He was like a star-struck teenager, taking stacks of video footage and generally revelling in his privileged position as travelling companion of his heroes. But who was the one to give Martin a reason to wish he'd stayed in the hotel and had a quiet drink on his own? We had returned to the hotel after a couple of drinks and were waiting for the lift to take us to our rooms. I noticed clusters of small black pebbles which filled the tall ashtrays beside the lift doors. I took one and bounced it off the floor in the direction of Martin, who was about 20 feet away. The little missile hit him right between the eyes, causing quite a nasty cut. There was blood everywhere, yet we were all laughing because the odds against this thing hitting him at all must have been pretty remote. We got him to his room and had to summon the doctor to stitch him up. To be fair to him, Martin saw the funny side, too, and he didn't drop me in it with Wilko. To this day, when I see him my gaze is instantly drawn to the scar on the bridge of his nose. I have probably left my calling card on the limbs of one or two players around the country after some crunching confrontations, but that was the first – and last – time I scarred anybody for life away from the football pitch!

Martin didn't let his mishap spoil his enjoyment of the match in the Dome, played in front of a packed 70,000 crowd. I couldn't help but be impressed – as all of my team-mates were – when the sponsors named their Man of the Match, one of the Botafogo players, and presented him with a sparkling Toyota sports car. On the plane home, we were all talking about the exciting incentive for winning the Man of the Match award at Elland Road in the return game. Imagine my sense of expectation when I was duly named star man after our 2–1 win four days later. I could barely contain my excitement as the sponsors made the announcement. Smiling politely, I was thinking: 'Come on, get to the nitty-gritty. Where's the car?' I didn't have long to wait; my prize was quickly produced. But I didn't have to be taken outside to receive it. They put the vehicle into the palm of my hand. It was a miniature, like a Corgi toy or one of those Weetabix vans you used to get from the cereal packets. Gutted isn't the word. I put on a brave face but I didn't know whether to laugh or cry. I had been convinced I'd be cruising away from the stadium in my spanking new Toyota Sports; instead, my prize was in my pocket. You can imagine how much stick I took from the lads. I never did get an explanation as to why there had been one rule for the match in Tokyo and another for the game in Leeds. I think I was too disappointed to try to find out. In the end, I was left to console myself with my Man of the Match rating. At least it was a good pointer to my form going into the season.

The campaign kicked off on 17 August; except for us and Crystal Palace, that is. Palace were due to play host to Leeds, but the match was postponed because ground improvements at Selhurst Park hadn't been completed. So the big day became Tuesday the 20th, and our home fixture with Nottingham Forest. It was a successful start, a 1–0 win that marked my first competitive match in the new role Wilko had devised for me, playing just in front of the centre-backs. Deep-lying midfielder would be the popular description; a job that entailed me acting as a minder to the central defenders, breaking up the opposition attacks and shielding the back line as much as possible. In the previous two or three seasons I had been accustomed to a free role, buzzing all over the pitch, so this new, restricted, more disciplined job was difficult to adjust to. I'm sure my dad and the fans found it as frustrating as I did; they were used to seeing me covering every blade of grass. But this was a different David Batty altogether. I didn't like it then. As the years went by, however, I was to play that part more and more often and grew to enjoy it. I know that, whoever I was playing for, the centre-halves always appreciated having me in front of them, fielding the flak. I think my initial frustrations stemmed from the fact that I was blessed with so much energy and I had trouble restraining myself from going in search of wider pastures to roam.

We drew at home to derby rivals Sheffield Wednesday the following Saturday and then went to Southampton and dished out a 4–0 drubbing. With hindsight, that result was an early pointer to the stunning accomplishments that were to follow that season. We gained more evidence of our growing status with back-to-back draws against Manchester United and Arsenal.

Yet all of this was only the backcloth to a cloak-and-dagger operation which ended in a top-secret meeting between me, my dad and a big-name manager, details of which I can now reveal for the first time.

There had been whispers about this club and me for 12 months or so, but I had never had reason to take them seriously until an agent telephoned my dad to say they were interested in exploring the possibility of a transfer. Dad said I wouldn't be averse to finding out exactly what was proposed and a meeting was arranged. Fans may find it hard to accept that I was ready to talk to another club. After all, I was the local hero in the Leeds side, the Player of the Year and the new recruit to Graham Taylor's England team. The world was at my feet, as they say. All of that is true; nevertheless, a harsh fact of life is that sentiment can cloud your judgement of what is right for you. In football, it could certainly cost you money. Though I was quite content at Leeds, I felt I had to explore options when they arose, especially when they involved such a big club. So, amid a background of furtive phone calls, a meeting between the manager, me and my father and the agent was arranged. Not surprisingly, the go-between insisted upon the utmost secrecy. I was, after all, under contract to Leeds United, although my deal expired at the end of that 1991–92 season. We agreed to meet at the agent's home near Doncaster the day after our 2–2 Elland Road draw with Arsenal early in September. I can recall the sense of anticipation that both Dad and I felt as we drove to the venue. We were equally excited at the prospect of shaking hands with the manager.

Over a cup of tea, he did an impressive job of selling

his beloved club to me. He talked about the unique atmosphere and the successes they had had that he was now desperate to recreate. He told me how I would be part of his dream midfield. I sat there, hanging on to his every word. I admit I was in awe of him; it was something of a throwback to my wide-eyed days at the feet of former Leeds manager Billy Bremner. I recall thinking: 'He's not as tall as I thought he'd be – but what a strong, commanding figure he cuts.' He told us about the many marvellous young players he had coming through and how he wanted me to join them. I was impressed. He wanted me to shake on it there and then, to give him my word that I would become his player the following summer. But there was one flaw in his tactics that morning: he wouldn't commit himself when we wanted to talk about money. And that is the bottom line. I wouldn't have been there if I hadn't been interested, but that's not to say I was unsettled at Leeds – far from it. I wasn't going to agree to leave Elland Road without knowing precisely what I would be leaving for in terms of money in the bank. If that sounds coldly materialistic, so be it. I have already underlined my indifference to the trappings of wealth, but that's not to say I don't have a need for the sense of security that money gives you. And, by then, I was developing an increasing awareness of my value to a club.

I was also aware that Leeds were on the point of asking me in for talks about a new contract. We had made a solid start to the season, showing every sign of building on our impressive first outing back in Division One. Just over two years earlier, Leeds had given me a very generous contract, so I had every reason to expect a similarly good offer this time. Another factor contributing to my refusal to give him any assurances that I would join him nine months down the line was the worry about what would happen if I were to get injured and hadn't signed a contract. That would have left me without any security. So we left without making an agreement. I had mixed feelings as we drove home to Leeds. Had my caution possibly cost me the move of a lifetime? Would Leeds come up with the goods and give me a deal that would match my new status as a fully fledged England player? I was soon to get the answer to these questions.

But first, I passed another significant milestone. I scored my second goal for Leeds. And, boy, had it been a long time coming: three years and eight months, to be precise. Dad recorded the damning statistic that it had been 161 matches since I previously hit the back of the net. Boxing Day 1987 had been the date of my first goal. Now, on 7 September 1991, I struck again. That clandestine meeting must have had a positive effect! Coincidentally, Manchester City were, for the second time, the victims of Batty's finishing prowess. When I hit them the first time it was at Maine Road. On this occasion, we were at Elland Road, and the fans raised the roof. I'm sure they didn't hold my lack of goals against me – at least, not like my dad did. But they were mightily pleased for me, all the same.

Somehow, I found myself inside the 18-yard box and with a shooting opportunity into the bargain. Peter Reid, City's midfield hard-man and player-manager, tried to block my shot after I swivelled and struck the ball. Goalkeeper Tony Coton, a good mate of mine since we forged a friendship on an England trip to Malaysia and Australia, couldn't stop the ball flying home. My first goal at Elland Road – and at the Kop end, too! The whole place erupted. The noise was deafening. It was a lovely, warm sunny day and, at that moment, I thought: 'Isn't life just wonderful!' I know I've said I don't worry about goals, but I'm not going to deny the buzz I get when I do pop the occasional one in. Contributing to my elation at that moment was a feeling of relief that a long-running saga had ended, for the time being at least. It had reached the stage when everybody – my family, friends, the fans and the press – was constantly harping on about when my next goal would be. Whenever I picked the ball up in the opposition half of the pitch, the home fans would scream 'Shoot, shoot!' It was all good-humoured stuff, but it was beginning to bug me. So, when I tucked away that chance to help us to a 3–0 win, my celebrations were tinged as much with sheer relief at the prospect of getting everybody off my back as with pure joy. That victory took us to fourth place in the table, behind leaders Manchester United, Liverpool and City after six matches played. It was very early days; even so, I can remember cautiously beginning to think that we might have the makings of an outfit who could become a serious threat to the big clubs.

I actually scored another League goal that season, five months later, on 1 February 1992, to be precise. And what a cracker it was, though I say so myself. Notts County were the latest unfortunates to feel the full force of Batty's scoring instincts. The ball was cleared from our penalty area and I won a 50–50 challenge for possession. That part was no surprise – I had developed a bit of a reputation for coming out on top in those situations – but what followed was a real eye-opener for the Elland Road crowd, and for me, too, I must admit. I set off with the ball at my feet and just kept running and running. I ran over half the length of the pitch, with County defenders backing off. I remember our centre-forward Lee Chapman in the middle of the pitch, taking a defender wide with him. To my disbelief I was now approaching the edge of their 18-yard box, and still there was no serious challenge in sight. It was the moment of truth. I let fly from around 20 yards. What a screamer! County's keeper Steve Cherry was clawing air as the ball fizzed past him and into the far corner. There isn't a centre-forward in the land who wouldn't have been proud of that one. I was dead chuffed.

Of the handful of goals I have scored, a few have been really spectacular, including a 30-yard stunner for Blackburn – my only goal for the Ewood Park club. Amazingly, that was also against Manchester City – City fans must be the only ones who worry when they see me approaching goal. One thing is for sure: because my strikes were so rare, I was always guaranteed maximum publicity. Throughout my career, people have told me they can't understand why I don't get more goals, especially as it is generally acknowledged that I can hit a ball as well as most, especially from long range. I have always replied that I don't see any point in letting myself get sidetracked by a perceived need to score goals. My job – unless someone tells me otherwise – has been to frustrate the opposition, win the ball and set up the moves from which my team-mates do the glory-glory part and hit the net. I have had no problem with that; I have very rarely been in a scoring position and, even when I am, my first tendency is to look for a colleague to pass to. This is no philosophy of self-sacrifice, just my genuine view of what my role is all about.

Within days of the goal against Manchester City in September, Leeds had approached me about a new contract. I asked Dad if he was willing to give the negotiations another go. After all, he'd done pretty well the previous occasion he went in to bat on my behalf. Dad agreed and duly went along to meet managing director Bill Fotherby at the club. This time, though he was willing, Dad decided he wasn't sufficiently able. He returned from his summit meeting to admit that Fotherby had baffled him with science and we agreed it would be more prudent of me to seek professional help in negotiating a deal. Dad and I realised that it might be pushing our luck to go in again on our own and expect to emerge with the best possible deal. I had a pretty good contract already; these negotiations were going to take it to another level. I decided to call in the Professional Footballers' Association, and Brendan Batson, PFA chairman Gordon Taylor's right-hand man, took on my case. I don't know if the club had got wind of my meeting. Neither my dad nor I ever breathed a word of it, for obvious reasons; there would have been hell to pay for me if word of it had spread. Yet, to our amazement, a newspaper reporter rang my dad some time later and bluntly asked: 'Is it right that your David had a meeting with another club?' God knows how that leaked or from where. But I do know that Leeds came up trumps for me in those contract talks. To be fair, they never gave me any reason to be suspicious that, as a home-grown player, I would be exploited. That seems to be the case at other clubs, where they feel they can get away with not paying local lads as much as they have to shell out for expensive transfer buys, but not at Leeds. I was already fairly confident that they had elevated me among the high earners with the deal that Dad negotiated so adroitly in 1989. Now, I was sure of my place in the pecking order because they nearly tripled my wages, with virtually no wrangling over the terms. I was very happy. We were in the big time and winning games. I was a fixture in the team and being paid more money than I would have dreamed possible two or three years previously. My flirtation with another club was quickly put to the back of my mind. I feel obliged to record that, despite my moans about Howard Wilkinson's methods, he must have rated me highly to sanction another first-class wages package. The differences that existed between us obviously didn't prevent him from recommending to the board of directors that I be given the best deal they could afford.

There was an increasing feelgood factor about the dressing-room at this time. After my disenchantment during the promotion season, I was now thoroughly enjoying my football and feeling as though I was a member of a team that was definitely upwardly mobile. I had no reason to think that life could be much better anywhere else. I was proud to captain the team for the first time when Gordon Strachan was injured and Wilko handed me the armband for the home match with Norwich City, which ended in a 2–2 draw. Wilko never gave me a reason why he chose to bestow the honour of leading the side upon me, but he repeated the gesture a few times. Then on 26 October we beat Oldham Athletic at Elland Road to go top of the First Division for the first time in 17 years. It was quite a day. Another milestone was Leeds's first victory over Liverpool – 1–0 – in 18 years. This really was a good time to be a Leeds player, especially for me. I had become a cult figure on the Elland Road terraces. Fans everywhere love big-name signings, but they really take to their hearts the lad who has come through the ranks of the youth teams, and all the more so if he is a local boy to boot. I was stacking up supporters' club awards and Man of the Match credits and I quietly revelled in the fans' adulation. Sometimes, when a player hits a stray pass the fans become unhappy and let the poor guy know their feelings. That can be extremely unsettling for a player, but there was never anything of the sort directed towards me. The crowd always focused on me, but always to give me encouragement. I think they were more relieved than I was when I got that drought-ending goal against Manchester City.

That November we went to Villa Park and recorded a 4–1 win. The match was televised live and I remember thinking we had won so comfortably that it might be significant for our prospects that season. It is hard enough to win at any away venue in the top flight, let alone cruise in 4–1 at a big club like Villa. We were on a bit of a roll and I was on a high: on 9 December, Mandy and I moved into our new house at Thorp Arch, Wetherby. The team maintained an unbeaten streak that stretched from 1 October to 8 February, when we lost 2–0 at Oldham. That date was significant for another reason; it marked the debut, as a substitute, of Eric Cantona. However, there was another crazy incident that could well have had serious, if not fatal, consequences for our title aspirations.

As a reward for the effort we had put in and in an attempt to recharge our batteries, Howard Wilkinson arranged a three-day winter break at the purpose-built Portuguese resort of La Manga. It was very much a sun and relaxation getaway and we were all delighted at the prospect. The season was going well; Leeds were vying for leadership of the League table and the players were enjoying their football. But it was a welcome change as we flew off to the Algarve, further boosted by Wilko's pledge that it was to be very much a foot-off-the-pedal few days away. It didn't take the lads long to take the gaffer at his word. The accent was on fun, not football, so we launched into the lager. We were staying in smart villas, four players to each one, and each group had a Fiat Panda to tootle around the complex in. On the very first night, our foursome had driven down the road the short distance to the bar, where we joined the other lads and proceeded to have a big drinking session for a few hours. I must admit that we had had quite a few drinks by the time someone decided we ought to get back to our beds. The decision to leave was unanimous and correct; the mistake was to get into the car. My big mate and left-sided midfield colleague Gary Speed clambered into the driving seat and started up the engine; I got in alongside with the other two lads in the back. We can't have been more than 200 yards from our villa and it would certainly have been no trouble at all to walk. If only we had. Speedo – appropriately named – set off as if we had half the Portuguese police force in pursuit. The little Panda roared up the road, approaching the bend on which our accommodation was sited. Through the lager haze, I was thinking: 'What the hell's going on? We're travelling too fast. Slow down, Speedo.' I don't know if I actually mumbled any words of warning to him, but if I did, they were either too late or unheard because he drove the car over the kerb and straight into a lamp-post. And I mean head-on. The little Panda – they aren't the sturdiest of vehicles – folded in half and wrapped itself around the lamp-post. Not one of us was wearing a seat-belt, yet we all stumbled from the wreckage unscathed and laughing like a bunch of 15-year-olds who'd just had their first experience of a beer too many. We stood, staring at the crumpled heap of metal that had been a smart little motor, turned and fell up the path and into our beds.

Next morning, I parted the curtains warily, hoping to discover that it had all been a dream. Dream! It was a bloody nightmare. There was the smashed Panda – and here were Sgt Major Mick Hennigan and physio Alan Sutton heading our way with faces like thunder. Through my hangover, I quickly rationalised the situation. I knew they would immediately assume that I was the culprit because of my history of getting into stupid scrapes. I could imagine that Wilko had already told Mick to go and bring that so-and-so Batty before him. Yet, for once, I could relax, safe in the knowledge that, though an accessory, I wasn't the one who had pulled the trigger. That was down to poor Speedo. So I lay back on my pillow and smugly pictured the scene as Gary took the rap – and the consequences. How short-sighted can you be? Gary was gutted as he prepared to plead guilty, but when the sentence was passed, it incorporated all four of us. 'If you can't behave yourselves you'll have to work instead of play' was Wilko's judgement. We spent the rest of our stay pounding the perimeter of the golf course on punishment duty. It was a nice break – for the first 12 hours.

In the cold light of day I couldn't say I was surprised by Speedo's dodgem-car antics, and I admit that if I had had the car keys, it would just as likely have been me who'd done the stupid deed. Gary and I were both daft in our cars when we were youngsters. He had a Ford Orion, I had my Marina and we drove them like Formula One stars, Ferrari versus McLaren. Gary was in digs in Seacroft, Leeds, and our routes into the ground would converge on the ring-road, near the *Yorkshire Evening Post* offices. Whenever the two of us saw each other there it was the signal for the flag to go up and a race to start. Stupid, I know. We had been lucky never to get ourselves into serious bother before. Mind you, recklessness behind the wheel – or, more specifically, an irresistible urge to drive quickly – wasn't confined to Gary Speed and me. The scene outside Elland Road when we returned from midweek away matches often used to resemble the grid at a Grand Prix. Several of us lived north of the city and we would have late-night races down the inner ring-road, starting from the big roundabout near the stadium. One midwinter night, I was first out and looking in my rear-view mirror to assess the competition. I saw Jon Newsome, our centre-half, lose it; his car spun in the middle of the road and ended up stuck on the central reservation. Luckily, Jon escaped unscathed, but we had to get the emergency services out. There were five of us at the scene, along with several other motorists who stopped to inquire why half the Leeds United team were parked and surrounded by flashing lights.

As the 1991–92 season passed the halfway mark, Leeds were flashing signals to the rest of the First Division. The message was: 'We mean business.' Our four-month unbeaten run, following a solid start, stamped us as serious title contenders. A booking in the top-of-the-table clash with Manchester United, which we drew 1–1 at Elland Road, earned me a two-match suspension going into the New Year and I missed the mid-January matches with Sheffield Wednesday – which Leeds won 6–1 at Hillsborough – and our home League Cup defeat to Manchester United. To my relief, I was reinstated to the side as soon as the suspension ended.

I remember the second week in February as being one that was full of Continental influence, for me and for Leeds United. The first, and most significant, development was the arrival of a man called Cantona. Little did we realise what an impact – albeit a brief one – Eric was to have on us going down the last stretch towards the title tape. He had been at Sheffield Wednesday for a matter of weeks, or even days, but none of us knew anything about him. We never did learn a lot about what made Eric tick, except in the one area that interested us the most: football. We quickly realised that, in a stroke of either pure genius or good luck, Howard Wilkinson had brought a rare and exceptional talent into our midst. Wilko's former club weren't at all amused when Eric walked out on them to join their local rivals. Whatever the ins and outs of the deal, one thing was for sure: Wilko had pulled another master-stroke. Ironically, Cantona's first taste of action with Leeds was as a loser. He was brought on as a sub for Steve Hodge in the 2–0 defeat at Oldham that brought our long unbeaten run to an end. Two days later, I was given more foreign fare to ponder.

Even though I probably wasn't playing as consistently well as I had the previous season, I must have been doing well enough, because word came through of yet more interest in me. In a phone call to my Thorp Arch home I was told that an Italian club was interested in signing me at the end of the season. The caller would not identify the club, but asked me for my reaction. In a nutshell, he said he needed to know if such a move would interest me. I said it would. Once again, that might shock Leeds fans, who have every reason to assume that, as a key player in the title-chasing team and one who had recently signed a new, generous pay deal, the last thing I would contemplate was parting company with the club I had been at since leaving school. I can understand supporters thinking along those lines. But you learn quickly in this game that players, while essential to a club one minute, are alarmingly dispensable the next. Just as with the other interest six months previously, I felt I owed it to myself and to Mandy to keep any window of opportunity open. I know I've stressed how much of a stick-in-the-mud I am and what store I set on putting down roots, yet you must remember that I was 23, and with no children to support. A move to Italy was something you would have to be either mad not to contemplate or afraid to consider. I may have been a bit daft in my younger days, but I wasn't mad! Several weeks went by without another word and I was beginning to think it had all been a bit of a hoax when my dad got a phone call from an Italian agent requesting a meeting. The agent asked Dad to meet him at a pub on the outskirts of Leeds and stressed the crucial importance of keeping the whole affair top secret. By now, Dad was getting used to all of this cloak-and-dagger stuff. He had cut his teeth on covert operations with the previous affair. In fact, Dad met the agent near Elland Road and took him home, where I was also waiting. We were told that, if Leeds would sell, more than one Serie A club would be keen to buy me that summer. Still no names, though. The agent left, apparently satisfied that he had established that, if all was above board with Leeds, I would be willing to listen to what the Italians had to say.

As it happened, I never heard another word about a move to the lira-laden Italian League: not directly, at least. Within days of the meeting with the agent, however, Dad got another phone call from an agent, who said he was empowered to inform us that clubs in Italy were becoming increasingly interested in the possibility of signing me. Dad told him we had already had a meeting with one of his countrymen. When he revealed the agent's name, the new caller exclaimed: 'What! He's supposed to be working for me!' I tell you, they say there's no honour among thieves. Though neither man ever got in touch again, I believe that the club originally making secretive inquiries about me was Parma. Just before the European Championships that summer, the newspapers reported that Lazio wanted to sign me to play alongside their English import, Paul Gascoigne. Leeds chairman Leslie Silver quickly announced that

David Batty would be wearing the white shirt of Leeds the following season. I still wonder if the Italian connection might not have ended had England – and I – acquitted ourselves better at the European Championships. Of course, we had a miserable tournament in Sweden. I ended up playing at right-back in one match. It wasn't an ideal advertisement for a player who was in the shop window. Not that I lost any sleep over the affair; I was happy enough at Leeds and wouldn't have dreamed of looking to get away. I had responded to the Italians' enquiries out of a sense of curiosity, and I would never have broken the terms of the contract I had signed with Leeds the previous autumn. Admittedly, I was intrigued by the prospect of playing in Italy, but it never became an obsession. What the whole episode did do, though, was give another insight to the behind-the-scenes wheeling and dealing in big-time football. The more middle men get involved in transfers, the more messy the whole business can become. Episodes such as this served only to convince me that I must do my best to find someone I could trust to look after my financial affairs.

Meanwhile, back on the home front, Eric Cantona was making an immediate – and indelible – imprint on Leeds United. From the minute I first saw Cantona train I knew I was in the presence of a very special footballer. He had fantastic speed of thought as well as action and, for a big man, his touch was unbelievably impressive. He was also the most supremely self-confident character I had ever come across on a football pitch; and off it, for that matter. We had some good players in that title-winning Leeds team: Gary

Speed, Gordon Strachan, Gary McAllister. But in comparison to Cantona, even those three were relatively ordinary. The thing about Cantona, like Paul Gascoigne, was that he had the God-given ability to do things that were extraordinary. I used to wonder if Eric surprised himself sometimes. His play was so off the cuff, so sensationally inventive. These impressions slowly became fixed in my mind as the weeks went by – along with another, nagging question that never left my head and to which, to this day, I don't have the answer: namely, what possessed Wilkinson, that most immovable, uncompromising of coaches, to sign a player who so patently flew in the face of his basic philosophy? The thought struck me virtually from the day Cantona arrived and it remained unanswered until the day Eric departed for Manchester United nine months later. I know people will say the obvious answer lies in the fact that Eric inspired us to title glory over the last laps of the marathon and that Wilko must have foreseen he would do exactly that. It might well be that Wilko identified signs of jadedness as we entered the last three months of the campaign; I have already admitted that I wasn't functioning quite as consistently well as I had the previous season. Even so, I still found it confusing that such a free spirit as Cantona should be introduced to the workrate-orientated system that Wilko had ruthlessly hammered home over the previous three years.

I can remember thinking: 'How on earth will this guy fit in? He's too skilful!' After all, as far as I could judge, skill wasn't exactly top of Wilko's specifications when choosing a player. If a player had stacks of skill it was often the case that he had a low workrate, and that was definitely a no-no where Howard was concerned. Still, Cantona came along, and the timing was perfect. He was in and out of the team in the first few weeks but he kept chipping in with crucial goals – and special ones – and there was no denying that his presence lifted the whole camp. He was always trying something unusual in the course of a match. Cantona could be counted upon to make something happen when you gave him the ball. I really appreciated that because, after risking life and limb to win the ball, the last thing I found amusing was to give it to a team-mate who didn't try to use it well. Believe me, if players don't use the ball well when I pass it to them, I soon stop passing it to them! That was never the case with Eric. He had a remarkable ability to turn an ordinary-looking situation into a dangerous one, to emerge, with one deft flick, from the tightest of corners, leaving defenders lunging in all directions. The crowd loved him and so did I. Yet Eric wasn't perfect. I have to say that, like most individual talents – especially foreigners in an English team – Eric did have a tendency to 'go missing' away from home when the chips were down. That happened once at Manchester City, where our title aspirations were made to look distinctly dubious by a 4–0 thrashing early in April. I had a good game that day, but Eric wasn't at the races and he was substituted in the second half. I put Eric's countryman David Ginola in the same bracket: a player who can be devastatingly effective and mind-bogglingly brilliant when the mood takes him, but who can also be a luxury, a passenger, when the going gets tough at a hostile away ground and the team is a goal or more behind. It is in those situations that you need all hands to the pump. You can't afford players who won't buckle down and do their share of the donkey work, tracking back and making tackles. I'm fairly confident that it was for those reasons that Wilko stunned the football world the following November by selling Eric to Alex Ferguson at Manchester United for just £1 million. For my part, I was sorry to see him go. Though there were times when he was a bit of a passenger, they were far outweighed by his match-winning abilities. I don't know what the word was from the Manchester United dressing-room, but the facts spoke for themselves. With Cantona in their team, United won four Premier League championship titles in five seasons, and a cup or two along the way. You have to say that if there was a knack to getting the best out of Cantona, Alex Ferguson had it.

True, Eric was a bit of a loner and could seem aloof at times. But he wasn't nearly so remote a figure as he appeared, though it was an image I think he was happy to promote. He was certainly no recluse; far from it. On several occasions he accompanied me, Gary Speed and Gary McAllister on nights out. We would go to Harrogate, which was far enough from Leeds to give us semi-anonymity. Also, we figured that, as senior professionals, it wasn't diplomatic to be seen around the bars of Leeds city centre too often. More often than not, Eric would volunteer to drive. He liked a drink – usually a glass or two of wine – though not nearly as much as we did, and he seemed to enjoy an evening out. He was always the quiet one, managing to maintain the air of mystery that became such a part of his cult image at Old Trafford, but he was sociable enough. He was also a complete nonconformist. I claim to be a man of moderate material needs, but compared to Eric, I was a raging yuppie. He lived in a modest semi-detached house in Roundhay, Leeds. Now, I don't believe in flaunting your wealth, but Eric went from the sublime to the ridiculous. To put it bluntly, his house, in a really ordinary suburban street, was a bit of a dump. The grass in the garden was knee-high and I never saw it looking any different. Eric didn't give a damn about appearances. It was clearly just a base for him and his wife and son, a roof over the family's heads and no more. Even my dad's work-mates on the bin round used to say: 'Have you seen where Eric Cantona lives?'

I later learned that when he moved to Manchester and eventually got a place over there, it was very similar. Eric was big time on the pitch, all right. But you couldn't accuse him of being a scene-stealer when he was away from football. His eccentricity was summed up for me by an incident that followed our fantastic 4–3 Charity Shield victory over FA Cup winners Liverpool in the curtain-raiser to the 1992–93 season. Eric scored a hat-trick at Wembley, his finest moment in the Leeds shirt, and there was no denying he was a proud man as he walked from the hallowed turf with the match ball in his hands. I was pretty pleased with myself, too, having played really well, though I did get booked. A few days later, Gary Speed and I called round at Eric's house. His young son was in the drive, kicking a ball against the garage door. I joined in for a couple of minutes and was gobsmacked when I saw, from the writing on the ball, that it was none other than the Charity Shield match ball. Gary was as astonished as I was when I told him later. Although I am definitely not the most sentimental of players when it comes to the game, I can assure you, if that had been my ball, there's no way I'd have let my lads belt it around the back yard. But that was Eric Cantona: an immense talent who had more than enough self-confidence and self-contentment not to be concerned with the trappings of his success.

He certainly didn't sit easily in the strict atmosphere of the Howard Wilkinson regime. Eric obviously hadn't been happy at being used as a sub so often during the title run-in, but he kept his own counsel and did more than his bit to spark us along the road to glory. His patience and self-restraint started to wear thin, though, the following season. Not surprisingly, after his Charity Shield triumph, Eric was a must to start in the side when the championship got under way. He stayed in the starting line-up for the first couple of months but I remember beginning to sense that he was growing restless with our direct style. He certainly couldn't accept being told, one day in training, that he wouldn't be in the side the following day. One moment he was sprinting, the next he suddenly pulled up clutching his hamstring, and simply walked off the training ground without a word to anyone. The lads looked at each other knowingly. He may have been injured for all we knew, but we suspected otherwise and admired his style. I'm not advocating such a reaction every time a player gets dropped. But, with some justification, Cantona couldn't accept that he didn't merit a place in the Leeds starting line-up. The cracks between him and Wilko were starting to appear. At the team meeting before our match at QPR, late in October, there was obviously an atmosphere between Eric and the manager. That impression was confirmed when, to our astonishment, Wilko suddenly produced Eric's passport – I don't know how he got hold of it – and handed it over to him. Eric took it and promptly flew to France for a few days. We lost to QPR in his absence. Within a couple of weeks, Cantona had been sold to Manchester United. The great adventure had lasted nine months. I believe Cantona's early exit was inevitable – he was a square peg in a round hole at Elland Road – but I also believe that the decision to let him go was a backward step.

One of my endearing memories of Eric is of sharing the sofa with him, Gary McAllister and Lee Chapman at Chappy's house in the Derbyshire dales the day we celebrated winning the championship. It had been a tense, seesaw four weeks since that day at Maine Road when we got battered 4–0, leaving Manchester United clear favourites to win the title. They were on top with 70 points from 35 matches. We were a point behind them, but had played 37. Perhaps the outcome of the General Election proved to be a good omen. I was amused to read the following entry in my dad's notes: 'The Conservatives have won the General Election. If Labour had been voted into Government they proposed to add an extra 10 per cent on high earners' income tax, plus higher national insurance contributions. So David is well pleased with the result as it will save him thousands of pounds. It is the first time in my life that I've wanted the Conservatives to win an election.' Oh, the hypocrisy! But I can't deny it.

Buoyed by that bit of good fortune, I did my bit to put us back on top of the League with a 3–0 home win over Chelsea and I had the thrill of captaining the side at Liverpool a week later, when Gordon Strachan was rested. Unfortunately, though we got a creditable goalless draw at Anfield, it wasn't enough to prevent Manchester United from regaining the leadership. They were now two points ahead with one game in hand going into the Easter period of three games in a week. When Ferguson's team lost their last game in hand – at bottom club West Ham – we were one point ahead with two matches to play. Dad and I were in the garage at our house when news of the West Ham result came through. I can clearly recall clenching my fist and thinking: 'Yes! It's still on.'

Sunday, 26 April 1992 was one of the longest days of my life. We went to Sheffield United for a televised morning kick-off. Manchester United were playing at Liverpool that afternoon, their match also going out live on TV. The situation was clear. If we won and United lost, the title was ours for the first time in 18 years, since Don Revie's great side beat Liverpool into second place in 1974. Such a scenario would put us four points clear with one match to play. Unassailable. And that's just how it turned out. We won 3–2 at Bramall Lane. It was a scrappy game and we were unconvincing, aided as we were by an own goal by the Blades' central defender Brian Gayle. In fact, we were lucky to win the match – but who cares? They say you need a bit of luck to win the big prizes. Howard Wilkinson returned to his Sheffield home for a late Sunday lunch, and I went to Chappy's place, with Gary McAllister and Cantona. A film crew from Yorkshire Television was there too. The cameras kept switching from the drama being enacted at Anfield to us four sitting nervously and somewhat self-consciously on Chappy's couch. Eric was beginning to act a bit dumb, coming the old 'I am sorry, I do not understand' routine as the TV presenter tried to coax words out of him once our triumph had been confirmed by Liverpool's 2–0 win. Chappy had played a bit in France and must have given the TV people reason to believe he was quite fluent in the language. So the presenter asked him to ask Eric how he felt at such an historic moment. Chappy drew a deep breath – and proceeded to repeat every word of the question in English, but with his version of a French accent. Eric looked disdainful and I roared with laughter, claiming quite legitimately: 'Bloody hell, Lee, I could have done that.' I don't think the harassed presenter got anything more than a few broken words of English out of Eric's lips, even though I know he was completely aware of what was going on. I have often thought how stupid we would have looked, sitting there in front of the cameras, had United won at Liverpool and we'd had to go through the whole torturous process again the following weekend. Perhaps Cantona was thinking that at the time.

We were only too aware that observers put the outcome of that title race down to the fact that Manchester United had thrown it away, rather than that Leeds United had won it. But that is unfair. True, Manchester United faltered over the final hurdles, but the championship is, as they say, a marathon, not a sprint. Every contender and every winner will have at least one bad spell over a nine- to ten-month slog. Ferguson's team happened to have theirs at the death. And I will always be impressed by Alex Ferguson's graciousness in conceding defeat. Though he must have been so choked he could hardly speak, he stepped in front of the camera at Anfield, and, when it was suggested to him that Leeds were lucky winners, he would have none of it. Ferguson made it quite plain that whichever team wins the First Division title deserves to win it. His message was clear: you can't win such a long, gruelling race by default.

We popped the champagne corks at Chappy's place before I drove home and picked up Mandy and all the players and their wives and girlfriends got together at a pub near Roundhay Park before moving on to the Flying Pizza restaurant in Moortown, an establishment owned by a big Leeds fan, and one which was frequently patronised by the players. We had a great time that night and the next, and the next, and the next. So much so that by the time we came to play our final match, at home to Norwich, I don't know how any of us were fit to walk, let alone play football. I can only assume that we were pumped up by the sense of occasion and that Norwich were equally deflated by it, because we won 1–0 to make it a fitting finale for the 32,673 fans inside Elland Road. We were presented with the championship trophy and our individual medals before kick-off, and I was again captain in the absence of the battle-fatigued Strachan, who was on the bench. It was a fitting climax for me. Though I think my form the previous season had probably been better overall, I was the proud recipient of the *Yorkshire Evening Post* Player of the Year award and the *Sunday People* newspaper's Merit Award. And, as if to consolidate my place in the affections of the Leeds public, I topped the *YEP*'s readers' poll for Most Popular Player.

More celebrations followed our final match, but Mandy and I spent an uncomfortable night on the drive of our house trying to sleep in the car. Returning from yet another social evening, we found that we had lost our keys. A neighbour who had a set had to let us in the next morning.

One of my first acts that day was to take both my home and away No. 4 shirts to my mum and dad's house, where they were added to the shirt collection being compiled there down the years. Then it was off to meet the other players and staff for our triumphant open-top bus ride through the city. An estimated 200,000 people hit the streets to salute us. They made for a wonderful, moving experience. Tears don't come too readily to my eyes – I'm not the most outwardly emotional of guys – but I was fighting to hold back the tears that afternoon, particularly as I got the feeling that, as the local lad made good, the supporters were reserving a special place in their hearts for me. I couldn't have been on a bigger high: I had a championship medal around my neck, a clutch of individual awards in my pocket, and every right to be optimistic that I would be in England manager Graham Taylor's squad for the European Championship finals in Sweden that summer. I was at the top. And yet, in retrospect, I have to pose the question: Did we win the title too soon? Were we really that good? The simple answer is yes. We won it and they can never take it away from us. But I can't hide from the fact that we couldn't carry the mantle of champions with distinction. The following season we finished only 17th in the inaugural Premier League. And the end of my first period with the club was in sight.

CHAPTER 10

leaving leeds

Although my joy at our championship triumph was diluted somewhat by England's dismal failure that summer in the European Championship finals in Sweden, there were compensations as I prepared for the 1992–93 campaign and Leeds's bid to defend the title. For a start, a 10 per cent pay rise, agreed in my contract negotiations, kicked in on 1 July. Later than month, Wilko again strengthened the squad, signing David 'Rocky' Rocastle from Arsenal, and Scott Sellars from Blackburn. Rocastle was experienced and Sellars a more than useful player to have on board as he was that rarity, a quality left-sided midfielder; Tony Dorigo and Gary Speed were our only natural left-footers so Scott's arrival was a welcome boost to the squad in that department.

I'm not so sure Dad thought so highly of me after the anticlimax of the European Championships. His depressing summing-up of my tournament reads as follows: 'I was hoping that if David was given an outing in these championships he would really lift his game and make a name for himself at international level. Well, he's had two games and, in my opinion, he hasn't enhanced his reputation.' It's a harsh assessment, but fair. I can't argue too much with it, but there were mitigating factors which I'll deal with when I discuss my England career later in these pages.

I returned from Sweden depressed, like most of my England team-mates, my mood exacerbated by a thigh strain that hampered my pre-season training. But, in typical Batty fashion, I was raring to go when Leeds hosted the Makita Tournament on 1 and 2 August, with Nottingham Forest, Sampdoria of Italy, and Stuttgart from the German Bundesliga. The injury meant I wasn't involved in Leeds's 2–1 win over Stuttgart on day one, when Sampdoria beat Forest 2–0, but once Wilko drafted me in for the final, against the Serie A glamour boys, I made up my mind I was going to make the most of it! It had been many years – not since the halcyon days of Don Revie's management, in fact – since Leeds fans had seen great teams from the Continent at Elland Road. I know this was only a warm-up event, designed as a loosener for the real battles to come once the League programme started, but I was in no mood for pussyfooting around when I took to the pitch that day. I suppose I was frustrated because my entry into the tournament had been delayed and, as ever, playing football was all or nothing so far as I was concerned. So, having taken one look at their team-sheet, which boasted big names like Lombardo, Mancini and Forest's former star Des Walker, I decided to have some fun. It was the ideal opportunity for me to indulge in my favourite pastime of getting stuck in to the so-called big-name players and that is precisely what I did. From the first whistle, I was up and at 'em like a new kid out to impress his manager. I can't remember the full-back's name, but he must have wondered what had hit him when I put him clean over the advertising hoardings at the side of the pitch. The crowd was loving every minute of it, and so was I. But Sampdoria's players weren't. Mancini got so riled that he grabbed hold of me. By then, I'd been booked and the referee was concerned I was about to spark an Anglo-Italian war. He went to the dugout and told Wilko that if he didn't take me off he'd send me off. At least, I assume that's what was said because, within seconds, it was a case of 'Come in No. 4, your time's up!' We lost the match 1–0, but the crowd loved it, and I like to think their pleasure was derived mainly from the fact that I injected some needle into the proceedings. These pre-season games are usually dull affairs, used only as a warm-up with no risk of injury, and I guess that's fair enough. But, as ever, the devil in me won the day.

We flew over to Norway where we won a friendly against Stroemgodset, then it was on to Wembley and the Charity Shield curtain-raiser against Liverpool. I picked up another booking but also had a good game, even though Eric Cantona understandably grabbed all the headlines after his hat-trick in the 4–3 win. For the players, this is really just another pre-season warm-up game, but it is a great way to start the campaign. I hadn't played for Leeds at Wembley before, and it is a great treat for the players and the fans to have the opportunity to go there, especially as there are no nerves, as there would be before a cup final or a key international.

We set out to enjoy the game. So much so that when Liverpool scored their third – going through Strachan's legs as he stood on the line – he and I just looked at each other and laughed. But although it might be a relaxed occasion, it can give you a key to how the season will develop. If you do well, you think you can take that form into the season, and as we had Eric scoring goals we thought we would be strong again. It was a big morale-booster for the team, and we cashed in by beating Wimbledon at home in our first Premier League match one week later and achieving a highly creditable draw at Aston Villa in midweek. We had made a pretty encouraging start to the defence of our title, but the cracks soon started to show.

Our title-winning side had largely been comprised of players at the back end of their careers who had won little before, and a few up-and-coming people, like me and Gary Speed. We all basically did what we were told, and followed Howard's instructions on how to play, though Eric was never really like that. He was very confident in his own ability to play off the cuff. There had been one or two other players brought in to give us an extra degree of imagination, players like Gary McAllister, who gave us extra guile in midfield, and Rod Wallace, whose pace (like Carl Shutt) caused opponents lots of trouble. Wallace and Shutt both had the happy knack of popping up with late goals when their pace could really tell on tiring defences.

The old back four had been very settled, with Tony Dorigo and Mel Sterland at full-back, and Chris Whyte and Chris Fairclough in the middle. But the following season Mel picked up an injury, and there weren't many good right-backs around, which is how Jon Newsome ended up filling in there. The midfield was a strong blend: Strachan was the natural leader, with his incredible will, fitness and determination; McAllister could unlock opposition defences; Speed gave us an extra dimension with his heading ability; and then there was me to break up the opposition and to feed the more creative players in the side.

Injury was to play its part in making my own season a particularly frustrating one. Already, I had had the thigh strain, quickly followed by an ankle problem that caused me to pull out of the England squad to play a friendly in Santander early in September. My Leeds team-mates Tony Dorigo and Rod Wallace were also named by manager Graham Taylor, but Wallace, too, had to withdraw. It was his first call-up and I recall being more upset for him than for myself. I struggled through several League matches with our big date, the European Cup tie with German champions Stuttgart on 16 September, in mind.

This was the first time most of us had played in Europe at club level, and it was a totally different feel. As Stuttgart is the home of Mercedes, all the players had their own Mercs. The whole set-up was an eye-opener, and we were about to find out how much English football had slipped behind the rest of Europe during the ban. A 38,000 full house turned out for what was without doubt the biggest occasion for Leeds since men like Billy Bremner, Johnny Giles and Allan Clarke had made the club's name one to fear and respect in England and Europe 20 years earlier. But, come the day, what a let-down we and the fans experienced.

To my alarm, Howard Wilkinson axed Jon Newsome and played me in his place at right-back. That is the only position I have ever occupied apart from central midfield, not counting my brief forays as centre-forward when I was a kid. And I didn't like it. The reason for my lack of enthusiasm for the role was straightforward: I wasn't any good at it. My one real weakness is that I'm hopeless when opponents take me on. I've never been the quickest, so all a speedy winger needs to do is knock the ball past me and go; believe me, usually he'll be away. Stick me in there, as Eddie Gray did during my early days as an apprentice, and I feel like a fish out of water. I never know where I should be in relation to the centre-half or whether I should be pushing on to the winger. I've always found it confusing.

The man in the street might imagine that a top-class footballer should be able to adapt readily to any position, but it really isn't the case: take Alan Shearer as an example. Alan, who I went on to play with at Blackburn and Newcastle and, of course, for England, was one of the best strikers I ever saw. But if he had been switched into midfield, he would have quickly become a very ordinary player. He is great up front, where he is used to playing with his back to goal and with a defender challenging him from behind, but I've seen Alan in training matches when he's been drafted back to midfield with everybody around him, front, back and sides. He looks baffled. He is a centre-forward through and through. It is the same for me when I'm at full-back. It is alien to me. I'm used to being in the thick of the action, and at right-back I feel exposed.

Exposed was the word for it that September night in Germany, when Stuttgart's tricky little left-winger took me to the cleaners. It was a hot evening with a capacity crowd, everything you would want for your European

Cup debut – except the result. After holding Stuttgart until half-time, the wheels came off after the break and we lost 3–0. We were battered. It was a rude awakening. I was even embarrassed by our revolting away kit, yellow with blue speckles. If we had performed well that night I'm sure I wouldn't have cared if I'd been dressed in pink with yellow dots on!

Wilko played me at right-back quite a few times that season, a factor that undoubtedly contributed to my growing unrest at the club. During our 2–0 home win over Everton later that September I was asking myself: 'What am I doing here? I'm just not comfortable.' I am normally so positive and I didn't mind a once-in-a-blue-moon outing as a defender, but it was becoming frequent and I was getting a bit depressed by it. After a 4–1 League Cup first-round home win over Scunthorpe that month, Dad penned another of his stinging critiques on my form.

However, there was a lighter side to that match against Scunny. Beforehand, I had decided to have my hair cut. And I don't mean trimmed, I mean shaved: a No. 1 they'd call it these days. Mandy wasn't happy about my intentions and I never said a word to the lads at Leeds. I called in at a barber's shop in Rothwell on the day of the match and told them to go to town. It wasn't quite as savage a hacking job as I did on Vinnie Jones a couple of years earlier, but it was a pretty ruthless cut nevertheless. I had grown tired of my hair; I wanted to get rid of my 'curtains', as the other lads described the wavy locks that drooped down my forehead. Obviously, a footballer has to wash his hair once, often twice a day and it had become a bit of a bind. I have never been one for spending hours in front of a mirror, unlike some of the guys I have played with. They make me laugh, the way they preen themselves like women getting ready for a night out. I remember watching David Ginola, at Newcastle, and Leeds striker Lee Chapman file their nails in the dressing-room and thinking: 'Bloody hell – what am I working with here!' One man who is the complete opposite to somebody like Ginola – and much more like me – is Stuart Pearce. 'Psycho' has longish, lank hair but absolutely no vanity. He would come down to breakfast in the Newcastle and England hotels looking like he'd been dragged through a hedge, with hair all over the place. I appreciated that. He hadn't been poncing around in the bathroom for ages.

Mandy's main objection to my plan was that the shaven-headed look gives you the appearance of a bit of a thug. Some people may have thought that I had it done in order to lend more credence to my hard-man image, but nothing could be further from the truth. So, many years before the look was made fashionable by lads like Roy Keane and David Beckham, I had the treatment. I walked down the corridor of the Hilton Hotel, Leeds, that afternoon with a towel wrapped around my head. As I approached our centre-back, Chris Whyte, I whipped off the towel – and he collapsed laughing. When I ran on to the Elland Road pitch that evening hardly a soul recognised me.

Though Jon Newsome had recovered from injury, I stayed at right-back in the coming weeks, a run which included the second leg against Stuttgart. Ironically, it turned out to be one of the best matches I have ever played in – even if, in that role, I felt as if I'd been a bit of an onlooker. We staged one of the great comebacks to beat Stuttgart 4–1, a scoreline whose impact was diluted by the fact that we went out of the competition 5–4 on the away goals rule. Or so we thought. Incredibly, though no one at the club realised it on the night, Stuttgart had contravened the rules by bringing on a fourth foreign player – the maximum then was three – 10 minutes from the end of the tie. The upshot was that UEFA ordered a rematch 10 days later at the Nou Camp in Barcelona. Our reaction to the replay verdict was one of joy; when we heard the venue, the mood was ecstatic. Imagine, a European Cup tie in front of 120,000 people in arguably the most famous club stadium in the world. What a bonus! Come the night, however, there was a crowd of only 7,400. It was like playing in a reserve match. But the big plus was that we won 2–1, and the bonus for me was that I was restored to my midfield berth. Six days earlier, at Ipswich, right-back Batty had given away a penalty, conceded a free kick which led to a goal and been booked. Then I was put back into mid-field, we beat Stuttgart in extra time and, suddenly, the world seemed a better place.

Carl Shutt, who came on for Eric Cantona, scored our winner that night. We were all shouting and singing in the dressing-room after the match when someone asked: 'Where's Shutty?' There was no sign of him. Mick Hennigan went in search and returned to tell us Carl was in the shower room. We piled in, to be confronted by the sight of Shutty, sobbing with his head against the wall. 'What's up with you?' we asked. 'I just can't take it all in,' he said. 'I can't believe what I've done. I've scored the winner in the Nou Camp – and it's my birthday tomorrow.' Boy, did he get some stick. 'Pull yourself together, you soft sod,' I told him, and we all went out to sample the night life of Barcelona, with former Bárca star Steve Archibald – who was a big pal of Gordon Strachan – as our guide.

Another irony of my misery at full-back during the build-up to that triumphant night – which earned us a second-round meeting with Glasgow Rangers – was that I was nevertheless selected for the England squad to play Norway in a World Cup qualifier in mid-October. Maybe I wasn't such a bad right-back, after all! Seriously, though, I played in midfield alongside Paul Gascoigne at Wembley in a 1–1 draw and was happy with my contribution.

One week later was the much-anticipated trip to Ibrox for the European Cup date with Rangers. If ever a night lived up to expectations, that was it. The newspapers had billed it as the Battle of Britain, and when I walked on to that Ibrox pitch, I wondered for a moment or two if there was, indeed, a war going on. I have never heard noise like it. You literally could not hear your own voice. Waves of sound and a persistent, shrill whistling that pierced our brains assailed us as we stepped from the tunnel. I loved it. It was everything you could wish for in terms of electric atmosphere. Any player worth his salt thrives on it, but there's no denying, that Ibrox roar was enough to crush the faint-hearted. Usually, in a ground with an intimidating atmosphere, you get it from two or three sides: at Ibrox there was no sanctuary from any angle. I could feel my eardrums vibrating. Leeds fans weren't allowed to make the trip for fear of security problems, but the players had tickets for family and friends. Mandy, my mum and dad and Mandy's brother Lee were there. Young Lee actually developed a headache because of the noise. But you could have heard a pin drop in the seconds after Gary McAllister whacked home a shot from 25 yards in the first minute. In the most astonishing transformation, the fanatical Rangers hordes were stunned into silence. Mind you, it didn't take them long to shake themselves out of their stupor and turn up the noise to ear-splitting levels again. Our keeper John Lukic had a bit of a nightmare, throwing in two goals to leave us beaten 2–1, but we would have accepted that before the match and confidence remained high for the return leg. Sadly for me, I didn't make the line-up at Elland Road.

A player's foremost concern is that the manager should pick him, but the underlying worry for every one of us is the fear of injury: not so much the niggles, the strains and the pulls, the bumps and bruises, that are an occupational hazard, but the serious problems like broken limbs, ligament tears and cartilages. I had been free of any significant injury setbacks until the afternoon of 31 October 1992, when Leeds met Coventry at Elland Road. I was starting to buzz again in my midfield role; near to top form, I was enjoying my battle with Coventry's Stewart Robson, who had recently joined them from Arsenal. I went down under a run-of-the-mill foul tackle from Stewart, who clipped me from behind. But I went over on my ankle and, immediately, I knew something was wrong, a feeling confirmed when I realised I couldn't get up. Now, I never stay down after I've been whacked because I don't want people to know I'm hurt, even if I am. But here, I had no choice. I was worried. I lay there thinking about the big game with Rangers four days later. My ankle bone had jammed into my foot, crushing the ankle, and it hurt like hell. The frustrating thing was that I was able to run within a couple of days, but as soon as I kicked a ball the pain was intense. The club was so desperate to get me into action against Rangers that I was taken to a medical centre at Horsforth which was equipped with a special oxygen chamber, like a diving bell in appearance. The idea is that you breathe in pure oxygen, thus increasing the blood supply to the injured part. I was in there for two hours, but it didn't have the desired effect and I was out of the tie. Leeds lost 2–1 and were out of Europe, beaten 4–2 on aggregate. I was gutted. I really did think we could have licked Rangers at our place.

The crazy aspect of the episode was that six weeks went by before I had a scan on the ankle. When I did, it revealed a hairline fracture. No wonder I had to pull out of the England squad for another World Cup qualifier and missed five club matches before going to Leeds Infirmary on 10 December. The ankle was put in plaster and I was out of action until Boxing Day, a total of 10 weeks. It was the first serious injury setback of my career; unfortunately, it was just the first of several over the coming years. Such circumstances would never be allowed to prevail nowadays. I was one of the most valuable, best-paid players in the team, a man who had helped us to win the League championship the previous season, hobbling around for weeks before someone suggested I go and get some expert opinion! I had grown up the hard way, in an era when you played through pain and kept going if you picked up knocks. I was a tough little so-and-so and I accepted that was part and parcel of trying to make it to the first team. But, with the benefit of harrowing experience, I now accept that those days belong in the dark ages.

I have no time for what I perceive as unnecessary modern methods in relation to training, diet and mental approach. Call me a dinosaur, but I have an unshakeable belief in an uncomplicated attitude to the game. I won the First Division title on a diet of fish and chips, for God's sake. I was brought up on fish and chips: my mum had a job in a chippy and was forever bringing home the leftovers. When I moved into my first house as a bachelor boy, I frequently called for fish and chips on my way to the stadium for a night match. In fact, they were often on the menu at the club canteen on Friday lunchtime. In those days, you were a dedicated athlete if you passed up on the battered cod and went for the breaded version. Most of us were on the batter, and took the mickey out of anyone who chose breaded. Ever since I was a youngster my attitude has been that, regardless of what you've eaten the night before, it's a poor look-out if you can't run around a football pitch for 90 minutes. I'm cynical about so much store being set by so many people on the value of so-called nutritional foods.

And I don't go a bundle on mental preparation, either. I have always been able to turn up, get my kit on and go out and play, regardless of how big the occasion. I've never even been one for warm-ups before kick-off, and the need to meet up a week before an international is beyond me. I live my life in as straightforward a manner as possible and that's how I approach my football: no frills, no unnecessary complications. Gordon Strachan had a foreign fitness guru who he brought over to Elland Road once. This guy gave a session at the banqueting suite, an exercise in the importance of mental approach. He had our striker Imre Varadi stand up and hold out his arms. Then he started making negative remarks, telling Ray how upset he must have been because no one gave him a warm welcome when he came to the club. He pushed Ray's arms down and they collapsed without resistance, weakened by the negative vibes! Next he made him hold out his arms again and started bulling him up, telling him he was the top man and a crucial member of the team. Now Ray's arms were immovable.

Strach thought this was wonderful. He would walk around the dressing-room before kick-off rubbing certain points on his body, like his forehead and his ribcage. By the time he put on his shirt to run out his torso was riddled with self-inflicted red marks. The process was designed, he said, to hone your awareness and your resolve, to make you mentally strong. You couldn't question Strach's application or his willingness to run all day, so I suppose it worked for him. As for me, I was happy to go out there after kicking a ball around the changing-room to release my nervous energy and downing a can of Coke. To me anything else was mumbo-jumbo. I don't have a problem with anyone else indulging in it, but I had always been blessed with enough self-belief to simply get out on the pitch and play. Everybody is different: John Lukic, the goalkeeper, used to lie in the bath for an hour and a half before a game. But I had no time for meditating; I just wanted to play. If anyone had ever tried to force me to adopt a so-called modern or sophisticated approach, I would have bluntly refused.

Maybe surprisingly, no one ever has. I know I've been a coach's nightmare for most of my career. To me, training is about using a ball. That is my job description as far as I am concerned. If training doesn't involve a ball, then I'm against it. I was a poor trainer in the later years of my first spell at Leeds and I became even worse when I went to Blackburn where Kenny Dalglish, more than any other manager I've worked under, was fixated by what happened on Saturday afternoon to the exclusion of the rest of the week. At Blackburn I became so lazy that I didn't even want to know about the Friday five-a-side. Whichever team I was picked for was the loser. 'Oh, no, not Batts' was the regular lament from my team-mates, because all I did was stand on the wing. If the ball came to me, so be it; I didn't go looking for it. But I played my heart out the following afternoon. Perhaps I'm fortunate to have so much energy that I have been able to outrun and out-tackle the majority of people while being so laid back on the training pitch; perhaps I'm narrow-minded about the benefits of a healthy diet and mental preparation. As far as I'm concerned, a plate of pasta isn't going to help me run any harder than haddock and chips. But the one change in the game that I embrace is the improvement in the treatment of injuries. If the modern methods had been used a few years earlier I'm confident that I would have been spared a lot of pain, uncertainty and frustration.

As it was, I made my return to first-team action on Boxing Day 1992. Significantly, as events proved, the match was against Blackburn at Ewood Park. Though we lost 3–1, I had a good game and Rovers manager Kenny Dalglish obviously took note. In the meantime, my form fluctuated – and Dad got increasingly frustrated with me and became more and more critical in his notes.

Dad had to eat a little humble pie when I scored in the 3–0 home win over Middlesbrough which followed. But, truth be told, I was having an up-and-down time that season. The injuries and my frustration at being played out of position so often were probably gnawing away at me, and I was getting more and more alarmed at the way the whole campaign was developing into a massive anticlimax after the triumph of the previous season. At least Dad wasn't the England manager! Graham Taylor kept picking me for the World Cup qualifiers. That, and my marriage to Mandy on 29 April, was consolation for a desperately disappointing showing in the inaugural Premier League season. Manchester United won the title, leaving Leeds trailing in an embarrassing 17th place. Even Billy Bremner, one of my biggest fans, said in a newspaper article that I hadn't been at my best. I don't want to make excuses, but it is hard to pick up your game when you are constantly coming back from injury and, in my case, a suspension or two. No doubt about it, I had got a bit stale, and I was struggling more than ever to come to terms with Wilko's training methods. I think he was well aware of my unrest.

Ironically, he and I had started to get along quite well

by then, despite my intransigence. He even asked me: 'If you ever fancy a couple of days off, let me know.' Initially, I was flattered and impressed that he should afford me such consideration, not that I would ever have contemplated taking him up on his offer. I never wanted preferential treatment and I certainly didn't want to have to owe him any favours! Later, I wondered if, in fact, he was testing me in some way. Had I said yes, would that have told Wilko I had lost my enthusiasm? Although I didn't give him the opportunity to come to that conclusion, I can't deny that I was annoyed. The bottom line is we were crap that season. From winning the title to 17th is nowhere near good enough. It was hard to believe that such a slump could occur under a manager as organised and disciplined as Wilko. In the final analysis, it was down to the players: we weren't up to the job of making a spirited defence of our title. We couldn't win away from Elland Road and I suppose that in itself put a big question mark against the mental strength of the squad. Yet I don't think we had a bad attitude. Whatever the reasons, the seeds of doubt had been sown in my mind and in Wilko's. For all I know, he had already decided that I might be dispensable.

Rumours that Liverpool wanted me surfaced that close season; Sheffield Wednesday, too. But I stayed on the roster and was joined by new signings Brian Deane, the big striker from Sheffield United who had been a Leeds Boys star, and David O'Leary, from Arsenal, who is now, of course, my manager. David had a nightmare with injuries, his Leeds career ending suddenly with serious Achilles damage – and don't I know all about that – in the 4–0 home defeat to Norwich on 21 August.

In September, during the warm-up for the home clash with Sheffield United, I sustained a freak injury. That 2–1 win against the Blades was to be my second-last appearance for Leeds before moving to Blackburn, but I should never have taken the field after breaking my wrist!

Gary McAllister and I had gone out to lash a few balls around before kick-off. I had gone into the net to retrieve a couple when Gary hit a shot – and he can hit a ball – which I punched away. There was a crack and an intense pain in my wrist. I was at the Kop end where the crowd were laughing at my ham-fisted attempts at goalkeeping. I knew from the pain that there was a more ominous side to the incident, but I daren't go back in and tell Wilko because I figured he'd go ape and accuse me of being irresponsible. I kept quiet and, because of the discomfort, played the match with my arm held at my side to minimise the risk of further knocks. I went out that night with Mandy but struggled to oblige the ever-present string of punters wanting to shake hands. Next day, after ringing physio Alan Sutton and telling him that I'd banged the hand during the match, I went for X-rays; they revealed that I had broken two bones and the hand was put in plaster. I never did admit what had actually happened. I wore a variety of casts made of different materials, but I missed four matches and ended up wearing a protective cover for the rest of the season. It was my own fault for not reporting the accident when it happened. That I didn't do so reflected the influence Wilko exerted, and my own stupidity. I knew he wanted me to play and I wanted to play. But with the benefit of experience, I wouldn't dream of playing on in such circumstances now; I would think: 'Big deal. It was an accident,' and come clean.

My comeback in the reserves was at Blackburn. Three days later, on 23 October 1993, I replaced David Wetherall in the second half with Leeds trailing 2–0 to Blackburn at Elland Road. And an intriguing thing happened. As I walked on to the pitch, their skipper Tim Sherwood said to me: 'You'll be at Blackburn next week.' I responded: 'I hope so,' because I was getting extremely fed up at that point. I don't recall how much of it was down to me but we fought back for a 3–3 draw. Then I had the chance to reflect upon Sherwood's out-of-the-blue message. No one else had mentioned any such development, but I was excited by the suggestion. I think I decided there and then that the time for change was upon me. Blackburn was the club to be at in the early nineties, when Jack Walker's revolution was in full swing; few players at the time wouldn't have jumped at the chance of going to Ewood. Nothing more was said to me that evening, but as I lay in bed at around 11 p.m. the following night, the phone rang. It was one of my team-mates telling me he had been talking to Kenny Dalglish, the Blackburn manager, who wanted to know if I'd be happy to join him. I said yes, though I couldn't be sure how serious this was. Less than a minute after I put down the phone, Dalglish called to tell me that Bill Fotherby had indicated that the board would sell me if the price was right. The two men had discussed the prospect at our match the previous day. Was this a dream? After all, I was in bed. I honestly wasn't sure if it was one of the lads winding me up. But I could hear Dalglish telling me how much he wanted me at Blackburn and asking: 'Will you come?' I replied: 'Yes. I would love to.' He said he would put in an offer and that I was to sit tight and say nothing. Once I knew Leeds were prepared to let me go I was on my way; I wouldn't want to play for someone who did not want me.

I couldn't sleep that night. The more I contemplated the possibility of a change of club, the more I realised how stale I had become and that the time had come for me to break from the only club I had known. Kenny rang me again on the Monday to say: 'I think I've got you. I've put in a bid and Fotherby said yes.' He told me to report for training as usual on Tuesday and act daft. I knew nothing! I was nervous the next morning, merely going through the motions – nothing new in that, mind – on the Fullerton Park training pitch a stone's throw from the manager's office. Of course, I was accustomed to being summoned to Wilko's presence, but this was different. I couldn't take my eyes off the gate as I waited for the summons from Mick Hennigan. I was concentrating even less than usual as I blasted balls around the park with Gary Speed. Suddenly, Mick was there shouting: 'Batts, the gaffer wants to see you.' The other lads must have assumed it was the usual Wilko lecture for me, but this time I knew differently; he told me that he didn't want to lose me but that the board had accepted a big offer from Blackburn. Did I want to go? Yes, was my unequivocal answer. Wilko phoned Kenny Dalglish there and then. By 1 p.m. on 26 October I was having lunch with Dalglish and his coach Ray Harford. I had telephoned

Brendan Batson at the PFA who drove to Blackburn that afternoon. By tea-time, we had agreed my contract and I had severed ties with my hometown club that went back to my signing schoolboy forms at 14. It had been a long and largely happy association, but I had no time nor inclination to wallow in nostalgia. I knew I had been ready for a change for some time. I was to play for the legendary Kenny Dalglish and the club that, almost overnight, had become the Bank of England outfit of the Premiership. It was all about the future, not the past, as far as I was concerned.

But that's not how the Leeds fans saw it. They were as stunned as my mum and dad, who heard the news while watching the Yorkshire TV regional news programme *Calendar* in a holiday flat in Scarborough. They hadn't given me and Mandy or my brother John their holiday address so we couldn't have got in touch if we'd tried. It was strange for my dad, and I did feel for him after all he and I had been through together during 13 years of non-stop football. But if he was surprised, the Leeds fans were horrified. There was outrage in the city. Radio stations were flooded with calls protesting about my transfer. Radio Leeds had a phone-in that lasted two hours and blocked their switchboard. The local papers ran polls. The result of the *Evening Post*'s was: in favour of selling Batty, 114; against, 1,952. Pretty conclusive, but there was no going back. I went into Elland Road on the Wednesday to collect my gear and there was as much disbelief among the lads as among the supporters. Brian Deane told me he couldn't believe the club had sold me. I went in to say goodbye to Wilko and Mick

Hennigan and despite all my run-ins with the two of them I was genuinely emotional. We parted amicably. I walked out of the door and made a conscious decision not to go back. I wanted it to be a clean break, never thinking for a moment that I would one day re-sign. Already, any remote possibility that I would regret making the move had been banished by the reception I received the previous evening at Blackburn. I was a big signing – £2.75 million was a hefty fee in those days – and was made to feel special by players and fans alike. I had sat in the stand and watched Blackburn play a League Cup tie. The fans threw me a Blackburn scarf and gave me every reason to believe I would be a popular addition – provided I did the business on the pitch, of course. That meant a lot to me. I had always known how popular I was at Leeds but, at the same time, I had taken a lot of stick from opposing fans, so it was reassuring to be welcomed with open arms the first time I ventured from my home patch.

When I checked in for training with my new colleagues, Tim Sherwood finally explained his pro-phetic remark on the pitch at Elland Road the previous Saturday. He said he had realised Rovers wanted me when he had been chatting to Kenny Dalglish's son Paul – later to follow in his dad's footsteps as a striker – who enjoyed chewing the fat with the senior pros. Paul had said to Tim: 'That David Batty gets better with every game.' Tim reckoned he could only have come up with that insight after eavesdropping on his dad. So Tim put two and two together and came up with four. Dalglish had obviously only phoned me the previous Sunday night after first making his intentions known to Leeds. He needed to know that I was interested in the move he proposed; there was no point in him and Blackburn suffering the embarrassment of a snub from me. But there was no danger of that happening: his call had brought my festering frustrations into sharp focus. I had no hesitation in agreeing to leave Leeds and I have never had any regrets about that decision. In fact, what followed was an exciting new chapter, full of fun, frustration and success.

CHAPTER 11

pub team millionaires

Like most footballers, I had admired Kenny Dalglish from afar for many years. The man was a living legend, one of the game's all-time great strikers. When a guy like that tells you how much he wants you in his team, you can't help but be flattered. After years of struggling to come to terms with Howard Wilkinson's philosophies, Kenny's straightforward attitude to the game was like a breath of fresh air. The man was a winner. What else could he be, after achieving so much with Celtic, Liverpool and Scotland? But his approach to management was uncluttered by tactical complexities and what I had come to regard as meaningless complications. To repeat another of the great clichés, football is a simple game. I really do believe that. The basic necessity is to get a group of talented players who are bound by team spirit and the desire to win, then tell them to go out and play. Essentially, that is what Kenny did in those roller-coaster years at Blackburn in the first half of the 1990s. He certainly made me feel special and the effect this had was fantastic. Kenny was no coach; he never pretended to be, leaving Ray Harford in sole charge of our training. But he commanded respect because of the sheer weight of his standing in the game. He never imposed any restrictions upon me on the pitch. He just let me play, confident that I would do a job for the team. And I revelled in the situation, producing one of the best and most consistent spells of my career in that 1993–94 season before a foot injury threatened to bring my exciting new adventure to a shuddering and final halt.

Blackburn was a laugh-a-minute experience. If the public – and the newspapers – had got to know half of what went on behind the scenes at the new club on the block, Jack Walker's revolution might well have been put down before the crowning glory of the Premiership title triumph of 1995. When you have just arrived at the millionaires' club the last thing you expect to find is a second-rate set-up. But that's what awaited me at Blackburn when I checked in for my first training session with Alan Shearer, Mike Newell, Tim Sherwood and the rest of the squad. I tell you, though Wimbledon originated the 'Crazy Gang' legend, we had our own version at Ewood. The strokes we pulled would have put us at the top of the poll in any contest. The incredible team spirit was probably forged in part by the pub-team facilities that existed when I arrived. We didn't have our own training pitch; we didn't have transport to and from training; we didn't even have a laundry. We had to take our kit home and wash it, something that I had never done in my life. Our expensive assembly of international and emerging play-ers would change in Ewood's crumbling dressing-rooms before getting back into their posh cars – except me, of course; I was driving an Escort – and setting off to the local public park.

From there, it got more and more farcical. If the pitches we used were bad, the balls were even more of a joke: heavy, battered objects that looked to me as if they had been thrown out long ago by a school team. I often wondered if Kenny thought that the use of such sub-standard equipment would make us appreciate the real thing all the more when we played on Saturday.

The pitches were unbelievable. One minute a dozen snotty-nosed kids would be ploughing up and down them, the next it was Batty, Shearer, Wilcox and co. I used to joke that we had dog-shit for goalposts. There was plenty of the stuff about. The pitches were either side of a long driveway leading to the crematorium, so our mud-splattered sessions, preparing to face Manchester United and Arsenal, were conducted against a backcloth of regular funeral processions. Many's the time we had to be careful not to let a stray ball bounce off the roof of the hearse. Then it was back into our cars, caked in all sorts of unmentionable stuff, for the drive back to Ewood and a desperately needed shower. I would often leave home in Wetherby for my 90-minute cross-country drive having already changed into my training gear; it was worth it to avoid using the dingy changing-rooms at Ewood. Although I was never once late for training at Blackburn – or, later, at Newcastle, to where I also commuted from my York-shire base – I'll admit that I risked my neck once or twice during the trip to Ewood. I took the A59 Skipton road and would frequently get stuck behind tractors and other assorted farm vehicles along the rural, winding route. I must point out that Jack Walker was, at that time, investing tens of millions of pounds in redeveloping Ewood Park into one of the Premiership's most up-to-date stadia and also building a state-of-the-art training complex at Brockhall Village, about 10 miles out of town in the heart of the lovely Ribble Valley, though that wasn't much consolation to us at the time. But our spartan situation didn't have a remotely negative effect upon the squad; if anything, it was exactly the opposite. The camaraderie and will-to-win mentality was as strong as I have ever known at any club. I suppose it came, in part, from a determination to rise above the pub-team facilities we had to endure.

The atmosphere within the squad was laid back. Dalglish had a free-and-easy, one-of-the-boys approach, a big contrast to the more regimented regime of Howard Wilkinson at Leeds. As far as Kenny was concerned, if you did the business on a Saturday, the rest of the week was up to you. And, boy, did we take advantage.

The capers on the team bus as it headed south were fantastic. How we ever made it to our destination on some trips I'll never know. For example, while speeding down the M1 someone had the bright idea that we should take it in turns to tap the emergency exit window with the little hammer provided for the purpose of breaking the glass in a crisis. The rule of the game was that you had to hit the glass a little harder than the previous man. Suddenly, to the loud noise of shattering glass, the whole window fell out. There was instant chaos. Kenny, Ray and the directors came rushing to the back as driver Paul Stone – 'Stoney' – pulled on to the hard shoulder. We insisted to Kenny that a stone must have caused the breakage. We carefully knocked all of the glass out and continued the journey on an extremely draughty bus!

We frequently had a supply of pies and sandwiches on long journeys south. A favourite pastime was to break the crusty edges off the meat pies, scoop out the jelly and mash the two into a thick, heavy paste, then hurl the home-made bombs down the bus. The missiles would fly over the heads of the staff and directors, frequently splattering against Stoney's windscreen. Another time we crept down the bus as it sped along the motorway and, using masking tape, bound Stoney's arms to his sides, from the shoulders to his elbows. He was steering God knows how many millions of pounds worth of Premiership talent in a strait-jacket! Even worse, for a few seconds he did it blind because one of the lads put his hands over his eyes.

Some of what we got up to in our hotels on away trips was even worse. There was one particular establishment in London – I won't identify the hotel – where we regularly indulged ourselves in our favourite water fetishes. Shearer, Newell, Sherwood, Wilcox – who has now rejoined me at Leeds – and I were the biggest culprits. As soon as we had checked in at the hotel, we made a beeline for the fire-extinguishers on our floor. Our favourite trick was to blast team-mates with a jet of water – or foam – through the peep-hole in the door to their room. I had discovered that you could unscrew the device from the corridor without the occupant of the room being aware of what was happening, and that the nozzle of the extinguisher fitted snugly into the hole. That done, one member of the two-man raiding party – Sherwood and I were room-mates and partners in crime – would knock on the door. As the lad inside reached for the door handle, we would hit him smack in the face with a high-power jet. How nobody was half blinded I don't know. Thankfully we never ruled anyone out of the following day's match.

When you'd been 'done' you got wise, of course. One trick some of the lads perfected was to open the sliding windows directly opposite the doors, get to the door and duck at the last second, with the result that the jet of water would fly across the room and out of the window. There must have been a time or two when an innocent passer-by copped for the lot. On one hilarious occasion we set the ambush for Billy McKinley, the tough little midfielder who had been signed from Dundee United. Our peep-hole punishment was the perfect prank to hit a new boy with, but Billy was wise to us; somebody must have tipped him off. After receiving the knock on the door, he left his bed and approached clutching towels, announcing triumphantly that he had rumbled us and wasn't going to be a victim of the watery indoctrination ceremony. He kept well out of the line of sight of the peep-hole and cockily insisted that our mission was a failure. But Billy reckoned without our schoolboy-like determination. He had prepared his defences, but they weren't watertight enough to stop a man as resolute as Mike Newell. Mike scaled a fire escape that took him on to the roof above Billy's room. There, clutching the fire-extinguisher, and for all the world like some intrepid SAS soldier, he managed to remove some ceiling tiles and blasted the unsuspecting McKinley from above. It was without doubt the water troop's most spectacular hit. And if an extinguisher wasn't available we were quite prepared to resort to more basic methods. On one occasion, Jason Wilcox was chasing defender David May – later to join Manchester United – through the hotel corridors armed with a bucket of water. May had only a towel around his waist. His flight eventually took him into reception where, in desperation, he grabbed a drinks waiter and used him as a shield. Wilcox had been thwarted.

After these soggy escapades the rooms and corridor used to smell awful. In one place, all the door mechanisms went haywire. None of them would work. There was a constant buzzing noise along the floor.

Looking back, it's hard to believe we got away with causing so much chaos. It reached the point where, on checking out, we would voluntarily slap down a £20 note apiece in compensation for the damage and inconvenience we had caused. Eventually one hotel would remove the extinguishers from the level we were booked on to. By that stage, our carryings-on had worn a bit thin – if for no other reason than we were having to live with a fire risk! But Kenny Dalglish kept a low profile; if he was aware of the goings-on he never said a word. But the club hierarchy must have become aware of it, because they must have had to pay for the damage.

I'm sorry to report that we showed no more respect for other people's property back at Ewood Park, where 'Uncle Jack's' multi-million pound refit was in full swing. First thing in the morning, before training, we used to go into the half-built changing-rooms, which had polystyrene ceilings about eight feet high. We loved to play cricket and something called two-touch, where the ball wasn't allowed to go above head height. If the ball hit the tiles building dust would fall. We made a new rule: if dust falls you stay in. By the end of our sessions lads would be deliberately launching balls at the ceiling, which was steadily getting ruined. Occasionally, the ball would stay up there; one of the lads got on another's shoulders one day and ended up bringing half the ceiling down. It was outrageous, really, and showed a marked lack of respect for the club's property. But it seemed that as long as we were winning matches, nobody was going to clip our wings. We took full advantage, often going in as early as 8.30 a.m. to start the mucking about.

I'm not proud of some of the daft things I was party to, but, at the same time, there is no denying that the bond we formed at Blackburn was a significant factor in the team's success. There was no question, for example, of Dalglish imposing restrictions on who you could room with, as Wilkinson did at Leeds. There, Wilko roomed me with Lee Chapman and my mate Gary Speed was put in with Gordon Strachan. Obviously, Howard perceived that Speedy and I together were a recipe for trouble. But so what? I have nothing against Chapman, but he and I were as different as chalk and cheese. For example, we were driving away from an away match one evening. Lee was on his mobile phone in the seat behind where I was playing cards with three of the lads, and he was saying: 'We are just departing the stadium.' Irritated, I turned and snapped: 'Don't you mean we're just leaving the ground?' His interests and mine were poles apart. He was into restaurants and wine; I'm a lager and fish-and-chips man. The result was that I would return to the room around midnight having played cards all evening with Speedy in Jon Newsome's room. It all seemed so petty. Now, at Blackburn, you mucked in with whoever you wanted to be with and got up to whatever you wanted to get up to, provided you got it right on the pitch next day. I remember playing a Sky game on a Sunday, flying to Ireland and drinking until Wednesday before coming back and winning the next match. It was a great time. We were all good mates, but I'm glad I didn't live near any of them. It was just as well I could beat a retreat back down the A59 to my Wetherby bolt-hole!

My debut for Rovers was in a 1–0 win against Spurs on 30 October 1993. I had a good game, but it was memorable for another, obscure reason. Spurs also had a debutant that day, a lad called Steve Robinson. Fourteen years earlier, on holiday in Torquay, my family had befriended a couple and their two boys who had travelled from Ireland. Mum and Dad kept in touch with the couple, who had once written to say that one of their boys had signed apprentice forms for Tottenham. He was Steven Robinson.

Something even more significant made an impression on me in that match: our centre-halves were actually passing the ball to me. That had never happened at Leeds; the lads there weren't encouraged to do that in case you had to give it back to them, so they hit long balls. At Blackburn, though, everything was geared to getting the ball to Alan Shearer and, subsequently, Chris Sutton – who signed in the summer of 1994 – as quickly as possible. The idea was to get it wide to wingers Wilcox and Stuart Ripley so that they could cross for the strikers, but we didn't hoof the ball as we did at Leeds. I loved it; with a new style and a fresh impetus, my enthusiasm and energy levels seemed to soar. It was like coming alive and I revelled in it. The Man of the Match awards poured in, most memorably for my performance in our 2–1 Ewood win over Leeds early in the New Year when I collected the Sky TV award and both of the sponsors' awards. By then I had started to amass a pile of prizes. I had so much lager from McEwan's, the club's sponsors, that my family and close friends started complaining and I had to start asking for bitter by way of a change. As for carriage clocks and wristwatches, there were so many of those I could have opened a market stall.

My form was an eye-opener not only to many of my team-mates, who hadn't realised from afar how much of a player I was, but also to me! The players seemed to really appreciate me and they were obviously surprised at the range of my game. I can understand that because I judge a player only when I see him in the flesh. Most of the time, your only basis for opinion is the papers or the TV pundits. If a player doesn't get mentioned in the media, he can be overlooked completely. The key is to see a man in action, playing either with him or against him, and I'm sure several of my new team-mates were pleasantly surprised when they got to play alongside me. Dalglish gave me a platform and I thrived on it, forming an instant understanding in midfield with Tim Sherwood. Each of us could rely upon the other to drop back instinctively if the other moved forward. Within two weeks of moving to Blackburn, I was wishing I had had the chance years earlier.

As our chase for the title hotted up, the high point

was a 2–0 Ewood victory over Manchester United on 2 April. Shearer – surprise, surprise – scored both goals as we cut United's lead at the top to three points. Two days later, I was voted into the PFA team of the year for the first time. That was especially pleasing as the ultimate accolade is to be recognised by your fellow players. My former Leeds team-mate Eric Cantona, then at Manchester United, was named Player of the Year and I wasn't going to argue with that; I was delighted to be named in the same company as the brilliant Frenchman. There is no doubt that it was a big boost for me. Although I have always played the game hard, I like to think that, by and large, I have been respected by my fellow professionals. An incident to illustrate that comes to mind. In my Leeds days I tangled with big Niall Quinn, then the Manchester City centre-forward, who is a genuinely nice fella. I clattered into him and as I sprang to my feet, Niall said: 'Hey, hey. Calm down. I voted for you as Young Player of the Year.' That took the wind out of my sails and I thanked him there and then.

As the season reached its climax, on 11 April, after another Sky Man of the Match display in the 1–0 win over Aston Villa, Dad was sufficiently impressed to pen this glowing tribute: 'What a player David is now. The move to Blackburn has done him the world of good. If Rovers could beat Manchester United to the title it would be down to two players, Alan Shearer, who scores most of the goals, and David, who has emerged as probably the best midfielder in the country.' As if to verify Dad's words, Graham Taylor named me in an England squad which was to have a get-together at

Bisham Abbey the following week. Ironically, pain in my foot meant I was substituted by Paul Warhurst towards the end of that Villa match. The next day, I was diagnosed as having two broken bones in my foot. It was the start of 12 months of misery and uncertainty about my whole future and a wretched anticlimax to a marvellous first season at Blackburn.

As we were still contesting the title with Manchester United, Dalglish was reluctant to lose my services, and I was willing to keep going. X-rays had revealed that a piece of bone had become detached from the main bone in my foot. The amount of calcification indicated that it was probably an old injury. The irony was that when I signed for the club, the doc studied the X-rays from my medical and told me I had broken my left ankle some time in the distant past. A significant piece of bone was missing, he said, and I was lucky to have played on. Apparently, it had happened when I was a kid. It was a miracle I had got this far. The next match after my grim discovery was at Southampton, where I went to a local doctor's surgery to have a local anaesthetic injection in my foot. It worked a treat; I jogged up and down the surgery thinking: 'I can cope with this just fine.' The same doctor came to The Dell next day to give me another injection before kick-off. I started the match but the pain became severe and I was substituted. Eight days later, on 24 April, I was wheeled out for action again, but it was to be the last time for nearly 12 months. We faced QPR at Ewood Park, and Manchester surgeon John Hodgkinson, who later performed surgery on my foot, arrived in the dressing-room to administer another jab. He brought a bloody great needle out of his bag; it was so big it looked more like a knitting needle. The one the doctor in Southampton had used was thin, but this was thick, and when he put it in the side of my foot the pain was acute. I went white and felt sick. In front of the Sky TV cameras I had a poor game in our 1–1 draw, a result which handed United the title. It was the end of Blackburn's tilt at the championship and the end of my season, with three games to go. My winning of the supporters' Player of the Year trophy – presented at half-time at the last match of the season, against Ipswich – was some consolation. But at that point, I didn't realise just how much misery I was going to endure in the following 10 months.

I had played all that season at Blackburn with a cast on the wrist I broke a couple of months before leaving Leeds. While I was hobbling around with my injured foot in plaster, in an attempt to see if the two pieces of bone would fuse, it was decided I might as well have an operation on my wrist. At the same time, I had surgery on the finger shortened in the church gate-slamming incident 20 years earlier. The reason for the operation, however, was a more recent incident. In March, I had gone to watch Mandy's brother Lee playing for Leeds Schoolboys at Thorp Arch – where Leeds United's training ground is now situated – and injured myself in typical Batty fashion. It was a wet and windy day and my golf brolly turned inside out. Carelessly, I threw it into the bushes, catching my finger and cutting it deeply. I played in a 3–1 win over Sheffield Wednesday on the Sunday with my finger nearly hanging off after stupidly administering my own treatment, namely a lollipop stick bound with Sellotape like a makeshift splint. After the match some butterfly stitches were put in it but it obviously hadn't been cleaned properly because, that night, it started throbbing with pain. I wouldn't let Mandy take me to hospital, and I drove to Blackburn the following morning with the finger killing me. The physio whipped out the butterfly stitches and, instantly, pus oozed from the wound. The tendon had rotted through. Talk about the walking wounded! I went into a private hospital in Rochdale to have the wrist and finger operations, with my leg already encased in plaster. When I emerged, people were looking at me in horror, as if I must be a car-crash victim.

The plaster cast was removed from my foot in June, but it hadn't had the desired effect. My disappointment was relieved only by the news that Mandy was pregnant, and due to give birth in February. I smiled to myself, recalling how the lads at Blackburn had taken the mickey out of me mercilessly all season because they knew we had been trying for a baby. 'Jaffa' – as in seedless – had been the frequent jibe. I might be hobbling around like an injured war veteran, but the good news was I was going to be a dad. A few weeks later – after I'd been on holiday with the cast on – the specialist decided to operate on the foot. I hadn't exactly treated myself with tender, loving care in the meantime. I had even been playing football with Lee at the Beetons' house, and by the time I checked in again at hospital, the bottom of the cast was all but worn away and my bare foot was nearly through. So, amid some concern as to what treatment to try, a small screw was inserted in a bid to connect the breakaway fragment to the main bone; the specialist had now realised that a tendon was responsible for pulling the bone away. If successful, I would be out of action for three months. If only that had been the case: I was in plaster for a further six weeks, during which period we learned that Mandy was to have twins. The cast was removed and I tried running on it. Sadly, I was still in pain. On 17 September I had another operation, when a bigger screw was put in. After another six weeks in plaster I cautiously decided the foot was okay. It proved to be yet another false dawn. After a week of rehabilitation at the FA injury clinic at Lilleshall I started training on 14 November. Within three weeks, the specialist decided to do a scan because I was struggling. The serious conclusion was that drastic action was necessary – amid fears that I might have no more than a 50–50 chance of playing top-level football again.

The next stop, decided upon only after much soul-searching by the medics, was to remove the piece of floating bone. The specialist admitted he was reluctant because once out there was no putting it back. After taking out the fragment, he then had to re-attach the tendon to the main bone, a procedure that might not work. The surgery was performed on 14 December, by which time I was getting pretty fed up with the inside of hospital wards. The two screws from the previous operations became gory mementoes, tucked away by my dad with the 1994–95 match programme collection! By now, Mandy was becoming uncomfortable carrying the twins and so, to help her, we brought forward our family Christmas party. Meanwhile, my concerns for my future surfaced again when I started getting more pain. A visit to hospital in Harrogate happily revealed that there was no infection around the area of the operation and it was decided to leave off the cast. That relief lasted only a few days before I picked up an infection and had to suffer an extremely painful injection, before the specialist put on another cast.

To make matters worse, on Christmas night, Mandy's BMW was stolen from outside our house. The neighbours rang the police after seeing two youths break into the vehicle. After a chase, the car rolled over on a bend and was written off.

But the New Year brought a double dose of good news. On 11 January the plaster cast was removed and for the first time in nine months, I didn't have any pain. I had spent a total of 24 weeks in plaster and it hadn't been funny. Throughout the season, Dalglish had been marvellous to me. Aware that Mandy was pregnant, he had been quite happy to let me stay at home, where I worked on my exercise bike whenever possible and did thousands of sit-ups. Just before Christmas, when I hadn't been near Ewood for six weeks, Kenny rang me and jokingly asked: 'Any chance we'll ever see you again?' After some haggling we settled upon a date of 10 January for my return to the fold, so I got another four weeks out of him. I will always be grateful to him for the way he handled the situation. I like to think he knew I was a good pro who wouldn't let myself go or abuse my body. I may have been a poor trainer, but I always appreciated the need to look after myself, especially when injured. The more work you do in those circumstances, the less you have to do to get fit when you start training again. I think Kenny knew I wouldn't be out eating and drinking whatever I pleased, and he was right. There was a lot of trust shown me and it was repaid when I returned to action late that season in pretty good nick.

Nine days after having the cast removed for the last time, Mandy gave birth to our twin boys, Jack and George, at 11.30 p.m. on 19 January 1995, in – where else – St James's Hospital, Leeds. It was the happiest night of our lives, but it was a really tough one, too, for Mandy, who spent many agonising hours in labour before Jack was the first to appear. George was a real struggle, because he was in the breach position. The midwife had hold of one of Mandy's legs, while the other was wrapped round my neck. I was shouting encouragement for the next half hour until George finally made his entry into the world.

Five weeks later, on 28 February, I played my first match in 10 months, for the reserves against Rotherham, and came through successfully. The first team were leading Manchester United by three points in the race for the Premiership title and the town of Blackburn was buzzing with excitement. By 15 April, I had made it to the subs' bench for the clash against my former club Leeds, a 1–1 draw. At that stage I had had no hint of it from Dalglish, but I was about to be reinstated for the run-in. It proved to be a four-week period fraught with mixed feelings as Blackburn stumbled across the finishing line to pip Alex Ferguson's United and win their first League championship in 81 years.

Though I was absolutely delighted for the club and for my team-mates and personally thrilled to be playing again after so much pain and worry about my future, my joy was tinged with sadness for Mark Atkins, the midfielder whose place I took in those final, nerve-jangling five matches of that historic season. Mark – we called him Arrow, because he looked like Formula One star Nigel Mansell, who drove for the Arrows team back then – had been simply magnificent that season as my stand-in. He and Tim Sherwood worked the midfield superbly and Arrow had chipped in with a few goals, something I still couldn't claim to do. I came off the bench to replace Mark during the shock 3–2 home defeat by Manchester City on 17 April and started the remaining four matches, to his exclusion.

My embarrassment at Dalglish's show of faith was heightened by the fact that we were hit by a massive attack of 11th-hour nerves. We managed to win only one of those games, a 1–0 home victory against Newcastle, and our keeper Tim Flowers had to pull out all the stops to ensure we took those three points although we were run off the park. That was the second-last match of the season, a result that left us two points clear of United. I remember Tim giving an interview on Sky TV, telling the world that we had the bottle to win the title. By then, a lot of people were doubting us and, I suppose, you couldn't argue as we staggered from defeat to defeat. We had lost at home to Palace and at West Ham in the previous two matches and we had to play at, of all places, Liverpool on the last day, while United were at West Ham.

I had got through my first couple of full matches on adrenalin alone but, against Newcastle, I felt my lack of match fitness. Yet I was in the starting line-up at Anfield; but Mark Atkins was left out of the side completely. We scored first but lost 2–1 and we were the most relieved bunch of players on earth when it was confirmed that United had been beaten at Upton Park and we were the champions. As it happened, I had an excellent game, confirmation that I was back and that I could look forward with confidence and optimism. But those thoughts were interrupted on the day by my sympathy for Mark. It wouldn't have seemed quite so bad if he had at least been on the bench, but to see him sitting in his civvies in the directors' box made me feel terrible about the situation. By and large, players are selfish and pretty ruthless when it comes down to team selection. But playing that day, with Mark out in the cold after all the effort he had put in that season, didn't sit easy with me. I couldn't get excited about the fact that we'd won the title; when they came on to the pitch with the trophy and the medals, I didn't feel as though I belonged. I walked past the table and shook hands with the officials, but couldn't bring myself to pick up a medal. Nobody loves winning more than I do, but I don't enjoy winning by default, which I felt I had done. The lads deserved their moment of glory; they had put in the effort and got the results over nine long, hard months. I had stepped in – at Mark's expense – only in the last four weeks, and we had won just one of the matches I played in.

My emotions were crystallised on the team bus afterwards when the Dutchman Richard Wietsge, who had joined us a few weeks earlier on loan from Barcelona, started telling us how he now had championship medals from four different countries. Wietsge had picked up a medal and he hadn't even been in the squad that day. What's more, the only match he had played in was the 2–0 defeat at West Ham, when I didn't rate his performance. We were saying to him: 'You nearly lost us this bloody success at Upton Park!' I remember thinking what a cheek the guy had. I want to win medals as much as the next man, but I couldn't feel I deserved it in his situation. If I was a sub in the European Cup final and didn't get on the pitch, I wouldn't take a medal. What would be the point if I hadn't played my part? To me, hollow success is like no success. These thoughts filled my mind as we pulled away from Anfield. But they were punctuated by one big plus: I was back in business after a trouble-torn period when my career had been on the line.

CHAPTER 12

exit from ewood

For the second time in three years, I went into a pre-season a proud member of the title-winning team, full of optimism for the campaign ahead. For the second time in three years, I was to be bitterly disappointed by events. At Leeds in 1992–93 we had failed miserably to live up to our status as champions, going through the following season without an away win. At Blackburn, in 1995–96, the fall from grace wasn't quite so pronounced, but it was bad enough. Rovers finished the season in eighth place – but there was a 21-point chasm between us and winners Manchester United. By then, I had moved on to Newcastle, where I had the dubious satisfaction of finishing much higher than my former team-mates, in second place after a tense and thrilling tussle with Alex Ferguson's emerging team. The story behind my move to St James' Park has been told in varied forms, the one consistent thread being that I was cast as the villain. I hope that the facts will finally lay to rest the misplaced suspicions and criticism of me on the part of so many Blackburn supporters, some of whom write to me to this day attacking me for 'deserting' their club after allegedly rebelling against the management at Ewood. I shall put the record straight over my acrimonious departure, which left me branded a trouble-maker in the eyes of the fans who had voted me their main man in my first season at the club.

It had all started to go wrong for Blackburn six months earlier when Kenny Dalglish stunned us all, and the rest of football, by announcing he had quit as team manager, just a few weeks after leading the club to its first title triumph in 81 years. Kenny seems, like Kevin Keegan, later my manager at Newcastle and with England, to make big decisions on the spur of the moment. Keegan opted out of Newcastle and, years later, the England job at short notice; Dalglish had already shocked Liverpool by leaving them in 1991. Now he caused a stir when he announced that he was handing over the managerial reins at Blackburn to Ray Harford, his first-team coach throughout the four-year glory ride to the Premiership title. But it might be that Kenny had given the decision a lot more thought than I imagine. Owner Jack Walker had alluded to a five-year plan. Perhaps, having brought the elusive title to Ewood, Dalglish reckoned that it would only be downhill from there on. If that is what he thought, he was dead right. Despite my recognition of the huge impact Dalglish had made at Ewood, I didn't fear the worst when he stepped aside and Ray was given the chance to run the team. It was disappointing that Kenny had chosen to opt out, but footballers, in the main, aren't too choosy about their manager, so long as he is picking them for the first team. Ray Harford was well known to every one of us; he had been our mentor and mate on the training pitch, one of the boys, really. And that proved to be the big problem.

Suddenly, Ray had to switch from being the man who put a consoling arm around a player's shoulder when he was out of favour to the one who was responsible for leaving a player out of the side. He struggled to make the transition. As coach, Ray had our respect, but we also took the mickey out of him, safe in the knowledge that he wasn't the man with the ultimate power over us. Now, though, he had that power and things could never be the same again. The onus was on Ray to bridge the gap between being No. 2 and No. 1 and, in my opinion, he didn't do that. We carried on treating Ray in the same familiar way that we had before. Slowly but surely, the relationship was undermined. The bottom line is that the gaffer has to be able to maintain a certain distance between himself and his players. You have to know that you can only go so far with the manager, even if, like Dalglish, he could be one of the boys on occasions. It might have helped Ray had Kenny simply left the club; instead, he was appointed Director of Football, a role which he was never properly able to explain. The fact was, though, that Kenny was still on the scene and that wasn't doing Ray any favours. We started the season unimpressively and the pressure was on Ray almost from the moment he took charge. On one occasion, down at the training ground, Ray gathered the national newspaper reporters and, in what I can only think was an act that betrayed his insecurity, summoned Kenny to come and tell them: 'Get one thing straight. I am not managing the team. Ray is.' Ray had enough on his plate trying to live up to the massive expectation generated by the title success, without worrying that the press and public perceived him to be a manager in the shadow of

Dalglish. The arrangement was destined not to work.

A home win over QPR got us off on the right foot that season but successive defeats at Sheffield Wednesday and Bolton followed, then a home defeat to champions-elect Manchester United. By the time we played out first ever Champions League match, against Spartak Moscow at Ewood Park, we had managed to add only one point to the three we won on the first day of the season. It wasn't the most encouraging situation for our entry on to the ultimate European stage. To follow that championship triumph we had to produce something special, not only put up a spirited defence of our crown but also seize the moment and perform like the proud champions of England against the cream of Europe. Our failure to deliver was emphatic. Signs that all was to end in tears showed themselves before we'd even kicked off against Russian champions Spartak. We had a crowd that night of only 20,940. I know we hadn't been pulling up any trees in the previous few weeks, but this was arguably the biggest night in the club's history! On our European Cup debut, the ground was 10,000 down on its capacity. It was an indication to me that the Blackburn public wasn't fiercely passionate about its football. I was starting to form the same impression about the club itself. We lost the match 1–0 and, three days later, went to Liverpool where we were lucky to escape with a 3–0 defeat. The writing was on the wall for the team that Jack built with his millions and that Dalglish had inspired with his sheer presence.

The defence of the League title was already looking like a lost cause, but the Champions League remained our big chance to cement our credibility as the new force. We had drawn Rosenborg, of Norway, and Poland's Legia Warsaw, along with Spartak: not an insurmountable group, surely? Sadly, that is just what it proved to be. We were beaten in Rosenberg and, increasingly, I felt the club was accepting the situation too easily, a feeling reinforced when we resumed Premiership action at Middlesbrough. Before the match, Ray Harford had a chat with the players in which he described the Champions League as 'just an adventure'. Although Ray was trying to take some tension out of our situation by playing it a bit cool, he left me thinking that he had already accepted we couldn't compete at that level. That wasn't the right attitude. It was an adventure, all right, but one that we should have been going into confident in our status as champions. We had four more games to play in Europe and I thought he should be ramming the belief that we could beat these teams down our throats. Instead, we went out at the Riverside and got beaten by Boro. Then Kevin Gallacher, our left-side midfielder, was injured. We signed Lars Bohinen from Forest and I was sent out wide left. I didn't moan, but I knew it wasn't the most effective role for me. Opponents did, too: after I joined Newcastle, their skipper, Rob Lee, told me of their relief when Blackburn played at St James' Park in November and they saw me lining up on the left wing. 'We all thought, "We've got these beaten today," ' he said, and Newcastle indeed won 1–0. By then, we had flopped yet again in Europe, losing in Warsaw. We had lost all three of our ties and the Champions League dream was in tatters. A scoreless draw with the Poles, in front of another 21,000 Ewood crowd, represented our first point in the competition. It was followed by the away leg in Moscow, on 22 November – and one of the most bizarre and controversial incidents I have been involved in.

We were halfway in the Premiership table and already no-hopers in the European campaign. Rumours were circulating that Leeds were interested in trying to take me back and that Arsenal were on the trail of our left-back, Graeme Le Saux. It was an unsettling time for all of us and, perhaps, for Graeme in particular. That is the only explanation I can think of, to this day, for his astounding behaviour on that night in Moscow. The temperature was minus 20 Celsius and we needed something to get our blood boiling, but I never bargained for what happened when Le Saux and I chased a ball out of play and across the touchline. Normally one of you shouts 'Leave it' or 'My ball' in that situation. Why neither of us did so, I don't know, but the result was that we collided a couple of yards out of play. In circumstances like that you expect to dish each other a bit of lip; I certainly didn't expect a smack in the face. But that's precisely what I got. Somehow we came together again, cursing each other, then Graeme clocked me one below my left eye. I couldn't believe he'd done it. I was gobsmacked. So was everyone else, including the referee; he took no action against either of us, probably because he'd never had to deal with two team-mates squaring up on the pitch and didn't know how to handle it. The same went for Ray Harford, who didn't mention the incident at half-time nor even after the game. I didn't retaliate when Graeme hit me; I was too surprised to react. Tim Sherwood stepped in to separate us, and with everyone in the stadium – plus millions watching back in England, as the match was televised live – asking each other if they'd actually seen what they'd just seen, we played on.

There was a weird atmosphere in the dressing-room at half-time. One or two of the lads were urging me to 'sort him out' as we walked off the pitch, but revenge wasn't on my mind. I'll state again that, despite my hard-man image, I get no kick out of seeking revenge or trying to carry on feuds that may develop during a match. I'll give you an example. The following season, when playing for Newcastle in a European tie against French club Metz, I got involved in a running battle with a Brazilian midfielder of theirs, Isaias. I barely recall the guy's name, but I can still feel his fist! We ended up on the floor, and as we disentangled ourselves, he caught me, splitting open my eye. He got only a yellow card and I got a lot of stitches and a lot of pain. Before the return at St James' Park the press, and some of my team-mates, were convinced that I was gunning for this guy and that he would live to regret taking liberties with David Batty. But nothing was further from my mind as I drove up for the match. As it happened, Metz were staying in the Gosforth Park Hotel, where I spent the night before midweek matches, and the player came over to me in the foyer, offered his hand and apologised for what he'd done a fortnight earlier. That was fine by me and there was no grudge carried over into the game. Whether people choose to believe it or not, I am not one of those cynical hard-case pros who are inclined to go out and 'do' an opponent on the sly. I wouldn't know how to leave my foot in. I'm not going to hold back when the action gets hot but I have no interest in rough stuff that isn't up front and honest. I've been a bit late in the tackle a few times, like any committed player, but never deliberately so.

As for Le Saux's actions, I couldn't understand why he had done what he did. People jumped to the conclusion that the fantastic scenes must have been provoked by something I had said to Graeme. The favourite theory, which did neither me nor Graeme any favours, was that macho man Batty had been winding up the more reserved, learned Le Saux. The mere fact that Graeme preferred the *Guardian* to the *Daily Sport* was sufficient reason for fans – and some players – to question his masculinity and to abuse him with cheap-shot insults. I was not one of those people and I deeply resented the insinuation. Graeme and I weren't big buddies, but we had no problem with each other. In fact, the night before the match, when I needed some clarification of our arrangements, it was Graeme whose home I rang. There was no history between us to spark such a strange incident. One of the lads did often bait Graeme a bit and the two of them had had a confrontation in the training-ground corridor a week before. Maybe that, plus the rumours linking Graeme with a return to London – he had joined Blackburn from Chelsea three years earlier – and our lack of progress that season had combined to leave him feeling frustrated and a bit on edge. Perhaps I was simply unfortunate to be in the wrong place at the wrong time. Or perhaps he felt angry at the way I'd also gone for the ball and thought I had deliberately collided with him.

There was an embarrassing silence between us at

half-time, and no one else mentioned the incident either. The whole business clearly affected Graeme more than it did me because he had a poor second half and was substituted. He never offered me an explanation, but he did apologise a couple of days later, before training. By then, I had quite a swelling below my eye but there were no hard feelings, only confusion as to why he did what he did. Graeme broke a finger for his trouble and was given a hefty club fine. What angered me more than the punch I took was the way the club handled the affair: they fined Graeme a fortnight's wages and me one week's. I refused to pay, insisting I shouldn't suffer for the actions of others. In the end, my stand earned a reduction in the fine to half a week's wages, but I was far from happy as the principle was unchanged. I think the club were as embarrassed as I was and felt they had to be seen to be taking action, but I saw it as a complete lack of support and felt it was further evidence of the slow but sure disintegration of the fabric of the place. My view was that the club didn't even need to say they were disciplining me, let alone actually do it. If I had been the one who had whacked somebody, I would have taken my punishment, but I hadn't done anything. To add insult to injury, Le Saux and I were banned for two matches by UEFA, so I got a double sentence for something I didn't do.

The whole sorry business was symptomatic of the increasing lack of discipline under Ray's management. The night before facing Spartak, most of us were sinking a few beers behind his back in our hotel room. I don't know exactly when we started having a drink or two the night before games that season, but we did and

I'm ashamed to admit it. That evening in Moscow wasn't the first time: I vividly remember being in a hotel at Newcastle on the eve of our match at St James' Park the previous weekend when one of the lads rang down-stairs with a drinks order. A few minutes later, the beers arrived – with the compliments of Arthur Cox, Kevin Keegan's coach at Newcastle, who must have been in the hotel, too. Maybe Arthur figured that it we were daft enough to drink on the eve of a match he would be daft not to feed the habit. And they did beat us the following day. Luckily, Cox's discovery obviously didn't count against me when Keegan came calling a few months later.

Four days on, in Moscow, we were indulging in our new habit of drinking a few lagers on pre-match evening – and deciding upon a prank that was typical of those days at Blackburn. In that hotel, you could tune to channel 12 on the TV set and watch closed-circuit pictures of the vast foyer. So we decided to brighten up the evening. Whoever pulled the lowest card had to go down to the foyer, position himself in the middle of the floor and do 20 press-ups. The range of exercises became more varied as different lads made the trip to reception, where flabbergasted guests and hotel staff could only stand and stare. All the while, the rest of us were rolling around the bedroom in fits of laughter. I must stress that we weren't getting blind drunk; far from it. Even so, I'm embarassed at the recollection of those nights. I was in my mid-twenties and at the peak of my fitness and it was utterly irresponsible of me even to contemplate having a drink on the eve of the match. I wouldn't do such a thing now and I wouldn't want any young player reading this to think that drinking before a game is a clever thing to do. It isn't.

Though there can be no excuse for it, I believe the creeping disintegration of the first-team set-up was the major, if subconscious factor, in our increasingly irresponsible behaviour. On the plane home from Moscow we were chucking the little face-wipe towels around. One of the lads hurled his down the plane and it landed on manager Ray Harford's head. There was silence. What would the gaffer do? Nothing. Ray never moved a muscle from the shoulders up as he slowly took the soggy little towel off his head. He never turned round to seek out the culprit, never said a word. The players exchanged meaningful glances. In that moment, I'm sure, Ray lost a little more control of a ship that was starting to run badly off course. In contrast, when our left-winger Jason Wilcox had hurled a fistful of table salt over his shoulder in a restaurant and accidentally hit Kenny Dalglish – when he was manager – flush in the face, we witnessed a far different reaction. Kenny, who could enjoy a practical joke with the best of them, sprang to his feet, confronted Jason and told him bluntly: 'Do that again and I'll knock you out!' We knew who was boss under Kenny. Ray never managed to exert that authority.

There was plenty of room for laxity under Kenny's management; I've already described some of the things that happened on away trips. But we were a team that was winning. As everyone knows, winning is everything. It masks a multitude of sins.

The big problems arise when results start to go wrong, and that's what happened after Dalglish stepped aside. The need for discipline and leadership is most vital when a team is struggling. Neither the players nor, presumably, Ray Harford had reason to think that it would all fall apart as we prepared for that season. We were quickly up to our old tricks in the country hotel we occupied before the Charity Shield curtain-raiser against FA Cup-winners Everton in August. The hotel had a golf course and a fleet of motorised buggies. We didn't use them on the course – we drove them around the hotel corridors, turning the place into a dodgem track, a game that stopped only when one of the lads got his buggy stuck at a bend and abandoned the vehicle there. As usual on trips to Wembley, we were all issued with new outfits: suits, shirts, ties – the lot. But not everyone was able to grace the big occasion in his finery; goalkeeper Tim Flowers and striker Chris Sutton, for example. They arrived at the twin towers in tracksuits, victims of the Terrible Trio of Batty, Sherwood and Shearer. Flowers and Sutton were rooming together. Armed with scissors, we entered through a window, took Tim's shirt off its hanger and cut off the sleeves. Chris had left his in its box: undeterred, we carefully removed it, gave it the same treatment, and just as carefully repacked it. When Tim discovered the sabotage, Chris triumphantly held aloft his shirt box thinking he had escaped, but he was just as annoyed as Tim when he came to get dressed. Kit man Alan Whitehead was a victim, too. He chose to put on the clothes, but spent the afternoon sweltering in the sticky Wembley atmosphere, unable to remove his jacket.

Those were heady days, of course. We were the champions, heading into the Champions League, and we had every reason to believe that another successful campaign lay ahead. By the time of our exit from frozen Moscow four months later, optimism was wearing decidedly thin. Ray Harford, presumably sensing that the situation was starting to get out of control, on and off the pitch, called a meeting on the training ground in a bid to assert some authority. But it simply didn't work. Ray said it was time to call a halt to our bad behaviour. After a speech which did little for me, he concluded – fatally – by asking, not telling us: 'All right, lads?' The response was a disdainful, collective shrugging of shoulders. The players hadn't got the message. Ray hadn't been firm enough. I do sympathise; exerting a proper measure of control over a bunch of footballers, at any level, isn't an easy task. When those players are highly paid internationals with fiercely independent streaks it must be extremely difficult. As players become more and more financially powerful and independent, the job of the manager only gets harder. The fact is, we were floundering by mid-season and clearly in no shape to make a respectable defence of our hard-won crown. A shameful 5–0 defeat at Coventry early in December was the clearest indicator yet of how things were going wrong at Blackburn. The pitch was frozen and the match shouldn't really have been played.

Nevertheless, the champions shouldn't be losing 5–0 to anybody – let alone Coventry who, with all respect, weren't the best team around. There was an almost total lack of spirit that day and it worried me. On Boxing Day I scored probably my best goal ever, the 30-yard screamer against Manchester City at Ewood Park. The fourth goal of my career preceded another home win, against Spurs, so we turned into the New Year in slightly better shape. But the beginning of the end of my Ewood experience was just around the corner, though I had no inkling until my room-mate Tim Sherwood imparted some intriguing information in the Royal Lancaster Hotel, Hyde Park.

We were playing at QPR in mid-January. Kevin Gallacher was fit after a lengthy absence and there was competition for places in midfield; Tim, Lars Bohinen and I were also in the frame. The night before the game, Tim and I had been debating what the manager might do for the match at Loftus Road. Early on Saturday morning, Tim told me that he had heard that the club had had an offer for me from 'a big northern club'. Both of us were experienced professionals, and as such we assumed that this information would not have been leaked by the club unless they were thinking of selling me. If a club isn't willing to sell then usually you would hear nothing about it until long afterwards. Tim and I spent the morning trying to work out which club had come in for me. Though Tim suggested Newcastle, I discounted them because they were flying at the top of the table and I couldn't imagine why they would want to change things. At that point, Leeds seemed favourites and I was happy enough with that thought. I went out that afternoon and had a blinder at QPR. As we headed for home I couldn't help but ponder whether my display had helped or hindered my prospects of a big move. If the interested club had been watching, I figured they could only have been impressed. On the other hand, Blackburn might think twice about letting me go. Already, I was mentally detaching myself from Blackburn. Once I had reason to think they were ready to sell me, my attitude was: 'If I'm not wanted, I'm ready to go.' Naturally, I assumed this meant that Ray Harford was willing to sell me and I have never seen the point of being at a club once there is reason to believe that the manager doesn't want to pick you. Assuming that Ray would call me promptly to put me in the picture, I told Tim on the coach journey north that I would let him know as soon as I did and hopefully by Monday the identity of the club who wanted me.

When the phone eventually rang at home later the following day, it was a former team-mate at Leeds, asking me if I would be willing to go to Newcastle. He told me that an agent had asked him to sound me out. Secretly, I'd been hoping it was Leeds, but you can't wait for things to happen in this game. You have to seize the moment and that was what I intended to do. I said I'd love to join Kevin Keegan at Newcastle. I still found it hard to believe they wanted me. When I moved to Ewood, Blackburn were the team players wanted to join. Now Newcastle, flying high under Keegan, were the club attracting all the attention. I took a call from the agent, confirming Keegan's interest and telling me to keep quiet. I then waited for Ray Harford's call. Next day, over the pool table at Blackburn's training ground, I told Tim Sherwood the club was Newcastle. I know I'd been sworn to secrecy but I owed it to Tim, who had been good enough in the first place to tell me what he had heard. So, now he knew and I knew that the club was Newcastle. We both assumed that the manager knew and that the manager didn't know that we knew; and, for some reason, the manager wasn't letting me know. By the end of Monday night I was on tenterhooks, thinking: 'For God's sake, Ray, where's this phone call?' When we kicked off against Ipswich – who we met in an FA Cup third-round replay at Ewood on the Tuesday night – I still hadn't heard from Ray. I was disheartened to say the least. Why the deafening silence?

As I walked on to the pitch that night I was in typical stubborn mood. My mind wasn't focused on the game; instead, I was consumed with frustration. I didn't do myself, or the team, justice as we went out of the competition. The tie went to extra time and I was substituted. We lost 1–0 and the truth is I didn't care; by now I was feeling badly let down. I drove home feeling increasingly angry.

At 7 a.m. the next day I called Ray. I said: 'I know about the offer from Newcastle.' He asked me: 'Do you want to go?' I replied: 'Yes, if you want to sell me,' and he said: 'Okay.' I put the phone down thinking we had sorted it out and that the move would be on, but I was stunned when Ray rang me later that day to explain that he had spoken to the chairman, Robert Coar, and that no one was for sale. I told him: 'You can take it from me, I won't be playing for the club again. So change their minds.' I was utterly disillusioned by now and I decided this was no time for sitting on the fence. Though I still didn't have an agent, I reasoned that the best way to get this move on was to involve the guy who had been in touch. He arranged a meeting at the home of the chairman, where I told Mr Coar that my heart was no longer in the club and that it would be in everybody's best interests if they sold me to Newcastle. I didn't want to play for Blackburn again. There was no shouting or arguing so I thought I had finally cleared the way forward. I was operating on the assumption that the manager was willing to offload me.

Unfortunately, Mr Coar came to the conclusion that I must have been tapped up by the agent, that I was happy at Blackburn and that I had been unsettled by the transfer talk. I had been unsettled, all right, but by the club. The directors held a board meeting at which it was decided I wasn't to be sold and that I should spend a cooling-off period staying away from Ewood. That much I agreed with because I did not want to be in the squad. By the end of the month, with the club clearly digging in, I rang the agent and explained that I couldn't see any progress while he was involved. I put the affair in the hands of Hayden Evans. In the meantime, Ray Harford rang and asked me to return to training, buckle down and maybe get my move at the end of the season.

Reluctantly, I agreed, setting to work with a will. A month had passed by and it was stalemate, so I got stuck in at training and really did myself justice for a week. But the final straw was in the wind. I walked into Ewood on the Friday morning, feeling pretty pleased with myself and savouring the prospect of being part of next day's first-team squad. Breezing through the swing doors of the changing-room, I saw coach Tony Parkes and Kenny Dalglish. 'Where are we training?' I asked. Tony told me: 'You're with the kids.' A surge of anger consumed me, growing in intensity as I turned on my heel and stormed to the other end of the stadium, where the youngsters changed. The chairman happened to be there, talking to the masseur. It was Mr Coar's turn to be in the wrong place at the wrong time. Weeks of pent-up frustration and fury poured out as I gave him both barrels, telling him where he could shove his club and insisting that I would never again pull on a Blackburn shirt. I was on my way out of the door when, on impulse, I turned, went back in and gave him a bit more. Mr Coar was up against the wall, probably afraid that I was going to get violent. Violence wasn't on my agenda, but I had kept all the intrigue to myself and I simply had to unload my frustration.

I went back to the first-team changing-room to pick up some gear and I was walking past the ticket-office when Ray pulled up in his car, having just completed his weekly press conference. He wound down his car window, but before he had time to speak, I yelled: 'And you can fuck off as well. I've had it up to here and you can all shove it!' Ray wasn't for taking that from me. He followed me back to the scene of my bust-up with Coar and we had a real set-to. In an hour, I had blasted both the manager and the chairman. You can't burn your boats more effectively than that! I rang Hayden Evans to put him in the picture and he got to work on the diplomatic front, to great effect. Later that day, Ray rang to tell me to stand by the phone. A couple of days later he told me Blackburn had accepted Newcastle's bid and I took a call from Kevin Keegan, confirming the situation. It was a satisfactory conclusion to a nasty, messy business; but it left me branded as the bad boy in the eyes of the Blackburn fans. I was portrayed as a rebel who refused to play or train and I received a stack of abusive mail from people who had no idea what the facts were. None of this would have happened if the information regarding the offer from Newcastle hadn't been leaked to Tim.

the newcastle experience

Late in February 1996, I passed a medical and joined Kevin Keegan's exciting revolution on Tyneside. That Newcastle team, sporting names like David Ginola, Peter Beardsley, Tino Asprilla and Les Ferdinand, was the best I ever played in. They were four points clear of Manchester United, with a game in hand, when I arrived. They were flying. But I had to keep my feet on the ground, in more ways than one. I went to the Gosforth Park Hotel the day before I signed in a £3.75 million deal and took a phone call from Beardsley, who said: 'Come out with the lads. I'll pick you up.' So, there I was, standing in a nightclub having a few beers with my new team-mates, and I hadn't even signed on the dotted line yet. Players were saying: 'It's class here, Batts. We're out every night! You'll be divorced in six months.' And I was thinking: 'Christ! Talk about out of the frying pan into the fire.' I enjoyed being one of the lads, as I had been throughout my career, but I was a happily married father and I knew I had to strike a happy medium. Just as at Blackburn, I was content not to be living on the doorstep. It was good to be part of a set-up where the spirit was so strong and the socialising such fun, but it was equally important to keep a balance between the lighter side and the serious side. That would have been hard to do if I had lived near to the majority of the players.

After completing the formalities the next day, I was jogging round the training complex at Durham with Keegan and his No. 2 Terry McDermott. The next match, home to Manchester United, was in 10 days. Keegan said: 'It's a shame you haven't played for six or seven weeks, Batts,' leaving me under the impression that I wasn't in his reckoning for the big game. I was disappointed, but I couldn't complain if he thought I wasn't fit enough to take on the team that had been steadily eating away at Newcastle's lead over the previous couple of months. So I was surprised and elated when, at 5 p.m. on the day of the match, Kevin announced his team and I was in it. The match was live on Sky TV and I had a good debut, winning the sponsors' Man of the Match award. The only problem was, we lost. We battered them in the first half, but Peter Schmeichel had a blinder and Eric Cantona scored the only goal after the break. If we had won that game we would have won the League, I am sure of that. But it wasn't to be: Newcastle had held a huge, 12-point lead before I joined them, yet we ended up four points adrift of United, who stormed to their third title in four seasons.

There was plenty of drama, on and off the pitch, in the climax to that season. Early in April, I took part in a match to rival the Leeds–Liverpool 4–5 epic of four years before. Newcastle lost 4–3 at Anfield in a thriller that they still love to show on the *Sky Classics* programme. It was a fantastic, see-saw match, wonderful to be a part of even if, once again, I was a member of the losing side. At half-time Rob Lee and I – Keegan's 'two dogs in the middle of the park' – slumped alongside each other in the dressing-room and said: 'We'll never keep this up for another 45 minutes.' Yet we did. I have an abiding memory of Keegan, draped over the advertising hoardings at the final whistle, looking as drained with emotion as we were from unrelenting physical effort. By now, Manchester United had taken over at the top and the heat was on. Kevin must have been feeling it when he produced an amazing outburst in front of the TV cameras after our win at Leeds in the third-last match of the season. He stunned everyone, including the interviewer, when he suddenly started ranting about 'that man' – clearly referring to Alex Ferguson – implying that the Manchester United boss had been winding him up. If Fergy had been indulging in his infamous psychological-warfare strategy, it wasn't apparent to us players. We were as baffled as most people – including Ferguson, or so he claimed – by our gaffer's excitable rantings. Our next but last match was at Nottingham Forest, where we had already arranged to play a testimonial for Stuart Pearce at the end of the season. Fergy had made some remarks in the newspapers, insinuating that perhaps Forest wouldn't pull out all the stops against us the following week. He may have also implied that Leeds – those well-known Manchester United-haters – would go easy on us, too. Whatever the reason, Keegan flipped his lid that evening, his outburst knocking reports of our victory off the back pages next morning. I don't know what Kevin's reaction was when he saw the tape of that interview, whether or not he was embarrassed. But I loved it; to me, it was Kevin through and through. He always wore his heart on his sleeve and I loved him for it. He is a passionate manager and I like that. The players joked about it, but not in a cynical way. We all appreciated Kevin for his openness and his passion for the game, which he desperately wanted us to play in an entertaining manner. At the same time, we did wonder if he was losing it a little.

Newcastle had been like a holiday club when I arrived, a bit similar to the scene at Blackburn. But, towards the end of the season, with our lead slipping steadily away, we were running through the woods one day when Kevin suddenly announced: 'Anyone who goes out tonight won't play for this club again.' It was the only time I ever saw him clamp down. There was a tremendous team spirit, and it was down to Kevin and Terry McDermott. Even so, it wasn't enough to carry us to title glory. We went into the last day of the season knowing not only that we had to beat Spurs at St James' Park but also that Manchester had to lose at Middlesbrough. They beat Boro and we could only draw. We were runners-up by four points.

The records show that Keegan's team wasn't quite good enough to last the pace in the marathon title race. Over nine months of competition the team didn't quite have the resilience, but we provided stacks of excitement along the way. David Ginola, who eventually fell foul of Kenny Dalglish, when he succeeded Keegan in January 1997, was the best example of the Jekyll and Hyde character of KK's Magpies. Ginola is one of those flair players who can often 'disappear' when the heat is on, especially in away games. But that isn't a big problem to me so long as he's doing what's required in attack. I have always loved the entertainers, the guys who can appear to be contributing little and who then suddenly produce a moment of magic to turn a match in your favour. Ginola, whose speed and skill for such a big man always amazed me, was a case in point. The manager must have a different perspective, though. His job depends upon results, not performances, and that is why the Ginolas of this world can be a weak link for the man in charge. I suspect that the weakest link in Keegan's managerial make-up is his idealism, but it is a glorious weakness. He really wants to produce attacking, entertaining teams, as he did at Newcastle. I remember how he raved down the phone to me just before I joined about 'this guy Ginola'. Sadly, we were always fractionally behind Alex Ferguson's fantastic Manchester United sides, even after Alan Shearer joined us in a world record £15 million move from Blackburn.

We were in Singapore on our pre-season tour in the summer of 1996 when Kevin approached me one day in the hotel and said, with a barely suppressed note of triumph in his voice: 'We've got him.' I said: 'Got who?' Kevin replied: 'Your mate. Alan Shearer.' He was dead chuffed. Paying that record fee seemed to show the world that Newcastle's ambition was undimmed and unlimited, even if the club had missed out on the championship. It was a statement that the club was determined to push on from the disappointment of being pipped at the post.

The way that Newcastle team played reflected the training at the club. It was marvellous. I actually started not only to take training seriously for the first time in four or five years, but also to enjoy it! Having said that, I didn't dare not to put my heart and soul into it. Thousands of fans turned up every day to watch us at our Durham training HQ. Those supporters were truly remarkable; with so many of them watching every day, you would have been a fool not to do your best to impress. It was an uplifting experience. The exercises were short, usually lasting no more than an hour, and varied, with the accent always on skill.

We had several routines, which proved to be quite daunting for some players, even men as self-confident as Shearer. Rarely do players have to train in front of the inquisitive eyes of so many fans. I wasn't fazed by it but it took some of the lads a while before they could step out on to the pitch without apprehension. Darren Huckerby, the striker who went on to Coventry, Leeds and Manchester City, was a typical example. Darren had joined us from Lincoln and he was particularly nervous about having to perform a series of skill exercises, incorporating head, chest, control and volley routines, in front of not only thousands of punters but also his much more experienced and famous team-mates. Even Alan, fresh from his exploits with Blackburn and already an established England star, was uncomfortable at first. If you lost control of the ball, you got instant stick from the other lads. But the atmosphere was superb, and Alan was quick to admit that his touch and technique steadily improved as a result of the completely different regime he had joined.

I was certainly delighted to be teaming up with Alan again. He has everything a manager wants in a player: attitude, presence, confidence, influence, character and ability. But there was one thing about the boundless praise that was heaped upon Alan which always amused and puzzled me, namely his workrate. The pundits used to go on and on about his phenomenal grafting in a game. It wasn't true. That impression might have been conveyed in part because of his habit of drifting wide and putting in the sort of crosses he would have loved to have been on the end of himself. But, in the main, Alan used to stand in the middle while we ran around him. Rob Lee and I took the mickey out of him for it. He wasn't as quick as you might think, either. But he had more going for him than most, including immense strength, physical as well as mental. He was at his most effective with a defender alongside him. If you put a ball over the top and Alan could feel an opponent at his side, he invariably brushed the man aside and won the race to the ball. I remember him getting the better of Manchester United's Gary Pallister in exactly that manner when playing for Blackburn at Ewood Park. Alan has a reputation for being deadpan and dour when giving interviews, but he is one of the biggest jokers in the pack. One of his favourite – and most annoying – tricks is to slap you through your sweat-soaked shirt after you've done the pre-match warm-ups. It stings like hell. If fans were puzzled to see us running out of the tunnel with our arms protecting our backs, it was because Shearer was up to his tricks.

I scored Newcastle's first goal of the 1996–97 season, a 40-yard chip against Wimbledon's Neil Sullivan, the keeper who had been beaten from 50 yards the previous week by David Beckham's incredible effort. We made a wobbly start, then took off after beating Sunderland in the big North-East derby, going on a great run that included a fantastic 5–0 win over Manchester United. The game showed off everything that was good about the Newcastle team of the time, the final goal proving to be a fitting finale when our big Belgian defender Philippe Albert – who sounded more like a Geordie than some locals – chipped Peter Schmeichel to complete the rout. Still, we didn't go on to outlast Ferguson's team that season, but they can never take memories like that night's display away from you. Our Champions League campaign foundered over two legs against Monaco, after we had seen off Ferencvaros, of Hungary, and then French club Metz in the tie during which the Brazilian guy split my eye open.

I have always been proud of the fact that I don't cheat on the pitch. I don't set out to 'do' opponents. I don't play-act if I get clobbered and I don't react, either. When the Metz player whacked me, I didn't weigh into him in violent retaliation, but I was disappointed that the referee didn't send him off. I am not a dirty player. I also believe passionately that many players' disciplinary records are made worse because of the disappointing actions of some of my fellow professionals. Talk about a 'players' union'! Too often too many of them don't do their opponents any favours whatsoever. Every follower of the game can remember occasions when players have taken a dive or exaggerated an injury and an opponent has been booked or sent off.

It might surprise you to hear that by November 1996,

I had never been sent off in eight years of highly competitive midfield action. We played at Chelsea shortly after the Metz match, when I did an un-Batty-like thing by inviting a Radio Five reporter up to my hotel room to do an interview. I have never been too hot on talking to the press and I agreed to Ian Payne's request because he's a Leeds fan. But I know it blew up in my face! The reporter asked me about my disciplinary record and I pointed out that, though I had received numerous yellow cards down the years, I was proud that I had never been shown a red. The next day I got sent off at Stamford Bridge. The following season, I took an early bath three times.

My first sending-off, after a tangle with Chelsea striker Mark Hughes, came when he and I were having a tussle when I let my arm rise and caught him in the face. I know it was careless and I admit I made contact, but I didn't think it was a vicious act, yet the end result was a red card. Keegan told the newspapers he would be disciplining me; in reality, we had a laugh about it and no action was taken. Early the following August, Villa's Steve Staunton fell over my leg. I got a second yellow card and was off again. Maybe I shouldn't have gone in for the tackle.

I can't deny, though, that I was picking up too many silly bookings that season. After another two yellows – for two daft trips – at Derby on Boxing Day 1998, I was trudging off the pitch when I noticed two stewards heading my way to escort me away. That kind of thing really annoys me: I can walk off by myself, thank you very much! So, just to be awkward, I veered away and walked behind them at the point when they moved in to flank me. The most annoying incident of all occurred in the last match of that season at Blackburn, when I shoved referee David Elleray in the chest. It was a game that had no meaning for either team. Blackburn were safe; we were heading for the FA Cup final and looking to avoid any injuries that might cost us a place at Wembley. We were all coasting through the match.

By then, I had played several matches without picking up a booking and was really making an effort to clean up my act. Their midfielder, Gary Flitcroft, and I were tangling for a ball that had run loose near the touchline. In those situations, it is impossible not to use your arms to some extent. Flitcroft went down and it looked as if I had thrown an elbow deliberately. I swear I hadn't done so. I went to Elleray, genuinely upset at the prospect of being booked. I was horrified when he brandished the red card. 'What for?' I demanded. He turned his face away at my question in a gesture that I interpreted as arrogant disregard for me. I was so angry that I gave him a push as I walked away. Talk about making matters worse for yourself! As I walked off the Ewood pitch I was consumed by a sense of injustice. I had to agree that it looked a bad incident when Flitcroft and I tangled but, logically, I wasn't going to risk suspension at the start of the following season by doing something so stupid, and deliberately smashing someone with my elbow is definitely not my style. I was summoned before the FA Disciplinary Committee in Manchester and took a PFA representative with me. As it had been my third sending-off that season I was given a five-match ban with an extra match for pushing Elleray. I went to the World Cup that summer knowing I would have an Achilles operation on my return and that I would be recuperating while the suspension was in force, but I was bugged by the principle involved. I could honestly claim I had not deliberately elbowed Flitcroft. I think I got my point across to the committee, but the video evidence looked conclusive and they had to be seen to be meting out 'justice'. The episode left me disillusioned.

After that first sending-off, at Chelsea, I came back from a three-month suspension to play at Blackburn where we lost after a performance devoid of inspiration. For the first time, I detected that all was not well with Keegan. Win, lose or draw, Kevin was always the life and soul in the dressing-room, an enthusiastic character whose zest for the game rubbed off on us all. Yet he was unrecognisable as he stood in the dressing-room after that defeat in late December 1996. He was standing near me as I got changed; normally, even in defeat, there would have been some banter between us. On this occasion, Kevin was lost in his own thoughts; he was miles away. I sensed that this was the beginning of the end for him at Newcastle and my instincts were proved right. A few of the senior pros were in the canteen at the training ground about 10 days later when Terry McDermott, Kevin's trusty lieutenant, came in and sat at our table. I'll never forget how, with a grave expression on his face, Terry announced: 'Forgive me for getting emotional, but Kevin has resigned.' Some of the lads were shocked; I was only surprised. It was as if Kevin had decided he had taken the team as far as he could and, not being a man to hang about in those circum-stances – as his subsequent, sudden exit from the England job in 2000 proved – he was gone without a word. Kevin did not say goodbye to the players, he just disappeared from the scene.

Within a week of Kevin's departure, I was returning from a shopping trip to Toys R Us in York, buying presents for the twins, when the radio broadcast the news that Kenny Dalglish was our new manager. Several weeks later my phone rang at home and it was Kevin. He had been driving through Wetherby an hour earlier and had seen me in my car and decided to give me a call. He seemed quite content with life and it was good to hear from a man for whom I had a lot of respect.

I had respect for Terry McDermott, too – we all did – but footballers can be hard at times. Following his melodramatic address in the canteen on the day Kevin's resignation was announced, Terry became Dalglish's right-hand man, and we took every opportunity to begin any remarks to Terry sarcastically with the words: 'Forgive me for getting emotional, but . . .' Though I had been sad to see Kevin go, I was delighted to know Kenny was moving in. I am always massively reassured by the certainty that the manager rates me, and Kenny rated me, I had no doubts about that. We did quite well under Kenny for the last four months of the season, again finishing runners-up to Manchester United, and above Liverpool and Arsenal on goal difference.

I went to Le Tournoi in France with England and came back suffering severe pain in my feet. Scans showed arthritic problems in my joints. It was suggested that I should have either injections, or an operation to fuse the joints which would put me out of action for six months. Unhappy with these options, I went to see a specialist who discovered that, when I planted my feet, they were rolling inwards, putting too much pressure on the inside of my soles. I was given orthotic insoles which tilted my feet marginally – but vitally – in the other direction. I had some to wear in my boots and some for the trainers that are my standard footwear. You won't see me in conventional shoes unless forced to wear them for official club duty or a formal occasion. The orthotics worked wonders. I was delighted: no injections, no surgery. I felt immense relief; there's nothing worse than pain in your feet when you're running on them all the time. I wouldn't go so far as to say those insoles – which I wear to this day – saved my career, but they saved me a lot of time and inconvenience, and spared me another visit to the operating theatre.

The momentum began to drain from the team slowly, but surely, the following season. Dalglish clearly wasn't as big a fan of David Ginola as Keegan had been. Neither, for that matter, was Alan Shearer. While Keegan was still boss I recall Shearer having a dig at Ginola, claiming that while at Blackburn, he had marvelled at the number of crosses he put over but that now, where were all those quality balls? I think Dalglish – in common with many other managers – regarded Ginola as too much of a luxury. David's days in the famous black and white shirt were numbered.

The omens for the 1997–98 season weren't good when Shearer suffered a serious injury in the Umbro Tournament at Goodison Park in late July that also involved Chelsea, Ajax and Everton. Alan did his ankle. I went to see him in the medical room where he told me he was knackered. I was rooming with him and went to the hotel to collect his gear while he went straight back to Newcastle, where he had an operation that night. He missed the first half of the season.

A few days later we went to Italy – where I had never played a match – to meet Juventus in a game to commemorate their centenary. Juve wore their original pink strip and, being an avid collector of shirts, I determined to do a swap after the match. There was a feeling that the Italians would be reluctant to exchange shirts because that strip was so special. I asked our Colombian striker, Tino Asprilla, to do his best on my behalf and I was thrilled when he persuaded Uruguayan star Daniel Fonseca to swap with me. That treasured pink item is with all the rest of my shirt collection at my mum and dad's house. The only full international shirt I haven't got is Malaysia's – because, at the final whistle after a friendly in Kuala Lumpur, their players all rushed off the pitch to keep an audience with the king and we never saw them again.

A successful start to our Champions League campaign – when we beat Croatia Zagreb 4–3 on aggregate in the qualifying round – belied the struggle we were to have in the Premiership that season. My abiding memory of the tie in Zagreb was the hostile atmosphere that hit you when you emerged from the long walk through the underground tunnel to the pitch. We had won 2–1 at St James' Park in the first leg and were under the cosh at 1–1 in Zagreb, going into the last minute, and with their crowd going wild. As usual, I was involved in confrontations with one or two of their players and thoroughly enjoyed myself. Until, that is, Zagreb scored with seconds to go, taking us into extra time. Their players screamed insults into my face as they came back to the centre circle. That doesn't bother me; I just find it a bit sad that players feel the need to go in for that kind of thing. But I had the last laugh. The match was petering out and looking certain to go to a penalty shoot-out when one of their defenders started messing about with the ball in the corner. His clearance went straight to our Georgian striker, Temuri Ketsbaia, who scored in the last minute to put us through to the competition proper. We were elated, they were gutted! Like I say, it's not my style, especially not the verbal stuff.

We drew Barcelona, Dynamo Kiev and PSV Eindhoven in the first phase. Fantastic! The opening match was home to Barcelona, and what a night that was. Keith Gillespie, the right-winger Keegan had brought from Manchester United as part of the deal that took Andy Cole to Old Trafford, was on fire. He murdered Barca's full-back Sergy by repeatedly knocking the ball past him and beating him for pace. Keith put over ball after ball and Tino Asprilla scored a hat-trick to put us 3–0 up. Admittedly, Barca battered us in the second half, pulling back to 3–2, but it was a superb start. Then we went to Kiev where we played in front of a 100,000 crowd. Again we got a bit of a battering, but we drew 2–2 thanks to an unlikely two-goal hero, full-back John Beresford. I was proud to captain the team when we arrived home, with Rob Lee out injured, and even prouder when I went off to help England clinch a World Cup finals place with a memorable goalless draw in Italy in October 1997.

My next match was at, of all places, Leeds, where I was given a tremendous reception as I got off the team coach. Then we were hammered 4–1. Back down to earth with a bang! The following week, PSV beat us in Holland. I was booked and so missed the return at St James' when, crucially, PSV did the double over us. After our heady start, the European dream was fading, to be finally dashed by a 1–0 defeat in Barcelona. Captaining the team in the Nou Camp was scant consolation. Nevertheless, I was happy at the club and pleased when Hayden Evans informed me that chairman Freddy Shepherd had indicated they were ready to offer me a new, five-year contract which would, in effect, tie me to Newcastle for the rest of my top-flight career. We weren't doing too well in the Premiership and we were now out of the Champions League, but the club seemed to be going places and I had a manager in Dalglish who had faith in me. However, one event overshadowed all else that December: the tragic death of my mentor Billy Bremner. Billy passed away on 7 December, aged 54. We ended our Champions League campaign on a winning note against Dynamo Kiev and the next day, 11 December, I attended Billy's funeral. It was the first I had been to and it was a highly emotional occasion for me. Billy's great friend Alex Smith, from Scotland, gave a moving address which brought tears from me and, I dare say, quite a few others in the church that day.

Newcastle's League season stumbled along. We signed my good mate Gary Speed, from Everton, in a £5 million deal in February. Everton had been our FA Cup third-round victims a month earlier. By the time Gary joined us, the Cup was our sole motivation – save for the need to ensure that we stayed in the Premier League! Our most memorable match en route to Wembley – though not for the best of reasons – was our fourth-round clash with non-League Stevenage Borough, which descended into an undignified mess. It all started to turn sour when Kenny Dalglish, for the logical reason that their ground wasn't up to scratch, suggested we play the tie at St James' Park. This was taken as an insult by Stevenage, whose manager Paul Fairclough was on TV every other day claiming we were running scared of an upset. I wasn't impressed with him. Unfortunately for us, Fairclough's team matched us at their place to earn a draw and a replay at St James'. We won 2–1 but, disappointingly, we didn't beat them convincingly. It was much the same when we scraped past Tranmere by one goal in round five, a tie memorable for the difficulty we experienced dealing with Dave Challinor's amazing 40-yard throw-ins, which rained into the goalmouth. I scored the last goal in our sixth-round KO of Barnsley. We were in the semi-final and a match against Sheffield United at Old Trafford, when Shearer scored the only goal.

Not long before the semi, our Premiership woes had deepened when we lost at home to relegation-bound Crystal Palace. Ours was a terrible performance. The atmosphere at St James' was funereal. We were booed off the pitch and deservedly so. I had signed my new contract by then and Mandy and I put in an offer for a house in the North-East. Thank goodness, in retrospect, that the deal fell through. Two weeks before we met Arsenal in the FA Cup final, we finally clinched Premier League survival with a 3–1 home defeat of Chelsea. At last, we could concentrate on the big day at Wembley. Sadly, not only the day itself but the whole build-up turned out to be a massive anticlimax. It is hard to put your finger on why a team starts to lose its cutting edge and its sparkle: all I do know is that, despite Dalglish's motivational powers, there wasn't a positive air about the camp as we prepared for what should be the most exciting day of a player's life, the FA Cup final. The crucial factor, confidence, was in short supply. Our 3–1 thrashing by our Wembley opponents a month earlier had hardly increased our optimism that all might go well on the big day. Like most boys, I had read with hard-to-suppress excitement players' accounts of their build-up to Cup final day, yet the glamour and sense of occasion didn't happen for me. I don't know if the fact that I had played many times at Wembley for England took the edge off it a little, or maybe the insecurity of our poor form leading up to Wembley left me feeling down: possibly it was a combination of the two. The fact is that we lost 2–0 and it could have been five or six, we were so poor. It was all sadly predictable. My dad has my loser's medal; I never even looked at it. I couldn't tell you what it is like. The team was poor; I was poor. I couldn't summon any energy. The whole week had been a damp squib. When my two brothers-in-law Lee and Mark couldn't find our hotel to attend the club party, and had to drive all the way back to Leeds in frustration, it just about put the cap on one of the biggest let-downs in my career.

There is one other vivid memory of that 1997–98 season, though it was a day that the participants would rather forget. The setting was Dublin. A favourite of Kenny Dalglish, the Irish capital had been a frequent destination for midweek breaks when I was with him at Blackburn. Tim Sherwood, Mark Atkins, goalkeeper Bobby Mimms and I used to frequent Davey Byrne's pub and often sat there all day, supping Guinness. We made so many visits that a code developed between us and the bar staff: a touch of the nose would mean you wanted a dash of blackcurrant in your drink, a flick of the ear and baskets of sausages and chips would arrive at the table. We'd be in there for 15 or 16 hours at a time. A guy standing next to me in the toilet one day said: 'Are you David Batty?' 'No,' I replied. 'Jees, you look a dead ringer for yourself, so you do,' he said. I think he must have been in the place as long as we had! Anyway, Kenny organised another trip to the 'Fair City' after coming to Newcastle. Unfortunately, it was to be the last. A group of the lads, Speedy, Shearer, Stuart Pearce, Philippe Albert, Keith Gillespie and I, were in a bar. Speedy and I nipped next door for a McDonald's – disciples of healthy eating, as ever – and on our return, we immediately detected an atmosphere between Alan and Keith. It seemed Keith had been getting on Al's nerves by repeatedly flicking bottle tops across the table. As we sat down, Al was saying: 'Do that one more time and I'll give you a good hiding.' Keith did it again. The two men got up and walked down the narrow aisle between the tables and out through the glass doors, but they had barely exited the place when I noticed a pair of legs in the air. We ran out to see Gillespie, spark out in the gutter; there was blood everywhere, and Alan was looking shaken. Allegedly, Keith had taken a swing as the two made their way towards the rear of the pub and Al had turned and decked him.

Matters went from bad to worse that evening as Pearce, Speedy, Albert, Andy Griffin and I made our way to another bar. Big Philippe had a traffic cone on his head and he and one or two of the lads began throwing the thing around. It hit a parked car, going through the windscreen and setting off the alarm. The woman who owned the vehicle emerged from a nearby apartment with her boyfriend and some mates, screaming in protest, and the Guarda rushed to the scene. Things didn't look good, but I told Andy Griffin to stay calm as I informed the cops that we weren't guilty and I didn't know who the culprit was. After some investigation, the police went into a bar further up the road and pulled out Stuart Pearce, who admitted he was responsible. The owner of the car emerged, Stuart telling her if she came to the team hotel the following day he would give her a cheque to cover the cost of the damage. He was as good as his word, but unfortunately the story reached the tabloids, one of which carried a photocopy of Stuart's cheque the following day. Keith Gillespie flew home the next morning. When we arrived back, Kenny held a meeting at which he read the riot act, telling us the chairman was disgusted and that we were a disgrace to the club. Any repeat, and the culprits would be transferred. It was strong stuff. But the heat was dramatically taken off the players a week later when the *News of the World* published a damning account that accused chairman Freddy Shepherd and director Douglas Hall – son of former chairman Sir John Hall – of insulting Tyneside women and Newcastle's supporters while on a jaunt in Spain. I felt sorry for Freddy Shepherd and his family because he was a good guy who genuinely had the club at heart, but it was a relief that the spotlight switched so rapidly from the players to the hierarchy.

that penalty miss

Late on the warm night of 30 June 1998, I took what is referred to in football as 'the long walk'. That is the description often given to the near 50-yard trek from the centre circle to play your part in soccer's version of Russian roulette, the infamous penalty shoot-out. This method of settling stalemate situations, after 120 minutes of normal play, can make the bravest of men go weak at the knees. Many of the best players in the world have been reduced to quivering wrecks at the very thought of taking such a crucial spot-kick. My former Blackburn and Newcastle manager Kenny Dalglish, one of the most prolific strikers of all time with Liverpool and Scotland, refused to be 'put on the spot' and openly talked about his sense of terror at the prospect of penalty-taking – and he didn't mean the ultimate test of nerve, the shoot-out! I simply didn't take penalties, ever. At least, not until that moment. And what a moment: England's continued participation in the World Cup hung on the outcome of my effort to beat Argentina's keeper Carlos Roa from 12 yards. A hit and the scores would be level at 4–4, a miss and England would go out and Argentina would progress to the quarter-finals. As every football fan knows, my shot was saved and England were on the plane home from France the next day. And I haven't lost a single night's sleep worrying about it since. In fact, though my failure will probably go down as the most famous missed penalty in history, I look back with pride on that fateful night in France. Let me explain why.

I don't suppose any footballer could be under more pressure than I was while I prepared to take that crucial swing of my right foot. Yet, as I took each stride of the 'walk' – towards the end of the stadium where the Argentine fans were massed – nothing but confidence was surging through my mind and body. I wouldn't have agreed to take the kick had there been any fear or doubt. If there is one quality I have been blessed with above any other it is supreme self-belief. I have never run on to a football pitch with negative thoughts in my head, no matter how big the reputation of the opposition, either individually or as a team. Though I was surprised to be asked by manager Glenn Hoddle to be one of our five nominated penalty-takers, I wasn't worrying about the challenge as I neared the penalty spot. Indeed, having come to terms with the fact that I had been asked to take the first penalty of my senior career, I was relishing the prospect of helping to put us through to the last eight. And I firmly expected to do that: already, I had talked confidently with Alan Shearer about the technique I would apply. The pressure of expectation from the tens of thousands of English supporters, coupled with the baying South American fans' bid to distract me from my responsibility, was no problem as I walked across the 18-yard line.

The thought that I would be faced with this situation hadn't entered my head after I replaced the shattered

Darren Anderton after 10-man England – David Beckham having been sent off, of course – held Argentina to 2–2 at the end of normal time. The England lads' spirit and determination after Beckham's dismissal was absolutely fantastic. There was a feeling of 'they shall not pass' as we thrust out our jaws and produced a display of British bulldog defiance. I remember with admiration how Shearer and his strike partner Michael Owen took it in turns to drop back and work to shore up the defences. We were absolutely united in our determination not to let Argentina score in extra time. There was never any chance that we might get a dramatic winner ourselves; everyone who had been out there from the start was on his last legs. Our clear-minded aim was to get to the end of extra time undefeated. But, strangely, it never occurred to me as the minutes ticked away that penalties would decide the match. Certainly, it never crossed my mind for a moment that I would be taking one. Some of the players, like Shearer, Owen and my fellow substitute Paul Merson, were obvious choices; Beckham, clearly, would have been another. The remainder were mostly defenders – and they were all knackered after their monumental efforts to keep Argentina out.

So, on reflection, perhaps I shouldn't have been as stunned as I fleetingly was when Hoddle, who had been walking among the players, suddenly appeared in front of me saying: 'Batts, pen?' For a split second I tried to take in the situation. In that instant I dispelled any doubts and replaced them with positive thoughts. 'All right. Yes' was my reply. I remember thinking: 'If Hoddle has the faith and the confidence in me to ask me, then I've certainly got the confidence to say yes.' As the implications of my decision sank in, I got a lift out of the situation. Never for a moment did I wish I'd said no. I had been relaxed after the final whistle because it never entered my mind that I would be put on the spot. When it happened, I was flattered. With hindsight, I admit I'm not sure if I'd put myself in that position again but, on the night, I quickly concluded that Hoddle must have had good reason to ask me. I figured it would be a big blow to him if I were to chicken out. The five men selected were Shearer, Owen, Merson, Paul Ince and me. Ince might have been a surprise choice to the millions of folk watching back home on TV but when my name flashed on the screen, I guess the public were flabbergasted. I can hardly argue with that; most of them had never even seen me have a shot, never mind take a penalty! I had often watched on TV as players were put through the shoot-out trauma, imagining that if I were ever in the situation I would do something completely daft like fall flat on my face as I ran up, or miss the ball altogether.

But there were no such thoughts on the night; at least, not in my head. My dad, watching back home in Leeds, didn't share my confidence. He wrote in his book: 'Mary and I got the shock of our lives when David was asked to take a penalty – and it turned out to be the last one, at that. Neither Mary nor myself really expected David to score. But we were still living in hope. It goes without saying he missed – and England were out of the World Cup.' But he added the touching postscript: 'Immediately after the penalty miss David held himself together well. And he gave a good interview later that night on *Match of the Day* when he seemed to be coming to terms with the situation. We are very proud of him.'

I had remained quite calm during the 15 minutes or so before the start of the shoot-out. The drama began with Argentina going first. Sergio Berti scored: 1–0. Then the supremely self-confident Alan Shearer for England: 1–1. Hernan Crespo's shot was saved by David Seaman to give Ince the chance to put us in front. His effort was saved and Juan Veron scored: 2–1. Paul Merson scored: 2–2. Marcelo Gallardo put his shot past Seaman: 3–2. Michael Owen did his job: 3–3. My time was coming. Still, I wasn't nervous, not even after Roberto Ayala made it 4–3 and I, as last man, was left with the task of keeping us in the competition. I had told Shearer I was going to drill the ball down the middle. That was the easy option, based on the theory that the keeper would move one way or the other. However, fatally, I decided at the last moment that I would place it. I opted to shoot to Roa's right; unfortunately for me, he decided to dive to his right. I hit the ball well enough, but at the ideal height for the keeper. If I had put it either higher or lower it would almost certainly have beaten him. The roar that went up from the Argentinians massed behind the goal was one of ecstasy, the silence from the England fans almost as deafening.

In an instant I took in the enormity of my miss: we were out of the World Cup, and people would say it was down to me. In another, I rationalised the situation. I had tried and failed to score from the penalty spot, something which I had never been asked to do even in League football. I gave it a go and it didn't come off. I wasn't ashamed of myself and I wasn't going to go for sympathy by breaking into floods of tears or collapsing to the floor, beating the turf in a gesture of agonised despair. Players who react like that, in the main, are doing what they think the fans expect them to do: 'Oh, look how the poor lad suffers!' That's just not my scene. In the final analysis, it was a football match we were involved in, not a war. I don't accept that you can get so upset over a game of football, even in the World Cup finals. Obviously, I wished my shot had gone in, leaving another poor sod with the responsibility of keeping us in, or shooting us through, a few moments later, but it didn't. I am just glad that I had the balls to take the penalty; I can hold my head high, knowing I did what was asked of me under the greatest pressure a player can ever experience. Had I said no when Hoddle asked me, I would be more upset with myself than I ever was for not scoring. I can't fully explain why, on that one night in all of my life, I felt confident about doing something which I never normally did. But I was up for it and the fact that it didn't come off will never detract from my inner satisfaction at having been prepared to answer the manager's call.

I don't like defeat any more than the next player, but I don't dwell on it, either. And I didn't dwell on that setback, even if, as my dad wrote: 'The country was in mourning.' A couple of players, Tim Flowers and Gareth Southgate – who famously missed from the spot for England on another occasion – came over to console me. It was decent of them, but I didn't need it. When we reached the dressing-room, there was an atmosphere of stunned silence. Glenn Hoddle's secretary, Michelle, was in tears. I felt sorry for her, for all of us, but I wasn't carrying the weight of the world on my shoulders. We had every reason to be proud of our performance that night. With 10 men from early in the second half we had battled to a draw with one of the best teams on earth. I am always one of the first into the shower and that night was no different: then I phoned Mandy and my mum and dad and her parents to reassure them that I wasn't the devastated wreck of a human being that some folk seemed to think I should have been. Mandy was more interested in the fact that this meant I'd be coming home the next day and wanted to know exactly what time I'd be arriving. That is what keeps my feet on the ground; it is basically the way I felt, too. I would have loved nothing more than to have scored and for England to be playing a quarter-final tie, but that didn't happen. So why not turn a negative into a positive? I was going home to my wife and kids the next day and I couldn't wait to see them, because I love them more than anything in the world and I'd rather be at home than anywhere else.

My rationalisation was put to the test when, in the bar later, I was watching the rerun on TV. Kevin Keegan, optimistic as ever, was asked as I ran up to the ball: 'Is Batty going to score?' Even though Kevin, like the teeming millions also tuned in, had never seen me take, let alone score, a penalty, he replied emphatically: 'Yes!' I sat there thinking: 'Oh, God!' As the players walked through the media area on the way to the team bus, however, I had no hesitation in agreeing to a request for an interview from a TV crew. It would have been easy to refuse; I'm sure the TV people half expected me to decline. But, by then, even if I was possibly still in shock, I certainly felt I had no reason to feel ashamed.

Heart-rendingly, the British public clearly felt that way, too. In the days and weeks that followed I received hundreds of letters. Not one of them was abusive, nor even critical of me. They were written by people from all walks of life and from fans of many clubs who would normally have been hostile to me as a Newcastle player. The only sour note in the aftermath of our KO came, for me at any rate, as I was standing talking to Hayden Evans and a couple of other friends by the bus. Argentina's coach was alongside ours and I wasn't amused to see their players at the back of the bus, with their shirts off, singing at the tops of their voices. They were rubbing our noses in it – mine in particular – and I found that distasteful. Had I been emotionally battered by my penalty miss, their gloating might just have pushed me over the edge. As it was, I consoled myself with the thought that they were doing themselves no favours – and of what I might do to them if I could get on to their bus! We went back to our hotel, drank beer until dawn and then went on to the golf course at first light. We climbed aboard Concorde for the flight home without going to bed.

Within days of getting back to England, it had become clear that, though I would be marked out forever as the man who missed the penalty that cost England its place in the World Cup finals, the real villain of the piece was Manchester United's David Beckham. As I have said, I had no trouble coming to terms with my part in the drama of that fateful evening in Saint Etienne. That isn't because I don't appreciate how much football means to so many people. Working men and women have it tough: the vast majority of them are doing jobs they don't like doing for a wage that doesn't relieve the strain that afflicts most people, a shortage of money. I know because I come from a working-class home. Professional football is a means to escape that lifestyle for the fortunate minority, like me, who play it for a well-paid living. I am well aware that, for the majority who can only dream of playing, the success of their team is their form of escapism. For that reason, if no other, I would have loved to have seen my penalty go past Carlos Roa and bulge the netting. But it didn't, and I couldn't afford to carry the burden of worrying about the nation's disappointment. There are more important things in life.

That is why I found it difficult to sympathise when I read that Beckham had, according to the papers, been upset that nobody except skipper Tony Adams had gone to console him after the match. Whether or not Adams was the only one to offer words of sympathy I wouldn't know, but that is more than likely the case. I, for one, didn't. Even if I hadn't just missed the penalty that would have kept us in the World Cup, it wouldn't have crossed my mind to offer consolation to Beckham. That will sound callous but it isn't meant to. If I had been Beckham I wouldn't have wanted people commiserating with me. If you have missed a vital penalty, or been sent off playing for your country, then you simply have to live with it, put it into perspective. Admittedly, Beckham took a lot of stick from the public and the press over his so-called red-card shame. I think some sections of the media took mischievous delight in giving the impression that Becks's act of folly had blackened him in the eyes of his team-mates, that the players were happy to have him as the scapegoat for our exit. That is nonsense. I certainly didn't judge David on the night and neither, to the best of my knowledge, did any of the other members of the squad.

We don't have the benefit of instant TV replays of these incidents; from the bench, where I was sitting, you don't see them even as clearly as you would if you were in the stands. But I do know that there was no malice in Becks's flick of the boot at Argentine midfielder Diego Simeone. It was a stupid thing to do – I'm sure he accepts that – but players don't condemn their fellow professionals for such occasional moments of madness, even if, as on that occasion, the team suffers as a result.

Most of us were no doubt pondering the fact that he was damned unlucky; a yellow would have been more than sufficient punishment for such a minor act of petulance. Players tend not to judge the action of others – not of team-mates, at least – because we all know we might do something similar in the heat of the moment. Beckham has that edge to his game, an abrasive streak that probably goes towards making him the good player he is. Patrick Vieira is similar in that respect. Their teams would probably suffer more frequently if that vein of competitiveness was stripped out of their players' make-up.

If you play this game, especially in a central midfield position like I do, then you would have to be a saint to go through a career and not get into trouble with referees, including the occasional sending-off. And there are very few saints who make it in top-class football. That is why I got really steamed up by a letter sent to me after I had been red-carded playing for England against Poland in a European Championship qualifier in Warsaw in October

1999. The match was a scrappy one and Poland were a physical team. In the closing minutes I went for a challenge, the way I had a thousand times before and many times since. It was a bit of a lunge, I'll admit, but the Polish lad writhed around on the pitch as if he'd been stabbed. I was so annoyed with his behaviour that I bent over him and pinched him. I expected a yellow card but got a red. In the dressing-room after the match, manager Kevin Keegan, obviously niggled because I had been sent off, snapped: 'You're going to have to learn, you daft so-and-so.' I was taken aback: I knew Kevin was a Batty fan and I thought he would have realised that I was guilty only of a fractionally late tackle and not of anything remotely reckless or vicious. My faith was quickly restored when, within a minute or two of his outburst, Keegan, who was eating some chocolate, came up to me and said with a grin: 'Here, Batts, do you want a piece? You're still my mate, aren't you?' I gave an interview in front of the cameras, during which I obviously wasn't contrite enough for a fella in London, who wrote to me suggesting I should be embarrassed and ashamed. He had seen the match and my interview and concluded that I was a bad example to his son! I was furious. I wrote back, asking him exactly what he thought I had to be ashamed of and suggesting that he get a grip of reality. I told him there were plenty of things happening in the world that merited his anger and frustration, much more so than me getting sent off in a football match. It was no surprise that he didn't respond to my reply.

I've had criticism in some quarters because I used to make a little gesture to the TV cameras for the benefit of Jack and George, watching at home. Once the boys were old enough to realise that it was their dad standing there in the pre-match line-up I decided it would be nice for them to get a wave from me, something for Mandy to tell them to look out for. From a straightforward wave, it developed into all sorts of quirky little gestures, like a flick of my ear or a scratch of my nose. It was just a little personal interaction between me and my kids, but from some of the things people have said and written, you would think I was committing treason! I've been accused of being disrespectful to the national anthem, to Her Majesty and to my country. But my kids come first. I know that they aren't going to be interested for long in the match, so I make sure they have something to watch out for before boredom sets in. If, in some people's eyes, that is irreverent to Queen and country, then tough! Where my kids are concerned, I don't care who I upset.

I have already said that I try to understand how much the success of their team means to the fans, but we mustn't turn a blind eye to the excessive reaction of some people to what happens on a pitch. I cannot tolerate people, like that letter-writer, putting me into some sort of morally bereft, criminal category just because I've been sent off for a late challenge. The fact that I was playing for England doesn't matter one jot in that context as far as I am concerned. That doesn't mean I haven't been proud to represent my country.

Ironically, that match in Poland was the last time I pulled on the white shirt; my red-card suspension meant I missed the England–Scotland double-header which gave us our play-off ticket to the European Championship finals in 2000. Keegan was a big fan of mine and I'm pretty sure I would have played in those matches and been well on the way to realising my ambition to win 50 caps. Now, I don't expect to play for England again. But after all my terrible injury problems since returning to Elland Road, I'm just grateful to have made such a successful comeback in 2001.

my england career

I would probably not even have been on the airplane to France in 1998 – let alone shooting for a place in the quarter-finals – had Glenn Hoddle taken a dimmer view of my walk-out on the England team during the World Cup qualifying campaign in October 1996. A combination of circumstances left me in the mood to show my rebellious streak when we took on Poland at Wembley in the first qualifying match. I had spent a couple of injury-blighted years, during which I missed out on Euro 96 and never had the chance to get to know Hoddle's predecessor, Terry Venables. I had started to feel more and more like an England bit-part player and that is one thing that I have never been able to settle for, for either club or country. I think I am a good team player but, I admit, only if I am actually playing. As I've said, I'm just not interested if I'm on the sidelines.

When that qualifying campaign got under way, our boys were 21 months old and I was more reluctant than ever to be away from home for long. Hoddle called me into his squad so I went down to Bisham Abbey and really buckled down in training. I knew I had trained well and I figured I'd done enough to earn a place on the bench, at least. So when Hoddle came to me on the day of the match and told me he wasn't even naming me as a substitute, I wasn't amused. The squad arrived at Wembley, with my mood darkening by the hour. As the match kicked off, I left my seat and went home. I found the players' courtesy cars outside the stadium and asked the driver to take me to Wetherby. I would have gone before the match, if the cars had been in place then, but they don't arrive until the games kick off. By the time I was home I was in the mood to turn my back on England. I had been away for the best part of a week and the thought of repeating the process, only to sit in the stand, held no appeal for me whatsoever. Next day, Hoddle's assistant John Gorman rang me to say that, if I turned up for the next squad, I would start the match. Now, I guess that wasn't a politically correct thing to do; you don't expect the England management to be making selection promises to players, particularly to one who has just turned his back on the camp. But that is what John said and it was good enough for me. The next match was in Georgia, in the grim city of Tbilisi. Hoddle was as good as his word. He picked me from the start and I was named Man of the Match in our 2–0 win. He never said a word to me about my walk-out.

For my part, all I can say is that I wasn't being stroppy or throwing my rattle out of the pram. I have never made a secret of the fact that I can't accept not being involved. I hate watching games. I certainly won't watch football when I've retired, unless Jack and George are playing. But I must admit, I might have to try harder to get used to not being 100 per cent involved as I get older. As the seasons go by I will have to accept that week-in, week-out selection is unlikely. That's a bridge

Messing about with Gary Speed at Lightwater Valley.

Popperfoto

Taking time out for a bit of fishing during England's tour to New Zealand.

Playing my first full international for England against Argentina at Wembley in May 1991.

Where I always enjoy being – right in the thick of action at the heart of England's midfield.

Rob Lee, Martin Keown, Stuart Pearce and I prepare for our 1997 friendly against Mexico.

The most important game I ever played: the England v Italy decider for qualification for the World Cup finals of 1998. A 0–0 draw was enough to see us through.

World Cup action against Romania. We lost the match 2–1, and after that I was dropped from the starting line-up.

Carlos Roa makes the save from my penalty in the shoot-out at the end of our second round tie against Argentina.

Gareth Southgate, who'd been there before, consoles me after my missed penalty. In fact I would have been more disappointed in myself if I had not had the courage to take the penalty than I was for missing it.

My late tackle on Radoslav Michalski earned me my first international red card in my forty-second match for England. Will I ever get another opportunity to play for my country?

With Mandy, Jack and George at the boys' christening in July 1996.

Mandy and me at our wedding – as soon as I met her, I knew she was the one for me.

When Mandy and I decided to take the boys to Lapland for Christmas 1998 to meet the reindeer, it was all too cold for them.

Mum and Dad enjoy the not-so-glorious summer of 2000! Their support throughout the years has meant so much to me.

With my brother John just as I was breaking into the Leeds side.

Going for a ride with Randy Mamola during the weekend of the British Grand Prix at Donington Park in July 2001.

David O'Leary warned me on my return to Leeds to cut out the rash challenges. So what happens on my debut? In typical fashion, I pick up a booking. Soon, however, I was to have much more serious things to worry about as my injury nightmare began.

Sliding in for a tackle on Valencia's Juan Sanchez in the Champions League semi-final. Sadly we weren't to make it to the final but it was a great run and things are looking bright for Leeds.

I'll cross when I come to it. Back in 1996, I wasn't prepared to go on week-long get-togethers just to make up the numbers. Happily, the England management obviously thought I was too important a member of the squad to ditch for disciplinary reasons.

I came to regard Hoddle as the best manager I had played for. I remained a key member of his squad going into the World Cup finals and I got on pretty well with him. He seemed to me to have the balance between tactical planning and organisation and man management just about right; he always seemed to make the picture clear to the players and you felt confident that he knew what he was doing. I have a lot of time for Kenny Dalglish and Kevin Keegan, but their philosophy was, in the main, to get good players together and let them get on with it. Hoddle wanted us to play good football, but he had a shrewd tactical brain, too. Despite his image when England boss, bogged down by quirky ideas, nothing could have been further from the truth in my experience. Take the Eileen Drewery debate, for example. Hoddle openly admitted that he had every confidence in Eileen's faith-healing abilities and the England players knew that she was available for counselling. But, contrary to suggestions in the media, there was no pressure on any of us, individually or as a group, to consult her. Hoddle certainly never asked me to go and see her, though I might suggest that he knew he would have been wasting his time. In fact, Darren Anderton, who had a lot of injury problems, was the only player I was aware of who consulted Eileen regularly. I laid eyes on her only once; she wasn't at our World Cup finals HQ at La Baule throughout our stay there. And, contrary to mischievous insinuations in the newspapers, there was no question that anyone would have a better chance of being selected by Hoddle if they had been to see Eileen. She was, indeed, such a low-key figure that I can never recall talking with any of the players about her.

My international career started in 1989 when I went to Switzerland with the Under-21s and roomed with Paul Gascoigne. I was selected for the squad that played in the annual Toulon tournament that summer, when we were based on a small island that the press boys nick-named Alcatraz. We didn't have the facilities you would expect when with a national squad; there were very few distractions and our frustration was deepened by the knowledge that the Irish lads were on the mainland in a plush, five-star hotel. Our tournament came to a prema-ture end when we were embarrassingly beaten by the United States in the second phase, but I left France feeling pleased with myself after being voted third-best player in the tournament. That remains one of the awards of which I'm most proud because there were a lot of quality players over there. I was 20 and I remember thinking that maybe I could go all the way and become a fully fledged England star. My last Under-21 match was in Poland – I made all of my appearances away from home – and the abiding memory is of the dreadful conditions on the trip and the animosity shown to us by the locals. We took basic foods like Mars bars and biscuits and it was just as well because the hotel food was almost inedible, especially the meat. The toilet paper had what appeared to be wood chippings in it! As we travelled to and from training, the local schoolchildren screamed abuse at us and stuck one finger up as we passed by. I don't know if there was a particular reason for them to be resentful of the English in particular, or if they simply disliked western Europeans. Certainly, they lived in grim conditions and I was glad when we headed for home.

I went on to play five times for the England B team, including a memorable night when I was captain against Czechoslovakia, on 24 March 1992. Alan Shearer and Matthew Le Tissier were in that side. I've still got the armband, which is one of my most treasured items of memorabilia. By then, I had been in the full squad nearly a year. My first call-up was as a standby for a game in Dublin in November 1990. John Barnes and Trevor Steven dropped out, injured, and although I didn't get on the bench, it was my first taste of the international big time, with a police escort to the stadium. I was 22 when Graham Taylor awarded me my first full cap, against Russia at Wembley in a friendly on Tuesday, 21 May 1991. Douglas Hurd, then Foreign Secretary, was introduced to the players before kick-off and I was quite chuffed when he told me he had been reading about me in the papers that morning. Fame at last! I played against Argentina the following Saturday and then it was off on my first overseas tour with the national side, to Australia, New Zealand and Malaysia. Sadly, my most vivid recollection of the trip was getting badly sunburned on the very last day in Kuala Lumpur. On the plane home I was dabbing damp towels on my scorched skin, which peeled off three weeks later: that was a lesson learned. The whole tour was a bit low-key, enlivened only by the comic antics of Taylor's assistant Steve Harrison, who is one of the funniest men I've ever met. Steve was forever pulling stunts, some of them unmentionable in these pages. When in New Zealand we went to watch *Silence of the Lambs* at the cinema. The lights came on at the interval and there was Steve, absolutely stark naked, staring at the screen as if nothing was amiss. On long trips, when boredom can be the biggest problem, a guy like Steve is worth his weight in gold.

Graham Taylor, who was pilloried so viciously by the press after our 1992 European Championship flop, is one of the nicest men I've known in football, along with John Gorman, who was Glenn Hoddle's No. 2. They remind me of my father-in-law Terry, who is really easy-going and doesn't have a nasty bone in his body. You might say that men like Taylor and Gorman are too decent to be in the cut-throat world of top-class football, so it's satisfying to see that they've had such good careers in the game. I was on a high going into Euro 92; Leeds had just won the First Division championship and my stock was high. But what an anticlimax the tournament in Sweden turned out to be. The omens weren't good when Taylor took us to Finland for a week of character building. It was red hot and there were mosquitoes by the million. And it never got dark: it took me several days before I managed my first real sleep. We had a psychologist with us, and we did orienteering and lots of other stuff which I don't think has any bearing at all on playing football. To cap a wretched week, when we played Finland in a warm-up John Barnes ruptured his Achilles and was out of the main event. It went from bad to worse in the tournament: we played two dire goalless draws, with Denmark – the eventual winners – and France, a match most memorable for the moment when their defender Basil Boli nutted Stuart Pearce; although it was significant for me because it was the first time I played against Eric Cantona, then my team-mate at Leeds.

The next game was against Sweden in Gothenburg and defeat would mean an early exit for England. The problem position was right-back. Keith Curle, Manchester City's central defender, had played there and had a nightmare. On the eve of the crunch match with the Swedes, Taylor went around the squad asking who was willing to play at right-back. Tony Dorigo, a natural left-footer, said no. I can't recall how far down the line I was, but when Graham got to me I agreed to fill the position nobody wanted. Actually, I had quite a good game until they brought on a big lad to face me on the left wing and he turned the tide of the match. David Platt put us a goal up – the only goal England scored in the tournament – but they came back to win 2–1 and we were on the way home. Taylor's reign ended after we failed to qualify for the 1994 World Cup late the following year. In the final qualifier we had to beat cannon-fodder team San Marino by seven clear goals to go through. I was back home, as a standby, and I have to admit I couldn't help but laugh when they went a goal up in the first minute. England won 7–1, but it wasn't enough and Graham Taylor was on his way. My progress with England had been interrupted by injury over the previous 12 months, during which time Paul Ince had emerged as a powerhouse midfielder whom I recognised as a real threat to my place in the side. But the real frustration was that, after playing my first full senior international alongside Gazza in the opening

World Cup qualifier against Norway in October 1992, when for the first time I really felt comfortable in an England shirt, I was then out for two months with an ankle injury.

Terry Venables succeeded Taylor early in 1994 and I was pleased to be in his first squad, coming on as a sub for Ince in a 1–0 win against Denmark. Shortly afterwards I went down with the crippling foot injury that put me out of Blackburn's team for 12 months. Even though Venables selected me for his Umbro Cup squad – against Japan, Brazil and Sweden – in the summer of 1995, only weeks after I returned to the Blackburn team, I wasn't able to establish myself in his squads in the coming months and I missed out on Euro 96 in England. Though I played well after my move to Newcastle in February 1996, I had probably burnt my bridges during the first half of the season, when I was played out of position by Ray Harford at Blackburn.

The departure of Venables later that summer, still dogged by controversy over his financial affairs and business dealings, turned out to be good news for me, for I enjoyed my most consistent spell as an England player under Venners' successor Glenn Hoddle – even if I had to stage that Wembley walk-out to make a point! The crucial matches of that World Cup qualifying campaign were against Italy. The pressure was on after Gianfranco Zola scored the only goal of the game at Wembley, when we simply weren't good enough on the night. But I was feeling more and more settled in the team, playing my part in our subsequent wins over Georgia, at home, and in Poland. We enjoyed a few days' break at the Mottram Hall Hotel in Cheshire, a favourite haunt of Sir Alex

Ferguson and his Manchester United players, before playing a friendly with South Africa at Old Trafford in May 1997. Ian Wright, Rob Lee, Gazza and I had a riotous time on the hotel golf course, Gazza acting the clown prince as ever. It had been raining heavily and Paul decided to do some press-ups in a water-filled bunker. We roared as close as possible in our buggy, half-drowning Gazza in the process. Then he got the buggy stuck in the sand and we all had to bend our backs to shove the thing clear. Hardly a glowing example of golf course etiquette, but it was hilarious for all that and typical of the fun you always had when Gazza was around. Then it was on to Le Tournoi in France, where I hardly played; I wasn't amused to be given the No. 17 shirt, while Paul Ince had No. 4, which I always regarded as my number. I told John Gorman I felt a bit second class. Twelve months later, when I was selected for the final 22 for France 98, I was given the No. 8 shirt and Gorman said: 'Will that do you, Batts?'

The biggest occasion of my international career was the night of 11 October 1997. The place, the Olympic Stadium, Rome; the match, Italy v England. It was our chance to clinch a place in the World Cup finals. We needed a draw: a tough task, to be sure. But of all the teams to face when needing a draw, Italy, to my mind, are as good a bet as any because of their methodical football. I love playing against that style. You can sit there and soak it up and that suits my game just fine. The night was everything I had hoped it would be. It was hot and an 85,000 crowd was packed into the fabulous stadium. We simply had to get a result against a truly world-class team, in a huge venue populated by hostile fans. There was no room for the faint-hearted; exactly the atmosphere I thrive on. It turned out to be the stuff that dreams are made of. We held the Italians fairly comfortably to a goalless draw and the only moments of nail-biting drama came at the end when Wrighty came off the bench and hit the post, to be followed by Christian Vieri's shot over the top of our goal. I was delighted for Glenn Hoddle, who was a picture of joy at the final whistle. He, like every England coach, had been under enormous pressure but he had organised us well and earned the respect of the players. A neat touch of his had been to have tapes made of us in training and playing games, accompanied by stirring background music. They were played on the team bus as we drove to the stadium. There is no doubt that we all found that a moving experience and it helped lift our mood. There was great self-belief in the squad that night: I felt we knew we were going to get the result we needed. What an atmosphere there was on the plane back to England! At take-off, drinks were being served, the lads were walking up and down the aisle, seats were pushed forwards and back. So much for all the regulations about in-flight safety! Dad wrote a cryptic, but meaningful note in his book. 'My son playing in such a game.'

Despite feeling reassured about the part I'd played in our qualification, I had to undergo some unease before finally nailing down my place in the final 22. I had played well in our final warm-up match on English soil, against Saudi Arabia at Wembley, but wasn't selected for either of the King Hussein Cup matches against Morocco and Belgium in Morocco. A hint of panic started to creep into my mind. After coming this far, and doing so well, surely Hoddle wasn't going to ditch me now. All was revealed on 31 May at our pre-France La Manga retreat. What a tense affair that was: all 30 players were given a time to go and see Hoddle in his room, where he would deliver his 'in' or 'out' verdict. All we knew was that eight of us would be taking an early flight home. Word kept creeping back that so-and-so was out, so-and-so was in. But we never saw any of the unlucky eight: they were put on a private jet and flown straight back to England. The biggest shock was the omission of Gazza who, as we read later in Hoddle's book, lost it and trashed the room. When I went in, Hoddle told me: 'Batts, you've done a good job and you'll be going to France.' I was relieved because, confident as I was that I had done a good job, I knew there had been bigger shocks in football than me being left out of an England squad.

The trappings of being a member of a World Cup squad were there to enjoy almost immediately. The day after the announcement of the 22, we had a golf tournament and were given sets of Taylor-Made clubs with our names printed on our bags. And there was a Lamborghini sports car for a hole-in-one. We heard a huge roar go up and learned that a golf writer had claimed that prize.

When the tournament got under way, our first match was against Tunisia. Hoddle again confused me: I hadn't figured in a behind-closed-doors friendly against a French Division Two side and I thought he would pick an attacking side and try to wipe the floor with Tunisia. So I was surprised, and delighted, to be selected for our opening match in front of a 60,000 crowd in Marseilles. Alan Shearer and Paul Scholes scored the goals as we got off to a solid, if unspectacular, start, but the wheels came off against Romania in Toulouse when we lost 2–1. Paul Ince was injured and replaced by David Beckham, who played well and kept his place – at my expense – against Colombia in match three. Becks scored a great free-kick goal against the Colombians and I came on as sub – Ince again the injured player to be replaced – to win another cap. Against Argentina I had to be content with coming off the bench once again. The rest, as they say, is history . . .

I had the satisfaction of discovering that my penalty miss wasn't being ranked as high treason, because I was on the invitation list for a reception at Buckingham Palace for the England lads just before the start of the next season. Mind you, that's no surprise considering Her Majesty the Queen isn't exactly a soccer fanatic. Though she approached me directly, she clearly hadn't a clue that I was the man who had left millions of her subjects in despair a few weeks earlier as she said, 'Who do you play for?'

I replied, 'Newcastle, Ma'am.'

HRH then said, 'It gets very cold up north doesn't it?'

I answered, 'Yes it certainly does, Ma'am.'

Rough-and-ready Batty's adherence to the protocol caused much amusement among my team-mates.

CHAPTER 16

back to leeds

That summer I had an operation on the Achilles problem
that had been troubling me going into the World Cup
finals. In the days that followed, I spent hours replying
to the hundreds of supportive letters I received on the
subject of my missed penalty and my public reaction to
it. I had been to Newcastle to have the stitches removed
when a bizarre incident threatened to set my recovery
back. Alan Sutton, the Leeds United physio, called at my
house to ask me to sign an England shirt, which he was
giving to his son for a birthday present. As I stood at the
gates, waving Alan off, young Jack clattered into my
heel on his bike. Of all the places for him to connect! I
pulled off my white sock, which was crimson with blood,
to find the operation scar gaping open. I admit that I was
shaken. I went into the house, shedding a tear or two
because I was concerned that serious damage had been
done. The older you get, the more vulnerable you feel
each time you are injured, and the last thing you need is
complications like this seemed to be. Alan, who had
stopped when he saw what happened, got his medical kit
from his car and put some butterfly stitches in. Luckily,
the surgeon who had performed the op wasn't concerned
when I explained what had happened: it was decided not

to try to stitch it up again and to let it heal naturally. That proved to be a time-consuming business: the wound was quite messy, with what looked like a worm-hole going right through to the tendon. I am squeamish about things like that and it turned my stomach a bit. Three or four weeks were added to my rehabilitation and during that period Kenny Dalglish was sacked as manager of Newcastle.

Kenny got the chop after only two games of the season – both draws – and the players were confused, to say the least. We couldn't understand how the club could give the manager considerable funding for new players during the summer – Kenny had brought in several new faces, mostly foreigners I had never heard of – and give him the boot before they had had a chance to settle in. On the surface, it didn't make a lot of sense. I wasn't happy about it and I know several of the senior pros felt the same way. I started to get the feeling of unease that tells me it might be time to move on. The very same day that Dalglish went, Ruud Gullit was named as his successor. When he first walked into the dressing-room at St James' Park, in his civvies, I was immediately struck by what a big man he was. I had played against Gullit when he was with Chelsea but, on the pitch, hadn't formed an impression of his size.

Gullit is well over six foot and he is big in more than the physical sense. He was extremely self-assured as he spoke to the Newcastle players that day; I thought of how much self-belief and confidence you need to walk in among a bunch of hardened pros, the great majority of whom you don't know personally, and talk with such calm authority.

I don't know just how much of an ego Gullit had, but I have to say that, contrary to popular opinion, I never had a problem with him. Even so, his approach to the job was completely different to anything I, and most of the lads, had ever known, and I think it went against him in the dressing-room. Men like Kenny Dalglish and Kevin Keegan adopted a more traditional, maybe more British, 'one of the lads' attitude to being in charge. Not Ruud: his was a more aloof, more distant stance. It was as if he was stating: 'I'm here to manage you lot – and it's do as I say.' A few of the players resented it. It didn't bother me, even if I had always quietly treasured my matey relationship with Dalglish and Keegan. My only problem with Gullit would have been if he had treated me one way and other players another. But he was the same with everybody and I never fell out with him, though some elements in the press hinted that he and I didn't see eye to eye.

Gullit's first game in charge was against Liverpool, who thrashed us 4–1 at St James', with Michael Owen scoring a hat-trick. What a rude awakening for Ruud! He must have wondered what the hell he had walked into. By then, I was nearing my complete recovery from the operation and I heard the first whispers that Leeds wanted me back at Elland Road. There had also been talk, in the newspapers, at any rate, of Chelsea, Spurs and Villa being interested. I hadn't been contemplating going anywhere before Dalglish's sudden departure; now, I was leaning towards a change. But despite the morale-boosting link with all of these Premiership clubs, the only one that grabbed me was Leeds. The club seemed to have got lost a little after the euphoria of the

1992 title triumph and its failure to build on that success. Howard Wilkinson had paid the price, his job being taken by George Graham, who was soon to be succeeded by David O'Leary. Now there were signs that Leeds were a club on the rise. And, after five years commuting first to Blackburn, now to Tyneside, the thought of living on the doorstep of, and playing once more for, my hometown club held huge appeal for me. I can understand my detractors claiming that I have always moved on at the first sign of disruption at my club. At the same time, I claim my instincts have always been proved right. I think I got out of Leeds at the right time, when I started to feel stale and my game was losing its edge; and, remember, it was Leeds's decision to sell me. I left Blackburn under similar circumstances. Now I was getting the same vibes about Newcastle, even though I had signed a new contract not long before. I always back my own judgement and I have always been ready to take advantage of a situation, I readily admit that. But I don't mean merely a financial situation: I mean in my career. My priority is to look after my wife and family, but I couldn't play for a club where I was unhappy, whatever the wage packet.

After recovering from my summer operation and serving a six-match suspension incurred at the end of the previous season, my first outing was at Rotherham in the reserves. It was a special occasion and not because we had a comfortable four-goal victory. What made the day one to remember with affection was that for the first and only time I was in competition with Mandy's brother Lee. He and I had often wondered out loud if we would ever face each other on the pitch. At last, we were doing that – even if for only the last 10 minutes, when Lee, a fellow midfielder, came on as a sub. Lee had great touch, good vision and good passing ability; he was an extremely capable footballer. But there is such a thin line between making it and not doing so. Perhaps his fitness level wasn't quite up to the exceptional mark you need to attain to compete at the top level. Lee is out of the game now and I felt really sorry for him when he decided he wasn't going to hack it. On the plus side, unlike so many young lads who fall by the wayside and become resentful and bitter, Lee has turned out to be a smashing young man who has enjoyed his life, doing the things that you can't – or shouldn't – be doing if you are a professional sportsman. I know the rewards are there if you get to the top. I also know football isn't the be-all and end-all and so, too, does Lee. Good for him. He's full of beans, a pleasure to be with and certainly not all screwed up about failing to make a lucrative living out of the game. He probably got out early enough to prevent the experience of being a pro from taking its toll.

I know a lot of lads who spent a few years in the cosseted world of professional football, only to be rejected and then feel like misfits in the real, hard world out there. Too often, lads like these can't cope with having to fend for themselves for the first time in their young lives. Make no mistake, players are mollycoddled. And the higher you go up the ladder, the more you are wrapped in cotton wool, no more so than when you become a full international player. When you travel with England you don't even have the responsibility of having to remember your own passport; the squad is covered by a collective arrangement. They do just about everything for you except wipe your bum. When I first went on holiday I was apprehensive at the airport because I wasn't sure about the procedure for getting myself through check-in and passport control. I had been used to being shepherded along like a sheep.

My initial appearance in Gullit's first team was on 1 October in the Cup-Winners' Cup at Partizan Belgrade. The lads had won the first leg 2–1 and the situation was nicely set up for us to progress. What happened? I gave away a penalty. We lost 1–0 and went out on the away goals rule. Talk about how to win friends and influence people! And I never knew what Gullit thought about the ad that Channel 5 used to promote their live screening of the match, a picture of my head superimposed on a body whose shapely legs were encased in black nylons and suspenders and high heels. The idea was to cash in on the 'sexy football' line that Gullit had promoted during his commentating stints at Euro 96. I was paid £5,000 to agree to it, though I admit I hadn't been prepared for the saucy picture that appeared. It was a bit of a laugh – and a well-paid one at that – as far as I was concerned, and it caused hilarious uproar on the plane coming home from Belgrade, when the English papers were on board. There was a full-page picture in one of the tabloids and the lads revelled in the mickey-taking. Hayden Evans rang the next day to assure me he had been on to Channel 5 and the newspapers, playing hell; I had to point out that it was all above-board and that I'd agreed to do it. Hayden even had magazines calling his office to ask if I was gay and people inquiring whether I had a high-heels and suspenders fetish. All I'm prepared to say is that I would have been more happy if those legs had been mine.

I was recalled to Glenn Hoddle's England squad that week and went on to play regularly in Gullit's team. The knowledge that Leeds wanted to take me was nibbling away at my mind. Newcastle chairman Freddy Shepherd told Hayden that the club had no intention of selling me. Then, on 14 November, I was dropped for the first time in my career. Howard Wilkinson had left me out towards the end of Leeds's promotion season, in 1990, but I was worn out then and simply in need of a rest. This time I was axed, pure and simple. To be fair, I wasn't playing particularly well and it didn't come as a total shock. Ironically, the team struggled in that home match against Sheffield Wednesday and within half an hour, I was off the bench and replacing Dietmar Hamann. Nevertheless, I took it as a clear sign that I wasn't a first choice in Gullit's eyes and I made up my mind that there was no future for me under his management. By now, George Graham had moved from Leeds to Tottenham and David O'Leary was locked in a battle with Leicester's Martin O'Neill for the hot seat at Elland Road. I knew O'Leary was a fan of mine: whenever our paths had crossed since I left Leeds, O'Leary had never lost the opportunity to tell me there would always be a place for me if I wanted to return. Now, I wanted to do just that. I was well pleased when Leicester blocked O'Neill and David got the job. When Newcastle played at Everton on 23 November I knew that Leeds had told Hayden Evans they were making Newcastle an offer for me the follow-ing day so I decided to confront Gullit after the match at Goodison. While all the lads were on the bus, I sat like a little boy lost on the steps of the coach, waiting for the manager to climb aboard. As I was steeling myself to ask him for a move, I could see him and the directors through the boardroom window discussing the deal that took Duncan Ferguson from Goodison to St James' Park.

I started to get fidgety and impatient. 'Come on. Get a move on. I need to talk,' I was thinking as the minutes dragged by. The situation needed bringing out in the open but the delay was making me nervous. Eventually, Gullit emerged from the stadium and I returned to the changing-room with him to talk. He knew what was coming. The signs had hardly been obscure; over the previous few weeks, each time the team coach had passed Elland Road on the M62 there had been a mischievous chorus from the back of the bus of: 'You'll soon be back there, Batts.' Gullit asked me: 'Do you want to go back to Leeds?' When I confirmed that I did, he said he would speak to the directors and recommend the deal. I climbed aboard the bus relieved that I'd broached the subject and delighted that Gullit had seen it the way he did, but there were two weeks of frustration and worry before the deal was given the green light. Not long after my conversation with Gullit, Hayden rang me to say that Real Madrid had joined the race for my signature. I told him I knew it was a marvellous opportunity for me – but to tell them to forget it. I must be the only player who ever turned down the most successful club in European soccer history! By then, my mind was set on Leeds and I'm sure you will have realised by now that when my mind is made up, a herd of charging rhinos wouldn't change it.

Newcastle, presumably upset by my desire to leave, told Leeds they wanted £6 million. Leeds had already improved their £4 million offer by £500,000. It was stalemate. I went in every day, voluntarily training with the kids as I'd made up my mind my first-team days at the club were over, and checking with Gullit if there had been any progress. Day after day, he or his assistant Steve Clarke told me 'No news', and I trudged off to train with the youngsters. There was no animosity and I never fell out with anybody. Then came the news I was longing to hear. Gullit called across the training pitch one morning to say the clubs had agreed terms; Newcastle had accepted an offer of £4.4 million and I was on my way. I thanked Gullit and Clarke for being so decent about the situation. Gullit could have made my final days difficult, ordering me to run every day and go in every afternoon; many a manager has taken such retribution in similar circumstances. But there was none of that and I was grateful to him for it.

That night I was in Jimmy's in Leeds having a medical, which included a scan on my Achilles. I was nervous as I lay there, because the Achilles had been giving me a bit of gyp and I was consumed by an 11th-hour concern that I might fail the medical. So I was relieved to get a clean bill of health and to be going into a press conference the next morning. Yet even after all the tension of the previous few weeks, I couldn't resist a mischievous thought of 'I could hold them to ransom here', as I read the papers the next morning. 'BATTY SIGNS FOR LEEDS' screamed the headlines, accompanied by quotes from chairman Peter Ridsdale. After all, I hadn't signed anything yet and I had only a verbal agreement at that stage. But my reaction to the premature reports was a spur-of-the-moment thing. Peter Ridsdale was clearly as excited by my return as I was and it was good to be coming home.

Nevertheless, I was a bit disappointed by some negative letters in the local papers from punters claiming I wasn't the attacking player Leeds needed and that I was too old! I have lived with accusations that I am negative all through my career and it doesn't normally get to me; wherever I've played, I feel I have been a key member of the side and I've always been appreciated by my team-mates. But because I'm not playing one of the eye-catching glamour roles I don't often get singled out in TV highlights and edited versions of matches. At the same time, I think I can claim that, since coming back from another career-threatening injury, I have added a dimension to the Leeds team, in that my presence has allowed other, more naturally creative players, like Olivier Dacourt, to express themselves fully. I have always said you shouldn't judge a player unless you see him regularly over a period of time. It is the only way you can reasonably assess a man's contribution. In the final analysis, if my team-mates and my manager appreciate the job I do, protecting the back four, winning the ball and giving it, then that's all that concerns me.

frustrated biker

If anything good came out of the horrendous injury problems that blighted my first two seasons back at Elland Road, it was that I found the time to indulge in my other great sporting passion, superbikes. Ever since I was a kid, standing starry-eyed alongside Ron Haslam in a Portaloo at Silverstone, I had harboured a fascination from motorbikes and their riders. As football took over my life, bikes had to take a back seat. But I followed the sport on TV and through magazines and always at the back of my mind was the tempting prospect of owning one of the monster machines. It was a temptation that was impossible to banish because my dad, who had introduced me to the thrill of the race track with those family trips to various venues nearly 20 years earlier, had owned a bike, leaving me to savour the possibility that I might one day actually ride one of the machines I found so intriguing.

One factor preventing most highly valued footballers from riding motorbikes is the risk of accident and potential problems with their clubs' insurance. Nevertheless, there are some famous players who have indulged themselves: former England stars Les Ferdinand and Des Walker, to name two. Les has owned two or three bikes at one time. A combination of circumstances led to me taking the plunge and buying a bike in the summer of 1999. Injury in my very first match back at Leeds had left me struggling for the remainder of the 1998–99 season and with time on my hands. Two months after returning to Elland Road, in February 1999, my brother John, who had never been as interested in bikes as I was, made me green with envy by passing his test and buying a CBR Honda 600, from Motor Cycle City, in Shipley. The bike was priced at £6,000 but was reduced to £5,350 after I agreed to have my photo taken, with John, on the bike. I had never ridden a bike and often pondered the difficulty of handling one of those huge machines, using the gears, the clutch, the back-brake with your foot. That curiosity was increased when John beat me to it. I asked him to bring the bike round to our house so that Jack and George could have a look at it, but neither of the boys was as fascinated as I was. By the summer, I had bought Dad a Triumph, which he later exchanged for a Bonneville. It seemed that everybody, except me, was revelling in the thrill of the one thing I had always wanted to do. I decided to take the plunge after being sent four tickets for the British Grand Prix at Donington Park, including four passes for the paddock area from the Modenas team. Dad, Mandy's younger brother Lee and brother-in-law Mark came along. We took the tent, as many fans do, but I guarantee there wasn't a bike fanatic there that week who was as star-struck as I was – with the possible exception of my dad. I thought he was going to faint with excitement when we were introduced to the great American rider Kenny Roberts.

Modenas looked after us really well. We ate in their hospitality suite and were invited to sit on the machines and talk with the riders and the mechanics. I was pleasantly surprised that many of the other teams recognised me and were similarly hospitable. It was one of the most thrilling days of my life. I received several invitations to go to other meetings and I had to keep pinching myself to make sure it wasn't all a dream. After I did an interview, which was broadcast around the circuit, we retired to the camping area where the scene was like something out of *Mad Max*. These bike fans are insane! They were performing all manner of tricks on their machines, such as burn-outs where you get in gear and accelerate with your hand on the brake, leaving the back wheel spinning. The atmosphere was superb – and I was completely hooked. Modenas invited us again the following summer and it has now become a regular event. On a visit to Brands Hatch, I went up to the commentary box to meet one of the top British riders, Jeremy McWilliams, and ended up presenting the trophies to the winners. I saw Les Ferdinand doing the same the following summer, immaculately spruced up in suit, collar and tie. Of course, I had been in my standard gear of tracksuit and trainers.

The biggest thrill of all was when I met my ultimate hero, the legendary Carl Fogarty, the Blackburn lad who dominated the world superbike scene throughout the nineties. Carl, who rode for Ducati, finally hung up his leathers in 2000. I had gone to Brands Hatch with the intention of meeting the man I had admired from a distance for so long. Hayden Evans assured me that Carl was well aware of who I was, but I was nervous and I felt all the worse when I arrived at the circuit late. I popped my head around the corner at the pits and there was Fogarty; he looked me straight in the eye and nodded at me in recognition. It was a marvellous moment and I felt pretty humble. Hayden had said that Carl respected me for my footballing achievements but my respect for him was simply immense – as it is for all of those guys, even the club riders. It takes a lot of raw courage to come off one of those machines, get on again and go into the same corner hanging on by the seat of your pants. Those men are a different breed.

Not surprisingly, having finally enjoyed first-hand contact with the sport I had loved from afar for so long, my longing for a bike of my own became a burning desire. I decided to go for it in the summer of 2000. Lee and I passed our Compulsory Basic Training test, which allows you to drive a 125cc or 50cc with an L plate. Then I applied for my real test. I put a lot of pressure on myself by ordering a huge Aprillia 1000cc, twin-cylinder super-bike and having it delivered the night before the test. I'd bought the leathers, helmet, the lot. Then I went off, climbed on a 500cc machine, and passed the test first time. Ecstasy! But talk about anticlimax. A few weeks later, I was pushing the boys on the swing in the garden when I snapped my Achilles tendon. I knew immediately what had happened. An operation followed and I was reduced to the second-hand thrill of videoing brother John riding my bike! I quickly accepted that the dream was dead and I sold the bike. I had owned it for only a couple of months and had hardly sat on it. I only ever had the chance to buy it because of the injuries that had left me with so much time on my hands. I've been itching to get back on a bike ever since, but I won't ride one again while I'm still playing football. Nowadays, I content myself with less risky hobbies, like doing crosswords and reading, mostly about crime-related matters. That somewhat morbid curiosity was aroused when I was a lad living in Harehills, Leeds, one of the areas in which the Yorkshire Ripper operated. I had a scrapbook on the Ripper when I was about 12 years old and I have been fascinated by criminals ever since.

At least I have the satisfaction of knowing that when I do finish with football, the good living I have made from the game will enable me to indulge myself in another bike, if I still want one by then. That said, the real pleasure I get from having earned a big wage since my mid-twenties is not the freedom to spend money but the security it has given my family. Like the majority of pro footballers, I am from a working-class background, as I've said, a lad who grew up watching his parents struggle to pay the mortgage and the household bills. And I like to think I have kept my feet firmly planted on the ground ever since. That isn't easy for some of today's players to do when they are catapulted into the £10,000-a-week bracket at 20 years of age. So many of the youngsters feel they have to live up to the modern image of the loadsamoney soccer star. Luckily, I never have. The fact is, I have everything I want in a material way and I see no sense in buying things that neither I nor the family need. Spending money for show turns me right off. Mandy and I get a lot of pleasure from spending money on people close to us, like our respective parents and other members of the family, but we are more than content with one house, one car apiece and a comfortable lifestyle.

Some of the lads I play with own two or three cars. What's the point? You can only drive one at a time, but they will have a posh sports car, a plush saloon and a four-wheel drive sitting outside their houses. The thought of either of my boys ever being so self-indulgent is repugnant to me. Our aim is to make sure Jack and George never take money for granted. There's not much that is more off-putting than the children of wealthy people who are embarrassingly aware of their parents' wealth; kids who are clued up to the cost of everything, often down to the last pound, and whose young lives are dominated by materialism. It makes me shudder. Mandy and I will do our best to ensure that Jack and George don't become obsessed in the same way.

One refreshing example of a young and successful footballer who hasn't gone down the road to rampant materialism is Leeds striker Alan Smith, who I first met all those years ago in Mandy's parents' front room. Alan has an old head on young shoulders. He is still not 21 as I write this, and he's been earning big money for a couple of years, yet he doesn't seem to feel the need to show people that he's got plenty of cash. I like that. My former Newcastle team-mate Stuart Pearce, still going strong at Manchester City in 2001, is as good an example as I can think of of a successful, well-paid player who has never let wealth go to his head. He is a working-class lad who came into professional football from the non-League game and the fame and fortune don't appear to have changed him. I hope that people who know me well would say the same about me.

One problem is that some youngsters think they are superstars while they are still in their teens. Though I wouldn't advocate turning the clock back completely, I do think there is room for a bit more respect for your elders – in society in general as well as in football. For example, the apprentices at Thorp Arch have responsibility for cleaning two pairs of the senior players' training boots. But all too frequently when I go in the lad responsible for mine hasn't done it. 'Sorry, I slept in' is usually the casually delivered excuse. That simply isn't sending me the right signals about this lad's attitude nor, as a result, his prospects of making it. Maybe, when I was an apprentice we were treated a bit too much like dogs but, if you had anything about you, you came through. Nowadays I think they get their bums wiped a bit too much. If you got tough with them, the PFA – the Players' Union – would be on the phone in a flash. You would quickly be accused of bullying. In my day a clip or two around the ear – and often worse – was part and parcel of coming through the early days. For my part, I console myself with dishing out the occasional kick on the training pitch, just to remind them who's boss!

injury nightmare

If I had known in December 1998, as I prepared to make my second debut for Leeds United, what I know now about the events of the following two years, I would most probably have made a voluntary early exit from football.

At just turned 30 and with 11 years of first-team experience, I was as genuinely excited about my situation as I had ever been. I was delighted to be back at Elland Road, where the whole adventure had started nearly 15 years earlier. I was made to feel like a returning hero. I had been gone five years, during which time I had amassed experience at the highest level with Blackburn, Newcastle and England. All in all, I reckon I was a better player than when I had left Leeds and I was bursting with anticipation at the opportunity to prove it. Not in my worst nightmare could I have imagined that it would be another two years – two years of hell – before I was able to put my new Leeds career on track.

In that intervening period, my emotions see-sawed from dismay to despair and back again so often, worse even than when I was out for nearly a year at Blackburn. At my lowest point, I simply couldn't see the club sticking with me. Had that happened, though, it would have reflected very badly on Leeds, in my opinion. My relationship with the club was strained almost to breaking point as I grew increasingly frustrated and angry at their refusal to recognise that I had serious problems. Fortunately, such a sad ending to my story was never written. But I wouldn't have bet against that during the long, dark months of doubt which dogged me throughout two career and, in one case, potentially life-threatening injury dramas.

The pain threshold differs from person to person, and I regard myself as a fairly tough character who has learned to cope with some significantly unpleasant conditions in my job. However, nothing I had experienced prepared me for the severity of the agonies I suffered – mentally as well as physically – following, first, a heart-related problem and, then, a ruptured Achilles tendon.

The supreme irony was that it all started to go wrong in my very first match, following that transfer from Newcastle, on 14 December 1998 at Elland Road against Coventry City. Mandy and both sets of parents were there to see me returning like the Prodigal Son. The occasion was all set up for a triumphant comeback. My dad wrote in his diary: 'David is very nervous about his debut but also very excited at the thought of playing for United again. There is a lot of pressure on him and I hope it turns out OK for him. He has a four-and-a-half-year contract and, if he does well, he could go down as one of the all-time great Leeds players.'

That final sentence expressed a lovely sentiment, one that, I like to think, I might yet fulfil. The welcome I received was summed up by one of the first remarks Leeds manager David O'Leary made to me, saying that I was such a good player that I didn't need to go around getting myself booked for fouling opponents. His attitude to young striker Alan Smith was similar when Smith forced his way into the side.

O'Leary told me he hadn't brought me back to behave like that. He wanted to see my value to the team unblemished by disciplinary problems. Lo and behold, my first challenge, in my first game, on Coventry's George Boateng, resulted in a yellow card! I really should have known better, but the adrenalin was pumping and, not for the first time – nor the last – I was momentarily reckless. 'See. That's exactly what I'm on about,' O'Leary snapped at me, indignantly, at half-time. I had no defence.

However, I was feeling quite deflated. No disrespect intended, but, in an ideal world, I would have had much bigger opposition than Coventry to make my long-awaited reappearance in a Leeds shirt. The first half was scrappy and we didn't start passing the ball properly until after the break. For me, though, it went from bad to worse. Early in that second period I competed for the ball with Darren Jackson and we both crashed to the ground. I landed chest down on his studs. And it really hurt. Usually, the pain from a bang like that wears off gradually as you run and the adrenalin kicks in and takes over. But my chest was getting more and more sore, to the point where I couldn't even shout. The simple act of breathing was giving me grief and I had to come off.

Now, I don't claim to be the toughest, but if I come off a pitch voluntarily, then it is because I've genuinely got a problem – I have even played with broken bones in various parts of my body. So I was almost disappointed when the doctor examined me in the dressing-room and deduced that I had merely winded myself. Arguably, I should have been relieved, but, mentally, you're looking for justification of your decision in those circumstances. I thought I had broken a rib, as I'd experienced that before. I began to ask myself: 'Surely I haven't come off for nowt?' However, next morning at the training ground, the physio Dave Swift examined me and said he could feel the rib moving and it was broken. I had played before with a broken rib but the danger in so doing is that, if you get another bang, it could puncture your lung. So I was advised to take a back seat while it healed.

We took advantage of the time off to take Jack and George to Lapland to see Father Christmas. What a mistake that was! It can get pretty nippy in Newcastle – where we flew from – but the coldest of days up there is like spring compared to those sub-zero temperatures in Lapland. Not even Moscow or Kiev, where I had played in December with Blackburn and Newcastle, were that bad. It seemed like a good idea at the time, but the kids were four years old and too young for such extreme conditions.

We returned to the relatively balmy Christmas temperatures of West Yorkshire, where I rested for a couple of weeks, before Alan Sutton, of the medical staff, took me for a training session. Everything seemed fine until I tried some shooting practice and I felt the rib go again. I was gutted to be back at square one, but not remotely prepared for the trauma that was to follow. On 9 January I awoke early, as usual, and went to play with the kids on the landing. I leant on my side and felt an unpleasant ache in my left shoulder. Disturbingly, it got worse with every heartbeat and every breath I took. Within 15 minutes the pain was agonising. It is difficult to describe the intensity of the pain that had consumed me so quickly and so frighteningly, but it was so bad that if someone could have jabbed a needle into me and ended it all there and then, I'd have settled for that. I wouldn't wish such torment on anyone. Confused, scared and hurting like hell, I stumbled to the car and, heaven knows how, drove to the nearby training ground at Thorp Arch. I was hunched over the steering wheel, reeling with the anguish brought on by every breath and heartbeat. If I moved forwards or backwards, the pressure on my chest worsened. As I staggered into the physio's rooms I leant against the wall and gasped to Alan Sutton: 'Sutty, I'm struggling.'

If it hadn't been so serious it would have been laughable as Sutty, thinking I was faking, replied with a nonchalant air: 'Just go in the gym, Batts, and get on a bike.'

I said: 'No, Sutty – I'm REALLY struggling!' At that, Alan got the message and gave me a strong anti-inflammatory tablet, which eased the pain, but only to some extent. I went back home and crawled into bed feeling worried and baffled.

I sat there until Alan arrived to take me to see Dr Feldman, the club medic, who referred me to the BUPA hospital at Roundhay, where a chest X-ray revealed I had pleurisy. By midday, I was under a cardiologist, who told me I had pericarditis, which is inflammation of the sensitive membranous sac which encloses the heart. When your heart beats, it rubs on this sac which, if damaged, causes great pain. Your hearts rests on your diaphragm and the nerves go from there to your shoulder, hence the terrible pain I was having in my left shoulder. When I broke my rib in that challenge with Darren Jackson, it had damaged the sac around my heart. I was put on steroids to ease the pain and told by the specialist I would be on them for quite some time, fifteen months, as it turned out.

During the worst times of that period I was thinking: 'Sod football. I want to live to see my kids grow up.' But the doctors reassured me I didn't have a problem with my heart itself, which was comforting as it is a fairly vital organ! Nevertheless, they did caution me that it might end my career. Right from the start of the problem, I decided I would pack in football if my life could be endangered by playing on. The trouble was, they didn't have any previous cases to refer to so they couldn't make any firm predictions. But they did say it was important to stop the pericarditis recurring as the more attacks I suffered the thicker my heart muscle would become by the time I was in my fifties – and that isn't good. The doctors also warned me that the steroids might weaken my skin tissue, thus making me more susceptible to injury and reducing my powers of recovery. It didn't exactly make good listening. But, if it didn't quite go in one ear and out the other, my attitude was: 'That won't be how it affects me.' In other words, I had blind faith in my own health. I had spent more than 10 years battling injury, like most players, on the basis that you just don't want to miss games. By and large, you get on with it. So, once the inflammation had settled down, I returned to training.

It was the start of a period, lasting until the present time, in which I have had more ECGs, echoes and stress tests than I can remember. To this day I go regularly for check-ups to make sure I'm ticking over – literally. I trained cautiously, but with steadily increasing confidence, for a couple of months, worried all along that I couldn't expect to survive at a top club in a stop–start situation. I played in two reserve games early in March and O'Leary asked me if I would turn out against Spurs at Elland Road in a night match. Although I felt I needed more time to reach full fitness, I agreed. It was a big match for Leeds, George Graham having left us in somewhat acrimonious circumstances earlier in the season to take over at Tottenham. Anyway, we battered them, playing them off the park, and I remember thinking: 'I'm back.'

A few days later I was in a winning team at Sheffield Wednesday and, to my amazement, Kevin Keegan then named me in his England squad. My delight at Keegan's faith in me was diluted when I woke up one morning – I'd been suffering from a cold – to feel the aching across my shoulders had returned. An echocardiogram revealed fluid around my heart. The club sent me to see a heart expert in London who specialised in treating sportsmen and women. He told me there was no sign of long-term damage to my heart and that I should 'keep taking the tablets'. I took this as a 'carry on and see how it goes' verdict, and certainly there were no alarm bells ringing.

Boosted by this, I returned to action and played the full 90 minutes for England against Hungary in the Nep

Stadium. I finished the season in reasonable shape, and was in Keegan's squad for the World Cup qualifiers with Sweden and Bulgaria that summer. Once again, I experienced concern when I came back from winning my 40th cap in Sofia feeling unwell. I had woken up on the morning of the match knowing I wasn't 100 per cent, but not feeling bad enough not to play. The continuing problem was fluid around the heart and the doctors believed that if I continued with the steroids, which would be gradually decreased in strength, I would make a good recovery. Against this background of constant concern that the problem was likely to flare up at any time, I did well in pre-season training and couldn't believe how smoothly everything was going in the first couple of months of the 1999–2000 season. But I was soon brought back down to earth.

It was early in November, when we'd travelled to Moscow for a UEFA Cup tie against Lokomotiv, that I noticed that my Achilles was sore. The thing that struck me was that the injury had come on so quickly. I know a bit about Achilles problems, having had an operation on mine when I came home from the World Cup in 1998. Normally, you have a week or two of niggling discomfort, warning you of impending trouble. Because that hadn't happened here, I was concerned. After the game we flew back from Moscow to London, where we played at Wimbledon on the Sunday, which was Bonfire Night. My Achilles was really giving me gyp throughout the game. However, because I had been sent off playing for England against Poland, I was suspended from the European Championship play-off double-header with Scotland and so I now had two weeks in which to get myself sorted out before the next Leeds fixture against Southampton. I felt sure it would clear up but I was about to be plunged into a saga even more miserable than the heart-related problem that had dogged me for the previous 11 months.

Through harsh experience, I duly rested for seven or eight days following the match at Wimbledon. When I trained it was still hurting and I was taken down to Leeds Infirmary, where I was given an injection. And that didn't rest easily with me at all. I have had what I regard as a healthy suspicion of injections throughout my career. I remember as a relatively young pro, in my early twenties, going home to Mandy really upset because I'd let them stick me with cortisone in the side of my knee. As it turned out, on that occasion it worked a treat. But, as a general rule, I steer clear of the needle because of the increasing evidence of the long-term damage that some have suffered; it often seems to me to be more of a quick fix.

After having the jab on Thursday, I trained on Saturday and played against Southampton on Sunday. My Achilles felt fine for 20 minutes, then I went to close an opponent down and it went again. This time, it felt like I had torn it, and I wondered whether enough consideration had been given to allowing it to heal properly before putting me back on the pitch.

A scan the following day revealed a slight tear where the calf muscle meets the Achilles tendon. I was out of action for 10 days and then trained for three days in the build-up to a Worthington Cup tie at Leicester. Come the day of the match I wasn't at all happy with my condition. I couldn't hop properly on my right leg. I went down to

Elland Road where I planned to tell Dave Swift that I had my doubts about the Achilles and that I shouldn't risk playing on it. That plan backfired because Dave, who lived in South Yorkshire, was being picked up en route to the Midlands. So I reluctantly boarded the bus and asked Dave for a meeting in the hotel, where I was rooming with goalkeeper Nigel Martyn. I told Dave I had no confidence in the injury and that I feared it would let me down if I went up for a header or closed somebody down. He reckoned it was just a scar tissue problem, so I said I'd play.

What happened? I shut a lad down out on the wing and the Achilles went. This time it was worse than it had been at any time previously. I couldn't even walk off the pitch. I was furious with myself – and with Dave Swift. As I stumbled into the dressing-room my frustration was deepening. A player wants to play, but there are times when you have your doubts about your ability to do so because of an injury. It is at those times that you have to put yourself in the hands of the medical experts. After all, they know more than you do and they are paid to take those sorts of decisions away from you. I am not the type who badgers physios on a whim. In the main, I shun treatment for minor knocks, preferring to let natural healing and my own determination be the cure. I am certainly no hypochondriac, but I guess they didn't appreciate that. And I sat there, fed up, and thinking that I deserved that recognition.

I went back to hospital for ultra-sound treatment which showed that the Achilles was torn again. I returned to the club and spent a couple of weeks resting, working on the bike and on weights before trying it again. Each time, I broke down. Within 10 or 15 strides of running I knew it wasn't right. So the club sent me off to Nice, in the south of France, for a 10-day visit to a specialist physio who had done a lot of work with the French players at Arsenal. I remember O'Leary telling me to get myself fit, because we had a big game coming up at Sunderland later that January. I had been out of action for the best part of two months and I was growing more and more dissatisfied with the reaction of people at the club to my complaints. Still, now they had sent me to France and perhaps, at last, a solution was to be found.

I was standing by the carousel, waiting to pick up my bags, and I was looking at the glass-panelled exit doors when I saw this bizarre figure of a fella with white bleached hair, orange-rimmed sunglasses and wearing a shell suit. I thought: 'No, please, don't you be my man.' He was. My first thought was: 'They've sent me to a nutcase.' But I grew to like and respect the guy, even though I was with him for only three of the 10 days that had been scheduled. After watching me break down after about 20 minutes on the trampoline, he agreed that the Achilles wasn't right.

I was with him morning, noon and night as he assessed my overall fitness. He even took me to a dentist who asked me if I'd ever been in a car smash! Apparently, my jaw and teeth weren't aligned. They found an abscess, and then told me how they'd taken all the bad teeth out of the French World Cup players in 1998. The theory is that infection in your blood leads to a longer recovery period after injury. So, if in doubt, whip it out.

To add insult to injury – literally, of course – the Frenchman then told me Leeds had asked him to find out if the problem was all in my head. He said I had been sent to him merely to get fit and that the plan had been for me and him to be pounding the beach every day. But he readily acknowledged that I had a real problem with my Achilles. I also had a problem getting any French francs, but the club was able to sort that out for me.

Despite that, I travelled back to Leeds fuming. I went straight to the training ground and to the manager's office, but he was off with a cold. I was stamping around the place, effing and blinding. I was insulted to learn that they hadn't believed me when I told them of my doubts. I could understand them taking that attitude with certain players, but not with me. I sought out Swifty and had a real rant at him. That Saturday, Leeds were at Manchester City in the FA Cup. On the way back, obviously having heard about my anger, O'Leary went to the back of the bus and said to Nigel Martyn: 'Tell your mate Batty if he's got anything to say to me, to say it to my face.'

Because the lads had a few days off, I didn't get this message until the Thursday. Furious, I stormed straight to O'Leary's office and told him bluntly: 'You needn't think I won't say to your face anything I'll say to anybody else.' As he had had three days that week in which to come and see me, I wasn't impressed that he hadn't done so, as I felt he should have made the time, however busy he was. It was the start of a period when I went into O'Leary's office on a very regular basis, demanding some positive action on my Achilles injury. I wanted it sorted out, but it wasn't getting better.

From mid-January until April 1999, I was basically left to my own devices in the gym. It was ridiculous: I would work on the bike for four or five days, try running and, within a few strides, break down again. I couldn't even walk afterwards. Then, I'd go through the whole, pointless process again. I was saying to the gaffer in despair: 'What more can I do?' But there was no answer forthcoming. I just couldn't understand what I'd done to deserve to be in such a farcical situation.

Increasingly, it became obvious that people thought I had a mental problem, not a physical one. I could jog without trouble and I could tell the lads were wondering why I wasn't training with them. They arranged a practice match for me, but I came off at half-time because I just knew I wasn't in good condition. I could probably have played on, but I thought 'sod this, I'm not risking myself for people who don't have faith in me'. I had a meeting with coaches Eddie Gray and Roy Aitken and they asked why, as an experienced player, I didn't just play through it. With increasing desperation, I responded: 'Because I know something is wrong.'

I had never brought football home, but I was getting to the end of my tether. I was moaning away at Mandy because the situation had gone on for six months and it was doing my head in. I had never been at such a low ebb, not even during my heart scare the previous year or while out for 11 months at Blackburn. You can only say so much, so often. And, if people don't – won't – believe you, despair and disillusionment set in. What got to me all the more was that these were people who had known me for years. Why wouldn't they accept that I am not a man who complains without good reason? I told O'Leary: 'You have played with me. You know what sort of man I am. I will play through a lot of things – but this isn't right! Do you think I take any pleasure from being in the treatment room all day. I just want to play.'

At that stage of my personal misery marathon, a terrible event occurred which put everything else into stark perspective. Two Leeds fans, Chris Loftus and Martin Speight, were murdered on the streets of Istanbul, where they had travelled to support the team in the UEFA Cup semi-final tie with Galatasaray. I wasn't out there because I was injured, so I was spared the immediacy of the shocking impact this dreadful, shameful crime had on the players and the club. But, along with young striker Alan Smith, I was one of only two local lads in the squad, so I was probably affected more than most by the deep sense of shock in the community. It was awful for the players on the trip because, when you go abroad, there is a special bond between you and the hundreds of diehards who travel. There is a sense of all being in it together in those situations. The players were watching the TV reports of the stabbings in their hotel on the eve of the match and then had to go out and play in a dreadful atmosphere in the Ali Semi Yen Stadium. It wasn't surprising that they lost 2–0.

As I had been out of the first-team picture for so long, I was never directly involved in the horrible episode and it wasn't a topic that was dwelt upon at the training ground. But I know that many of the lads' attitude had been that they just wanted out of there and that the match was rendered meaningless because of the tragedy that had befallen the families of the two supporters. Without any doubt, had I been in Istanbul my only thought would have been to get home to the safety, security and love of my family. Leeds's exit from the competition after the 2–2 result in the return leg at Elland Road was insignificant. Not for the first time in my career, I had reason to reflect that the basic facts of life, like a loving family, good health and good friends are much more important than football.

After the trauma of that sad episode, I soon found myself wondering what, if any, future I had in the game, specifically at Leeds. A footballer's life is easy when he's fit. You train, go home, play, train, go home, play. What could be simpler? A great life. And why would I want it any different? But, for some mysterious and infuriating reason, the club just couldn't see it my way. And because of that they certainly wouldn't grasp the nettle and get it sorted. Meanwhile, I was bumbling along, getting nowhere.

Then I had another problem when a scan revealed trouble halfway up my calf, where there was bruising developing. The guy at the hospital said I was nipping my joint and he gave me a cortisone jab, which wasn't even hitting the spot. The idea of cortisone is that you pinpoint the problem and zap it, but he wasn't anywhere near. He was fiddling around with the needle, though I told him the problem was higher up in the calf. He said it would 'track around' and hit the spot! I was thinking: 'This guy is clueless and my career is on the line.' I limped into the hospital and I limped out again.

As the end of the 1999–2000 season approached, I was probably an expensive nuisance for Leeds. They had paid a big transfer fee and good wages and they weren't getting anything in return. I knew what they were saying to my face, so God knows what they were saying to each other. I kept asking if I could have an operation. For some reason, the answer was no. And I grew more and more convinced that they would hit me with an ultimatum: 'Are you going to be fit or not?'

That worry was reinforced by what I considered to be a disgraceful remark made to me a few days later by Dave Swift. Two days after having the cortisone jab I tried to run. Run! I could hardly walk. It was another complete waste of time and I was coming to the end of my tether. For the umpteenth time I complained to the staff at the club. Another scan was arranged and Swift said to me: 'Well, after this you'll either be training or painting the garage.' What the hell was that meant to mean? Was he telling me I might be packing it in altogether? A physio talking to a player like that is outrageous. I was so desperate, I went for the scan actually praying it would show some serious damage. It had become so bad I couldn't even put my foot down in comfort. Yet, to my astonishment, the results showed only that I had a bit of inflammation and that I had what Harry Kewell had been playing with all season. It was another situation where I might so easily have gone ballistic, but I restrained myself. I told Swifty: 'Don't talk to me about tendonitis. I had that at Newcastle and I played with it.' I had one more cortisone jab which again made no perceptible improvement – I was sure I needed surgery, but they still wouldn't agree. It was the end of April and I was resigned to my fate. What an inglorious end to the big Batty comeback at Leeds.

Then our Dutch defender Robert Molenaar made a suggestion that was to set me, at long last, on the road to recovery. Rob – who was later transferred to Bradford City – had been out for a long time with a cruciate ligament injury. He told me he had a friend called Rinus Waerts over from Holland, a physio who runs a clinic in Amsterdam and specialises in deep massage. He suggested that Rinus take a look at me. I was only too happy to accept any help. Rinus gave me some deep rub treatment and decided there was so much scar tissue he needed to use his expertise to get at the muscle and really work on it. The massages were excruciatingly painful but, in conjunction with strengthening exercises, I started to feel stronger as the weeks went by. I was also boosted psychologically by the feeling that this was the first time I had received the personal attention I thought I had merited all along. Maybe there was light at the end of the tunnel, after all.

Then, on 28 May – I'll never forget the date – I stepped back from pushing the kids on the swings in our garden and felt the Achilles go! It was horrendous. Actually, I did it twice. I stepped back, felt the pain, rocked forward and back and felt it go again. I pulled down my sock and saw a big depression in the back of my calf where the Achilles should be. I was in agony, as if electric shocks were shooting up my leg.

Luckily, Rinus was staying down the road at the Wetherby Hotel. I went straight over and will always remember the grave look on his face as he looked at my leg and pronounced: 'Big damage.' The club doctor said I had ruptured my Achilles. As it was a bank holiday weekend, I had to wait until the Monday before going for a scan at Sheffield Children's Hospital. Confusingly, the scan verdict was that it was not ruptured. I had hopped into the hospital because I didn't want to risk doing any more damage, so I tried to walk out. That didn't do me any favours. They said the Achilles was intact but that I had torn it a bit more on the original site and that the tear was lateral rather than horizontal, which is the more serious of the two.

At long last, surgery was recommended, and the club asked who I wanted. I said simply: 'Just get me the best in the business.' John Lawton, an orthopaedic surgeon at Leeds, suggested a man called Nicola Mafulli, an Italian working in Aberdeen, who specialises in Achilles injuries. Rinus had read up on him and was impressed, so I said yes. I can now state unequivocally that Mr Mafulli saved my career, though I must give special mention also to Dave Hancock, who succeeded Dave Swift as club physio at the start of the 2000–01 season, and Rinus Waerts. Mafulli was in the United States on a lecture tour so I had to wait a week, but I wasn't particularly concerned at the delay because I had been told I hadn't ruptured the tendon.

When the specialist flew in from Detroit, the club sent a driver to pick him up at the airport and take him to his hotel. I was impressed that, almost straight away, he sent for me. After a brief examination he announced it was ruptured. He said he could tell that simply from the trouble I had standing properly, and that it would be a bigger job than he had anticipated. He even admitted he had no real idea what he was going to find when he 'went in'. Bafflingly for the layman, the Achilles was clinically ruptured while showing up intact on the scan, which was how the confusion had arisen.

The operation was performed on 4 June at Leeds, where Mr Mafulli had had to get clearance to work. As soon as I came round, he was by my bed telling me straight that it had been a major job and a real mess and that I should have a long, hard think about playing on. Some people might say that was insensitive, but I appreciated his no-nonsense approach. It had been eight months of misery and I was grateful to have an expert hit me with some straight talking. Indeed, my first thought as I lay there contemplating his words was: 'Right, I'll damn well come back from this.' It would have been easier to think I was finished but, after all I had been through, my immediate reaction was to prove to myself – and maybe a few other people – that I could still be a big-time footballer. Mind you, when Mr Mafulli came in the next day to explain what he'd done, the gruesome details were enough to overturn even the staunchest of convictions. At the same time, the ingenuity and expertise he had used on me was of the highest calibre.

When you rupture your Achilles, speedy surgery is of the essence. It is important to go to work while the tendon retains its elasticity. In my case, because a rupture hadn't been diagnosed, the delay was more than a week, in which time I had worsened the problem by walking on it. The result was that the severed tendon had almost disappeared up my calf. The surgeon had to keep cutting and cutting until he found the end of the Achilles, which is why I have a 10-inch scar. Apparently, two nurses were pulling on the tendon, desperately trying to stretch it down. After 10 minutes of effort, they managed only to gain about a quarter of an inch, which wasn't sufficient. There was a four-inch gap which had to be bridged, ideally with something with a blood supply, which heals quicker. So, the brilliant Mr Mafulli took a tendon from the outside of my foot – the one which keeps your ankle in place and prevents your foot from turning over – and one from high on the side of my leg, called the plantarus, an anatomical relic from our original species, which only a small percentage of people now have. Fortunately, I was one of that minority, for if I hadn't had the plantarus he would have had to take some of my hamstring. Using these two tendons, Mr Mafulli built a new Achilles by weaving the two new sections and the stump of my original Achilles together. It was a masterpiece of surgery and one for which I shall remain eternally grateful. He told me I would be out of action for another six to nine months, but I was only too pleased to have the prospect of playing again to cling to.

After undergoing such specialised and crucial surgery, I was in no mood to be messed around. I had lost faith in the club physio Dave Swift and I insisted that Rinus Waerts took charge of my rehabilitation. That was politically sensitive at Elland Road, but I stuck to my guns and chairman Peter Ridsdale agreed that I should have my way. In the event, Swift left the club before the start of the season and was succeeded by Dave Hancock. I told him: 'I'm sorry, but I don't know you and I want Rinus in charge of my programme.' Dave listened politely and asked me to give him a chance. There was something about his manner that I liked so I decided to go with him. It was a good decision. I simply can't speak too highly of Dave. He will work all hours to get a player fit, dedicating his time and energy to your personal requirements.

Dave gave me a programme which was nine to five, six days a week, and it was bloody murder! He also gave me a warning that I would be cursing and swearing in pain and frustration. He was dead right there. The worst aspect of the rehab was its mind-blowing monotony. From Monday to Saturday my days were filled with a seemingly endless round of stretching and strengthening exercises, specially designed for my Achilles, plus work on the bike and with weights and other fitness routines. Often, I would go in at 8 a.m. to get some of my programme done early and in welcome solitude. It's a massive understatement to say the work was tedious. But I'll say one thing for it, it made me sleep well for the first time in my life. I was so knackered when I got home that I would kip like a baby. My philosophy on getting to bed early has always been: don't bother, there's plenty of time for sleep when you're dead. But the daily grind in the gym was so gruelling that I was glad to feel that pillow on my face every night.

The all-important thing was that Dave's programme worked. He not only got me back on the pitch again, but also three months ahead of schedule. On reflection, I would say that the toughest part of those last few months was the mental side. When you have been through as much doubt and despair as I had, to be confronted with such a tough fitness regime – and with no guarantees of a successful comeback – was daunting, to say the least. I had to be totally focused, completely dedicated. And I'm not sure I would have sufficient mental strength left to tackle such a challenge again. The first six months of the saga were desperately frustrating. The second six months, after the operation, were tortuous. But, throughout that subsequent period, I was boosted by the belief that, at last, I had been given the best of treatment and sound advice. I rang Rinus in Holland to thank him for his help in the initial stages. But there is no doubt in my mind that, but for Dave Hancock's rehab programme, I wouldn't have got back anywhere near as early as I did – if at all.

As I got stronger during those early months of the 2000–01 season, the most tantalising experiences were the big Champions League occasions. It was tough, being on the fringe as the lads came in, still buzzing with excitement, after those European matches. However hard you try to be involved, and however long you have been in the game, it is virtually impossible not to feel like you're on the outside looking in, in those situations. The first Group Stage draw was a real kick in the nuts for me: Besiktas, AC Milan, Barcelona! Three months later I remember running at the training ground with Dave Hancock and saying: 'Wouldn't it be unbelievable if we came out of the hat this time with Lazio – and Real Madrid?' And we did. I went home that night wondering if maybe, just maybe, I would be able to get back for some of those games. In the event, I played in all four of the post-Christmas Champions League matches in Group Two. That followed the moment I wasn't sure if I would ever experience – when I pulled on the Leeds shirt to play my first senior match since breaking down in that Worthington Cup tie at Leicester exactly 12 months earlier. It was against Sunderland at Elland Road in front of a full-house 40,000 crowd. I came on as a sub and was given a tremendous reception. The thrill of it will live with me forever.

glorious comeback

On the night of Wednesday, 9 May 2001, Leeds's fantastic Champions League adventure came to an end in the atmospheric Mestalla Stadium, Valencia. Though that 3–0 semi-final defeat also signalled the slightly premature end to my season, after being banned for the last three Premiership matches, at the same time it brought down the curtain on arguably the most rewarding few months of my career. How could it be any other way after I had gone into the season not knowing if I had a future in football? Though the players, fans and officials of Leeds United left the Mestalla deeply disappointed to have had their dream of a place in the final of Europe's premier competition dashed at the last hurdle, I returned home from Spain a winner. Though as deflated as anyone on the night, I was able to go home to Mandy and my children and reflect upon my elation at simply playing first-team football again – let alone featuring in a Champions League semi-final. The effect of the whole, wonderful experience only started to sink in once I had kicked my last ball in anger after that defeat to top-class Valencia.

My two years of injury misery had ended when I played the last 20 minutes of the Elland Road clash with

Sunderland the previous December. Just getting on the field was sheer relief after all the pain and uncertainty I had endured, but I couldn't possibly have imagined that I would go on to enjoy such an action-packed second half of the season. Nor, indeed, could I have thought that I would play my part in one of the most remarkable turn-arounds in the club's history.

At the beginning of the season such things seemed so improbable, especially when I read the screaming tabloid headline 'BATTY FINISHED' as I embarked on my training regime. Manager David O'Leary had told the press boys that I wouldn't play that season, which would make it a third successive campaign out of the frame. The papers reasoned I was all washed up. I had lived through enough anguish since returning to Elland Road not to be completely shocked by what I read. But, considering my determination to prove a lot of people at the club wrong and play again, it was still an unpleasant surprise to read that my efforts were, apparently, already deemed to be in vain.

I hadn't been given any warning by O'Leary that he was going to make this statement to the media and I wasn't too thrilled by how they interpreted it. The thought which immediately nagged me was that the manager had deep-rooted doubts about my injury saga. I had known that for two years, and I was also aware that those doubts were shared by others on the staff. Some months later, after re-establishing myself in the team, physio Dave Hancock told me that when he had seen pictures of the aftermath of my Achilles operation, he couldn't envisage how I could play again. Obviously, he had passed on those thoughts to the gaffer.

As I contemplated the reports of my 'retirement' in the newspapers, I pondered – not for the first time throughout that whole period – how dispensable every player is, no matter how experienced or able a competitor he might be. I have never been romantic about my role in this game, but I've always been realistic. I have no problem digesting the fact that, despite such a long career at the highest level, I'm as expendable as anyone if the feeling is that I'm crocked. I would be just another piece of dead meat, like all footballers, whether they like it or not. We are only of any use to our managers and to our clubs if we are fit to be out on the pitch. You increasingly become a forgotten man. If I was a manager – which I never will be – I like to think that I would make time for the lads who are on the injured list. I also accept that that is probably easier said than done. I'm not saying O'Leary is particularly harsh in that respect. Like all managers, his focus has to be on the men who he can select in the hope that they will keep him in a job by winning matches. When I read the newspaper reports, I was left to believe that he no longer thought I would be in that category. So, it was with some relief that he took me aside to point out that he had said what he had to nip in the bud growing pressure on me to make my return. He assured me his statement was made purely to deflect attention from my comeback bid. And I was happy to accept that explanation.

In fact, I started urging Dave Hancock to let me play from around mid-November. I eventually got my wish with appearances in one or two behind-closed-doors games and then in the reserves. It felt good to be running around a pitch with a ball at my feet again and winning tackles, but I was impatient for the real thing. Even when you've been out for 12 months, playing in those sorts of games quickly loses its novelty value. In my case it does, anyway. O'Leary knew this, too. He could see I was champing at the bit. So, before a Thursday evening reserve match against Sheffield Wednesday, he told me that, if I came through OK, I would be on the bench for the visit of Sunderland two days later.

He was as good as his word and I experienced the joy of stepping across that white line and into Premiership action with the result against Peter Reid's team more or less sewn up. It was a special moment. The crowd gave me an ovation and I felt a mixture of relief and elation at being back in business. Apart from a niggling concern that I might have been left behind stamina-wise – the game moves on so rapidly in terms of general fitness – I didn't feel I had anything to prove to myself. But, certainly, I had something to prove to a few doubters around the club. Aside from the sheer joy of playing, the best emotion was feeling a part of the scene once again. When you're not in the squad you are aware of how you slip on to the fringe. You can go to games and try to be involved but you become more and more of an outsider looking in. And, when you are reporting for rehabilitation and spending all day in the gym, you can't get involved in the dressing-room banter which is such an integral aspect of the footballer's daily life. Throughout my long absence I hardly watched a game. To be fair to O'Leary, he told me he could order me to be there, but he acknowledged there would be no point because I simply didn't get a buzz from that. In an ideal world, all players would happily turn up to support the team. But it just isn't my thing and I've never been one to do something for appearance's sake. A lot of people will disapprove of that but I come back to my previously stated philosophy, which is that I rest easy in the knowledge that I give every ounce of blood, sweat and tears when I play. Every manager I have played for and the players I have played with know that. Most crucially, I know it.

In a bizarre twist, my progress back into the side was hampered by a problem in my chest that must have had the doubters raising their eyebrows. I had been told I would start the next match, at home to Aston Villa, as fellow midfielder Olivier Dacourt was suspended. Though raring to go, and no longer concerned about my health, I wasn't entirely convinced by my fitness and I told Dave Hancock I would have preferred another stint coming off the bench before going for the full 90 minutes. Then, by the Thursday, I started getting pain in my chest. Immediately I feared that, after my successful battle against the Achilles, my previous serious problem had returned to haunt me. Despite being disturbed by a tightness in my chest, I knew it wasn't the dreaded pericarditis because I wasn't getting the tell-tale and dreaded pain in my shoulder. Nevertheless, it was a worry. Dave Hancock knew I was strong-willed and determined from my months of grinding rehab, but he didn't know me as a player. He suggested I could be suffering from a bit of stage-fright. I firmly told him that that wasn't the case, as I never had been, and wasn't then, nervous about playing. But I insisted something was amiss. At 9.30 on match-day morning I went for a scan and though the cardiologist said it was clear he also indicated that there were symptoms of a sort and that I should act on my instincts. After all I had been through, I wasn't risking everything for the sake of playing against Villa. So I told the club I wasn't playing and went home. On the Monday morning I had blood tests and an ECG. The tests revealed high readings in my liver, so I was taken off my tablets and recovered almost immediately.

So my first start was delayed until the New Year's Day home match with Middlesbrough. I had been on the bench for the previous match, at my former club Newcastle, where I got a heart-warming reception from the Toon Army, though I didn't get on the pitch, despite the fact that we were poor and were beaten 2–1. Against Boro, another side near the bottom of the table, we were sub-standard again. It was the first time Olly Dacourt and I played together in central midfield, and it just didn't work. We were too similar, with me slipping instinctively into my role as the anchor man and Olly unable to free himself from the same job, which he had been doing for months in my absence. We were both playing too deep and I had instant misgivings about our ability to play together. Now, I've never been short on self-belief, but I admit that the thought flashed through my mind that one of us would have to go if we didn't sort this out – and that it might well be me.

Olly had been forced to adopt my deep-lying role throughout the first half of the season and he had performed well. I also figured that he had been bought the previous summer because O'Leary thought I might not play again. Our next appearance together, against Barnsley in the FA Cup, was a slight improvement, but the overall team performance was a shambles – one of the worst I have ever been involved with. We scraped through 1–0 against a team – no disrespect intended – we should have wiped the floor with. Yet, in the second half – at Elland Road, mind you – we couldn't get out of our half of the pitch.

I was even more embarrassed afterwards when a steward came to the dressing-room to tell me I had been voted by the sponsors as Man of the Match. Man of the Match in a game like that! There simply couldn't be any such person, in my opinion. It didn't rest easy with me and, despite the group waiting outside the door to escort me to the sponsors' lounge for the champagne presentation, I refused to go. The stewards and other officials were nonplussed and pleaded with me to reconsider, but when my mind is made up, there is no changing it. I went home, leaving them in a right state. They got themselves out of the awkward situation by persuading Robbie Keane, who had come a close second in the voting, to go and accept the bubbly. That didn't prevent Keith Hanvey, the club's commercial manager, writing to tell me I had made life extremely difficult for him with the sponsors. Although I had some sympathy with Keith, I felt he could have turned a negative into a positive with the punters by explaining that I couldn't justify accepting their award after such a poor team performance. Not for the first time and, hopefully, not for the last, I wasn't up for being a hypocrite.

Ironically, after my accolade, I was dropped for the next game, at Manchester City. I was disappointed to have my comeback interrupted, but, to be fair, Olly Dacourt would have felt even more hard done by if he had been the one to give way. Before the Barnsley game, O'Leary had urged Olly to try to get forward more because he and I were playing too square, just in front of the back four. Still, he had found it hard to change and O'Leary decided to break up the partnership at Maine Road.

What I did object to on the day was being told to pound round the pitch with the other subs after the game. There were punters in corporate hospitality boxes yelling 'go on, Batty' sarcastically, as I slogged it down the touchline. I decided I hadn't come through all my trials and tribulations to run my nuts off in front of a bunch of boozed-up berks whose only intention was to take the piss. So, after a couple of laps, I left the others to it and walked in. Dave Hancock had done a great job supervising my rehab, but pounding around a track isn't the type of running I do on the pitch and I objected to being asked to do it. I told Dave: 'If you want me to run I'll come in and do it tomorrow, but I'm not having half-cut punters taking liberties while I'm sweating my socks off.'

Another frustrating day on the bench followed as we lost at home to Newcastle and the prospects of a relegation fight started to loom large. But the tide started to turn with an away win over Villa, when I replaced Dacourt for the last 10 minutes. Olly stayed out of the side for the FA Cup visit of Liverpool, when I and the team played well, despite being mugged by two late goals from substitutes Emile Heskey and Nick Barmby. I stayed in for the home game against Coventry, which was the beginning of my long, unbroken run in the side, and the second match in a 13-game run that took us to the brink of Champions League qualification, a prize denied us by Liverpool's last-day win at Charlton.

Me and Olly were paired together again for the trip to Ipswich early in February. Ipswich had stunned us with an early season win at Elland Road, but, by now, the promoted Suffolk outfit was recognised as the shock team of the season. So our win at Portman Road was a significant one and, with me and Olly gelling properly for the first time, the day was a turning point in our season. We played Everton off the park, despite only drawing, before coming to the next big milestone, the European double-header with Belgian champions Anderlecht, who had famously beaten Manchester United in the first Group phase before Christmas.

The first meeting, at Elland Road, was my first European match since returning to the side and a situation that was more than I would have dared hope for six months previously. We went a goal down and rode our luck for a while, but came back to win 2–1, a result which prompted some sour grapes from the Belgians, whose coach Aime Anthuenis dismissed us as 'very average'. That comment wasn't lost on us as we travelled to Brussels, where Anderlecht were unbeaten in 20 matches in the Vanden Stock Stadium. Among their victims were Manchester United and Lazio, and I think they thought they were going to wipe the floor with us. They were in for a rude shock. By half-time a double blast from Alan Smith and a goal from Mark Viduka put us 3–0 ahead. In the dressing-room, I reminded the lads of Tranmere's amazing 4–3 FA Cup win over Southampton the previous night after being three down at the break and urged them not to let the same disaster befall us. Though Anderlecht pulled a goal back, Ian Harte killed them off with a penalty. It was a very big win, one which fired us and gave us the belief that we could take on and beat the best. And me and Olly Dacourt were getting better and better as a midfield pairing.

By that match, we were starting to complement each other. Olly knew, instinctively, that I would be in position behind him if he moved forward, and I had similar confidence in him. We were working hard for each other, a crucial necessity in the centre of the park, which is always the hardest area of the pitch to control. If you get that control you usually win, and we were starting to do that. Yet it was something we never discussed, not even during our sluggish start in the side together. I think that good players – if I can immodestly describe myself as one – have an innate ability to know what is required of them and to produce it. That is what happened with us. We followed up that morale-boosting double success, which clinched our place in the quarter-finals, with good displays at Spurs and at home to Manchester United before going to Real Madrid, where we lost 3–2, and two of their goals were ridiculous. A Raul handball was somehow not seen by the referee but was picked up by the Leeds players and the television cameras, and Luis Figo scored after his cross hit a divot and was deflected past keeper Nigel Martyn. This double dose of injustice followed a stunning opener from Alan Smith, who maintained his amazing record of scoring in all of the top stadiums in his European debut season. Though Mark Viduka pulled a goal back to equalise, Raul put Real back in front and, to be honest, I felt they could have stepped up a gear if they had felt the need. I was rested, along with Dacourt, for the now meaningless return with Lazio at Elland Road, but we both returned to the team as our impressive domestic run continued with victories at Charlton and Sunderland. Then we faced Deportivo La Coruna in the Champions League quarter-final.

Of all the three other teams in our section of the draw, Deportivo, Valencia and Bayern Munich, it is fair to say we would have chosen Deportivo. But what a gifted set of players they were. We won 3–0 in the first leg at home, a result which was trumpeted as one of our best performances of a magical journey through Europe. But, in truth, the scoreline flattered us a little. We played very well, but the professional in me felt some sympathy for the Spanish side, who were technically superb and who must have felt aggrieved to be going home with such a mountain to climb in the return. I don't think our cause was helped when we went over there with everyone back home saying we were already through to the semis.

I knew that these Deportivo players were class acts and that the danger in that situation lay in erring on the side of caution because we didn't want to concede an early goal and put ourselves under pressure. There was a tremendous atmosphere in the Estadio Muncipal De Riazor. The pressure on us intensified after Brazilian midfielder Djalminha scored from the penalty spot after only 14 minutes. I don't know if it was a nervous reaction to the fear of blowing such a big lead, but I honestly believe a few of our lads froze on the night. Too many of them were giving the ball away, particularly in the first half, and I was thinking: 'What the bloody hell is happening here?' When Deportivo scored a second, it looked really ominous, but we hung on and made that semi-final date with yet another Spanish club.

I actually thought we had done a lot better than most people gave us credit for when we drew 0–0 with Valencia in the first leg at Elland Road. Goals, of course, completely change people's view of matches. The fact that there weren't any left commentators talking down the performance and writing us off. Listening to the radio reports as I drove home I wondered if they'd been at the same game, because I was confident that we'd played pretty well without getting a break. The vital thing was that we hadn't conceded an away goal. What we couldn't foresee, not even in our worst nightmares, was that we would be hit by a second handball goal in three visits to Spain when we played at the Mestalla. Juan Sanchez, the Valencia centre-forward, 'did a Raul' on us when he clearly knocked a right-wing cross past Nigel Martyn with his arm early in the match.

Sadly for Leeds, neither the referee nor his assistant saw the offence. Despite this setback, we rallied to play some decent stuff and I felt we were in good shape at the break. But, in only the second minute of the second half, Sanchez got clear again and, despite the efforts of myself and Eirik Bakke to shut him down, he scored from around 25 yards, with Nigel Martyn left unsighted. From that point, we were fighting a lost cause. Deep down, I sensed there was no way back against another superb, technically gifted team. The fact is we never looked like getting the better of their excellent Argentinian centre-backs, Fabien Ayala – who swapped shirts with me afterwards – and Mauricio Pellegrino. When their skipper Mendieta scored the third, the tie was well and truly dead for us but, in truth, we had had 43 minutes to get used to the idea. We had come a long way against all the odds, but the final glory was denied us and we couldn't really complain because Valencia were an admirable side.

Unfortunately, Alan Smith let his frustration get the better of him. Alan lunged in on one of their players in the closing moments and was shown the red card. He took a lot of flak for that and there is no doubt he is going to have to clean up his act if he isn't to damage the reputation he is rightly building as an England striker of the future. If I were a manager, he'd be the player from Leeds I'd most want in my side. I, of all people, am not knocking Alan because he goes in hard and picks up the odd yellow and red card. What I am telling him is that he must realise that he is much more likely to get punished for that type of challenge than I was at 20 years of age. I was one of the toughest tacklers around – and still am, I hope – but I didn't get sent off during my first seven years as a first-teamer. That was mainly because you could boot opponents up in the air and get away with it up until five or six years ago, but not any more. And, to be fair, the game is better for it. So Alan will have to learn to curb his recklessness. I told him later that, as the minutes ticked away, I could see the signs in the way he was lunging at players and losing it. But I was never close enough to him to tell him to cool it. He was left to sit out the first three UEFA Cup ties of the following season, a sobering lesson for anyone.

That was my last involvement of the season because,

ironically, I had been sent off at West Ham and received a three-match ban, which ruled me out of the last three Premiership games. Now, though my words to Smithy might sound like the pot calling the kettle black, I can only say in my defence that my red-card offence, following an incident with the Hammers' Joe Cole, wasn't nearly as nasty as it might have appeared. Nevertheless, it was the sixth sending-off of my career, all of them since 1996 when I was with Newcastle. I had actually earned praise from the gaffer at half-time for a first-minute tackle on young Cole which set the tone for another dominating display from the team as we pressed our claims to finish third and clinch the Champions League place which accompanies that.

We had the points comfortably sewn up when I went in for another challenge on Cole as he turned away from the touchline, having just won the ball. I always go in with my arms held high, not with the intention of hurting anyone but for the dual purpose of maximising my balance and the strength of the challenge, and, though I won the ball, I did catch Cole, even if I honestly didn't realise it at the time. O'Leary went on TV afterwards saying I had told him there had been no contact. It was what I thought at the time. Later that night, watching *Match of the Day*, I realised I had, in fact, clipped the lad with my elbow and I rang O'Leary to apologise for possibly embarrassing him. He didn't hold it against me. I played only one more match, apart from the Valencia semi-final, before drawing the curtain on what had been a personally triumphant four months. I had been back at Leeds nearly two and a half years but had become a regular player for that latter period alone.

At last, I had been able to fulfil the purpose which O'Leary had recruited me for, namely to bring my experience to bear on his emerging young team. By the time I got into the side on a regular basis, it simply couldn't be described as a young team anymore. The lads who were emerging when I arrived, like Smith, Jonathan Woodgate, Eirik Bakke and Lee Bowyer were all battle-hardened by the time I finally pushed my nose in and the 'young team' thing was vastly overplayed in the press that season. Obviously, the lads I have mentioned still have much to learn, just as I did when I was in my early twenties, but I look forward to the day when the 'emerging' label is dropped and we are recognised simply as a good side. For my part, I do believe the foundation has been laid for even more exciting times over the next few seasons. I am proud of the fact that we did not lose one of the Premiership games I started after coming in, full-time, against Coventry on 31 January up to losing at Arsenal on 5 May, which was the first of my three-match ban.

The most significant of all those games was, in my opinion, our mid-April win at Liverpool, the team which eventually squeezed us into fourth place. I suppose if one team emerged as a genuine potential challenger to Manchester United's supremacy – apart from ourselves – it was Liverpool, who plundered a unique cup treble in 2000–01. We were fighting them for that valuable third place for the last couple of months and we knew we *had* to win at Anfield to keep alive our chances of bridging the gap with them. And it lived up to its 'Match of the Day' billing – especially for us. We dominated the first half, with me and Dacourt bossing the midfield, Steven

Gerrard and all. Liverpool couldn't get the ball off us, the crowd went quieter and you could sense their fans thinking that this Leeds team was a pretty mean outfit. We went 2–0 up and, though Gerrard scored a few minutes into the second half – and was later sent off for a second bookable offence after clipping my leg – we were fairly comfortable winners. That performance should have proved to our players that they can go on to even bigger and better things, to challenge the very best in the Premier League. In my book, it was more important than any of the Champions League successes of the season. For me, it was a clear signal of our capability and intent, and I have every reason to believe that the big clubs should be aware that Leeds are back as a force.

We went into the game on the back of a home win over Southampton, which was more memorable in the Batty household for the fact that it marked the addition to our family of Jimmy, our Blue Roan cocker spaniel. Typically of me and Mandy, though we had talked for quite some time about getting a dog for Jack and George, when the decision was made it was on the spur of the moment – and the night before a game! Mandy's mum had called with a list of places where you could buy dogs and we ended up 40 miles up the A1 at Scotch Corner at 9.30 on Friday evening. We all fell in love with Jimmy and he was added to the family. In fact, Jimmy became a part of our domestic set-up so quickly that we cancelled our family holiday. It must have been 11.30 p.m. before I got my head on the pillow in preparation for facing the Saints at Elland Road next day. Thankfully, we collected the three points almost as easily as Jimmy has settled into our household. We are fortunate to live in a lovely part of the world where there is a lot of open space and plenty of riverside walks, ideal for a dog and children to stretch their legs. And that is where me and Mandy, Jack and George are frequently to be found, with Jimmy in tow.

Of course, there was a cloud hanging over the club throughout the season and during the last couple of months in particular: the much-publicised court case involving Jonathan Woodgate, Lee Bowyer and Michael Duberry, who all faced serious charges relating to an incident in the city centre in which a student was badly injured. Now, obviously, I cannot comment on the charges facing the players – Duberry was acquitted before the trial was halted and rescheduled for the autumn following an article in the *Sunday Mirror* – but I will say that it did not distract me from training or the matches.

I am sure that for the manager and the club officials it was a difficult period, given all the media attention. But, for my part, I kept my nose out of the whole affair. I made up my mind from the outset that I wouldn't be asking either of them any questions. And I stuck to that principle. In my opinion, people ask more out of morbid self-interest than genuine concern, so I decided my conscience was going to stay clear. Once the case got under way at Hull Crown Court, young Woody elected to stay at home in Middlesbrough and we didn't see him at the club until the end of the season. Bowyer, famously of course, not only commuted from Leeds but continued to play, more or less twice a week. Sometimes, he would be flown in by helicopter, often arriving within an hour of kick-off and never training with the squad, which is a marvellous testimony to the lad's natural fitness. What Lee did strengthened my long-held belief that, if you have strength of mind and purpose, those qualities are more important than the modern mania for special diet and training methods. I eat pasta, fish and chicken when on club business because I don't have any choice, as opposed to the good old fish-and-chips staple of my first years as a pro. Yet, when I'm home, I refuse to live like a monk. If the kids are being served fish fingers and chips then that's what I'll have, too.

Bowyer's decision to attend court and then play amazed so many people around the country. But it didn't surprise me because I figured it was his best way of finding a release from the incredible pressure he must have been under. He was concentrating on doing the one thing he is good at and which he enjoys. And he certainly played his part in our push for success in the Premiership and in Europe.

Woody dealt with the tension of it all by staying at home and I didn't see him until he turned up at the training ground after the trial had been halted. He was having some treatment for dry, flaky skin on his hands, for which we use E45 cream. As I popped in to the physio's room, Woody was asking, in all innocence, for some P45 cream! It reminded me of the day he made his England debut, in Bulgaria, and he decided he needed a massage, as many players like a rub-down before a match. Phoning for a massage service from your hotel room can be a delicate thing to do in any western European country. But in Bulgaria ... Well, Woody went ahead and he was saved from scandal only when a member of England's security squad intercepted a young lady whose credentials definitely extended beyond kneading one's muscles. Hooker was a more appropriate job description and she was sent packing before the unsuspecting Woody got himself into a real spot of bother. Now, Jonathan and Lee must face trial all over again and I can only say that I hope justice prevails. When it all gets under way once more, I will do as I did the first time around: go to training and matches, keep my mouth closed on the subject, and go home to where I am happiest.

But previously I had had to deal with a weird episode at home which, I suppose, was a classic example of the price of fame. We had just returned to pre-season training in the summer of 1999, when I got a message at home one day from the club's PR girl, explaining that she had had a strange call from a woman who was staying in a hotel in Wetherby who wanted me to telephone her there. The PR was obviously baffled, but said this mystery woman seemed to know me and had assured her that I would know what it was all about. In fact, I was completely mystified.

Events quickly took an even stranger turn when, as I sat there puzzling over the message I'd received, I noticed a car pull up outside the gates to our house. It was a taxi. A youngish woman got out and started talking to Jack and George, who were playing in the garden. Mandy went to the window and, as soon as the woman spotted her, she scarpered. We rushed out to the boys, who told us she had been asking if this was my home. Now, the alarm bells were really ringing. I telephoned the police in Wetherby, and told them this woman was staying in the Jarvis Hotel which, conveniently, is bang opposite the police station. They went straight over and spoke to her. But her story left me even more baffled.

She said I had been bombarding her with e-mail messages, assuring her of my feelings for her and telling her that I would be there for her if things didn't work out in her marriage! This had been going on for three months. I was stunned as the police relayed this to me. Apart from the obvious, that I wouldn't dream of going behind Mandy's back, I didn't – and still don't – own a computer. So, I couldn't have been winging off e-mails to anybody. I had to make a statement to the police and they went to this woman's address to interview her husband.

He thought that I was, indeed, courting his wife through cyber-space. The husband admitted that their marriage had been under considerable strain. And he told the police how he had discovered a pile of e-mails, from me to his wife, when she accidentally knocked her handbag off the table one day. Many of these messages were vile, and most of them contained information about me which, while accurate, was the sort of stuff the average fan could have known. I had my solicitor on the case by now and he got an injunction to stop her coming anywhere near our home.

Within a few days of that being served, we were in the house when we heard a loud, persistent scraping noise out on the road. We looked out of the window to see a car, with a traffic cone stuck underneath it, driving up and down past the gates. It pulled up and, to our amazement, a woman in a dressing-gown got out, rang the buzzer on the electronically controlled gates and gave some obviously false name before jumping back in the car and driving off. Both of us were beginning to get very angry – and concerned about the safety of Jack and George.

So Mandy got into her car in pursuit of her. She saw a car parked near the motorway, memorised the registration and came back and rang the police. They confirmed that the number she gave them was almost identical to the woman on whom the 'keep clear' notice had been served. I was becoming increasingly worried about the whole situation when the police got in touch to tell me they had traced the address of the senders of these e-mails to a married couple in Hull. These people were absolutely unknown to me and had, apparently, latched on to this woman via the Internet. In one of their messages to her, they told of a visit to her workplace and described how her clothes had suited her on this particular day. No wonder the woman believed I had a crush on her and that all of this stuff was genuine.

It seems this couple had started something that became a dangerous obsession – imagine going to the trouble of travelling to this woman's place of work in order to authenticate the next message. The whole episode went on for about two weeks, and it left me and Mandy with a disturbing awareness of how being in the public eye can have its dark side. I took my solicitor's advice not to prosecute the couple, on the basis that it wouldn't be worth the huge publicity it would bring. I gave a statement to aid the woman in her case against them. And, I must admit, I feel I let that couple off the hook. For all I know, they are back at their sinister games, making somebody else's life a misery.

CHAPTER 20

the future

My successful return to first-team action brought with it a marvellous end-of-season bonus when the club agreed to extend my contract by 12 months – with a generous pay increase to boot – taking me through to 35 years of age. When I signed the new deal, my intention was to complete the contract and then retire, completely, from football. It will mark 20 years in the game for me and I think enough will be enough. I know one of football's most popular sayings is: 'Never say never.' I am mindful of that, but it was always my hope that I would be able to play – at the highest level – until 35. The club have generously given me the opportunity to do that and, the way I feel as I write this, I will be more than happy to play on for another three seasons and then quit.

I can categorically rule out any possibility of my being tempted to try management or even coaching. As I've already stated, management and all the hassle that goes with it has no appeal for me whatsoever. I am sure that I don't have the touch of arrogance I believe you need to be a team boss, someone who can stand in front of a bunch of strong-willed fellas and tell them what's best for them. I haven't got that kind of mentality. Although I play with arrogance and, some might say, too much of a swagger, off the pitch I am not like that at all. As for coaching, I couldn't remotely entertain the thought – because I hate training so much.

I'm not as bad a trainer in my twilight years as I was in my mid-twenties, especially at Blackburn, if only because I have to work damned hard to keep up with the younger guys around me. But I'd be lying if I pretended to get any pleasure out of it. I love playing as much as I ever did and my big regret is that I can't play four times a week and avoid training altogether. Games are great but the bits in between can be tedious. There are an average of 50 games a season interspersed with 250 training sessions. I'd prefer the figures to be reversed. And I have no hang-up about admitting to my dislike of training. I have seen so many players who were world-beaters on the training ground but who didn't reproduce that form when it mattered on Saturday afternoon. My contention has always been that I do the business when the whistle blows. So, though in my dreams I'd like to play till I'm 50, I don't fancy more than another three seasons of pounding that running track. What I do relish is the prospect of continuing to play a key role in a Leeds team which I would dearly love to help win trophies. There is no doubt in my mind that we have the potential to improve on our 2000–01 season, albeit with the addition of a few players – including midfielders.

Competition for places is not only important, it is also essential in the modern game where a manager needs to be able to freshen things up once in a while to keep the momentum going. And I have never been scared of competition for my place, believing as I always have that I can see off anybody when it come to the crunch. What I do want, and I'm sure David O'Leary does too, is to see the squad get bigger and stronger so we can mount a sustained challenge to Manchester United in the years ahead. You need top-class men on the bench as well as on the pitch and the more players we sign the better, so far as I am concerned. I can only hope that I stay injury-free and fit enough to go on trying to boss the best midfielders in the country and in Europe.

Having played for three of the country's leading clubs, and played against the others, I know that the atmosphere we have at Leeds United right now is very hard to get and few other clubs have it. But at Elland Road everything is in place. There's a tremendous amount of confidence. A great example of what confidence can do for a player is Danny Mills. That chant 'Danny Mills Is Fucking Brilliant' was originally ironic, but now we even chant that at him in training now when he does something good, because he's come on so much and that's just down to his confidence improving.

Then there's Harry Kewell, who I first got to know and like through our time spent together recovering from our injuries. People say he's a bit stand-offish but he's not, he's just very confident and he knows what he does and doesn't want to do. The other big Aussie Mark Viduka is a great bloke – 'the Fan's Man' we call him. They used to say it about me, but I turned it on him after he came off early in one game and had to warm down in front of the crowd, and he was just milking it. Since the rumours about Real Madrid being interested in signing him have started, I've been calling him the 'Real Fan's Man'.

The great feeling stretches all the way down to the

apprentice level. We get them to perform a Christmas carol on their own, or in little groups of two or four, singing in front of everyone from the club, not just the squad. I wouldn't do it now, never mind as an apprentice, but it does make them feel a part of the set-up. At other times, Gary Kelly is the main organiser for days and nights out. He's always joking, diving in bins and stuff, doing things you wouldn't even do drunk, never mind sober.

Nigel Martyn is the oldest in the squad, but you'd think he was the youngest from the way he behaves. We call him 'Village' because he's the village idiot. We have water fights against Woody and Al. And, with Jason Wilcox, we have recreated some of that old atmosphere from the Blackburn days. Because I see him so often I'd say that Nigel's the best keeper in the country, whereas I might only see Seaman on the TV. He's just been unlucky with the timing but you have to credit him with being patient.

Finally there's the manager, David O'Leary. It seems so long since I played with him that I can't really remember him as anything but the boss. He's done a great job – especially distancing himself and setting himself apart from the team to ensure he holds our respect.

One thing that won't change – and hasn't since I was a kid – is my simplistic philosophy that the bigger they are the harder they fall. Whether I am facing Roy Keane, Paul Ince or whoever my attitude is the same: I'm going to show him who's boss, or damn near die in the attempt. It is my job to establish the pecking order from the first whistle. That means winning the early tackles and knock-downs in the midfield. It is no place for the faint-hearted, and that is one thing I've never been. Even as an apprentice, I got stuck into my peers with a relish that once earned me a clout around the ear from senior pro Gary Hamson after I'd dished out the rough stuff in a training session. I start every match with the basic premise that every professional footballer deserves my respect, but I fear no one and never have. Reputations don't impress me. Every opponent is there to be conquered. And I think I've had more than my share of conquests. I suppose I have a sort of 'look after No. 1' approach. I'm safe in the knowledge that if I do what's best for me, if I sort out my personal battles, it will be to the benefit of the team as a whole. And I think that is why I have played for three top-flight clubs many hundreds of times over the past 13 years.

But playing on as my powers dim holds no appeal for me. Not for me that steady decline in speed of thought and action which sees so many players ploughing on into their mid to late thirties at an ever-falling level. After so many years at the top, performing at Old Trafford, Highbury, Anfield and Elland Road, I don't fancy the prospect of playing in front of a couple of thousand fans at places like Scunthorpe and Rochdale. Right now, about the only job in football I could envisage for myself would be some sort of part-time scouting role assessing a player.

What I do know is that I have absolutely no plan to go into any other career or form of work. My Holy Grail is to complete my contract in good health and retire to spend my time with Mandy, watching Jack and George grow into fine young men. From a professional perspective, my dream is to bow out as a member of a winning team, one of the best in Leeds's history. But my biggest wish is to lead a happy and healthy life along with Mandy and the boys. Many friends say I'll be bored rigid within months. Who knows? They may be right. But I don't see it that way. I have always had plenty of spare time on my hands as a footballer and I have never been restless as a result, even though I don't have any all-consuming hobbies or pastimes. Since marrying Mandy and having the boys, I find they completely occupy my time.

The way I figure it, the average bloke, who has worked nine to five for 30 to 40 years then suddenly retired can find all that spare time a real problem to cope with. They often desperately need something new to fill the void. But I get seven weeks every summer in which to do nothing, and it isn't a problem. I have dedicated myself to playing football at this level for 20 years and my position is: when it's all over I'll be happy to do nowt. That may seem smug or self-indulgent, but I don't mean it to. It's just the way I feel about the future. I am well aware how fortunate I am to be in a position to be talking of retirement at the age of 32. I know that every adult in my family and in Mandy's would love to be in that position. Most folk would love to be facing the big poser 'will I be bored if I pack in work at 35?' All I'm saying is I've got the opportunity to put it to the test. And I'm going to.

career statistics

Statistics up to the end of season 2001–02:

Summary of Appearances

Season	Team	League	FA Cup	League Cup	Others	Euro Cup	UEFA	ECWC
1987–88	Leeds U	23	1	–	2	–	–	–
1988–89		30	1	3	1	–	–	–
1989–90		42	1	2	4	–	–	–
1990–91		37	6	6	4	–	–	–
1991–92		40	–	4	1	–	–	–
1992–93		30	3	2	1	4	–	–
1993–94		9	–	–	–	–	–	–
1993–94	Blackburn	26	4	2	–	–	–	–
1994–95		5	–	–	–	–	–	–
1995–96		23	1	4	1	5	–	–
1995–96	Newcastle	11	–	–	–	–	–	–
1996–97		32	3	2	1	–	7	–
1997–98		32	6	2	–	7	–	–
1998–99		8	–	1	–	–	–	1
1998–99	Leeds U	10	–	–	–	–	–	–
1999–00		16	–	2	–	–	4	–
2000–01		16	2	–	–	8	–	–
2001–02		36	1	1	–	–	6	–

Totals

Team	League	FA Cup	League Cup	Others	Euro Cup	UEFA	ECWC
Leeds United	289	15	20	13	12	10	–
Blackburn Rovers	54	5	6	1	5	–	–
Newcastle United	85	9	5	1	7	7	1
Complete Career	426	29	31	15	24	17	1

Others include: Simod Cup (1987–89), Zenith Data Systems (1989–92), Charity Shield (1992–97)

Summary of Goals

Date	For	Opponents	Venue	Goalkeeper	Score
26/12/87	Leeds U	Manchester C	A	Perry Suckling	2–1
07/09/91	Leeds U	Manchester C	H	Tony Coton	3–0
01/02/92	Leeds U	Notts Co	H	Steve Cherry	3–0
30/01/93	Leeds U	Middlesbrough	H	Steve Pears	3–0
26/12/95	Blackburn	Manchester C	H	Eike Immel	2–0
08/04/96	Newcastle	Blackburn R	A	Tim Flowers	1–2
21/08/96	Newcastle	Wimbledon	H	Neil Sullivan	2–0
01/02/98	Newcastle	Aston Villa	A	Mark Bosnich	1–0
08/03/98	Newcastle	Barnsley	H	David Watson	3–1 (FAC)

International Appearances

Date	Opponents	Venue	Result	Competition
21/05/91	USSR	Wembley	3–1	
25/05/91	Argentina	Wembley	2–2	
01/06/91	Australia	Sydney	1–0	
03/06/91	New Zealand	Auckland	1–0	
12/06/91	Malaysia	Kuala Lumpur	4–2	
11/09/91	Germany	Wembley	0–1	
16/10/91	Turkey	Wembley	1–0	Eur Champ Qual
12/05/92	Hungary	Budapest	1–0	
14/06/92	France	Malmo	0–0	Eur Champ Finals
17/06/92	Sweden	Stockholm	1–2	Eur Champ Finals
14/10/92	Norway	Wembley	1–1	World Cup Qual
17/02/93	San Marino	Wembley	6–0	World Cup Qual
09/06/93	USA	Boston	0–2	
13/06/93	Brazil	Washington	1–1	
09/05/94	Denmark	Wembley	1–0	
03/06/95	Japan	Wembley	2–1	
11/06/95	Brazil	Wembley	1–3	
01/09/96	Moldova	Chisinau	3–0	World Cup Qual
09/11/96	Georgia	Tbilisi	2–0	World Cup Qual
12/02/97	Italy	Wembley	0–1	World Cup Qual
29/03/97	Mexico	Wembley	2–0	
30/04/97	Georgia	Wembley	2–0	World Cup Qual
24/05/97	South Africa	Old Trafford	2–1	
31/05/97	Poland	Katowice	2–0	World Cup Qual
07/06/97	France	Montpellier	1–0	
10/09/97	Moldova	Wembley	4–0	World Cup Qual
11/10/97	Italy	Rome	0–0	World Cup Qual
11/02/98	Chile	Wembley	0–2	
25/03/98	Switzerland	Berne	1–1	

Date	Opponents	Venue	Result	Competition
22/04/98	Portugal	Wembley	3–0	
23/05/98	Saudi Arabia	Wembley	0–0	
15/06/98	Tunisia	Marseille	2–0	World Cup Finals
22/06/98	Romania	Toulouse	1–2	World Cup Finals
26/06/98	*Colombia*	*Lens*	*2–0*	*World Cup Finals*
30/06/98	*Argentina*	*St Etienne*	*2–2*	*World Cup Finals*
10/10/98	*Bulgaria*	*Wembley*	*0–0*	*Eur Champ Qual*
14/10/98	Luxembourg	Luxembourg	3–0	Eur Champ Qual
28/04/99	Hungary	Budapest	1–1	
05/06/99	Sweden	Wembley	0–0	Eur Champ Qual
09/06/99	Bulgaria	Sofia	1–1	
04/09/99	Luxembourg	Wembley	6–0	Eur Champ Qual
08/09/99	Poland	Warsaw	0–0	Eur Champ Qual

Matches in italics are substitute appearances

index

PSYCHO
The Autobiography

STUART PEARCE

The bestselling football autobiography of the year

With the whole nation willing him on, Stuart Pearce took two famous penalties – and no one can forget what happened next. But what was it like for the man in the middle of it all? In *Psycho*, Pearce reveals all. Not just about those penalties, but about life at the top over the past two decades. This is a remarkable story from one of the most popular and charismatic footballers of our time. Packed with brilliant anecdotes, this updated edition will fascinate and inspire all who read it.

'Unputdownable . . . Pearce's honesty shines through' Sarah Edworthy, *Daily Telegraph*

NON-FICTION / AUTOBIOGRAPHY 0 7472 6482 1

THE WAY IT WAS
My Autobiography

STANLEY MATTHEWS

The number one bestseller from football's
greatest hero.

Sir Stanley Matthews was a legend, the first superstar
of world football. In this, his long-awaited and
definitive autobiography, completed just before his
death in February 2000, he recalls the untold stories
about many of football's most famous characters and
games. The camaraderie, humour and tragedy are all
revealed in this remarkable memoir from a man who
was loved and respected around the world.

'A fascinating and amusing insight into the inner
workings of football during its golden era'
Daily Telegraph

'A ticket to a different era, when the game wasn't
saturated with money and men like Sir Stanley upheld
sporting ideals' *The Times*

'Brings vividly to life some of the greatest games of the
time and features his perceptive analysis of the
characters who illuminated the age' *Independent*

NON-FICTION / AUTOBIOGRAPHY 0 7472 6427 9

More Sports Writing from Headline

BEYOND THE PIT LANE
The Grand Prix Season from the Inside

LOUISE GOODMAN

The Formula One World Championship is one of the greatest sporting spectacles in the world, testing men and machinery to their limits in a high-speed contest packed with excitement and intrigue.

Louise Goodman has travelled the world with the Grand Prix circus for more than a decade and *Beyond the Pit Lane* is her insider's account of life behind the scenes of this complex and fascinating sport. She explains how Formula One operates and what challenges the Grand Prix teams face.

Race by race, Louise Goodman reveals the stories behind the personalities, and captures the ups and downs of the 2000 Formula One season. No fan can afford to be without it.

NON-FICTION / SPORT 0 7472 3541 4

Now you can buy any of these other bestselling non-fiction titles from your bookshop or *direct from the publisher*.

FREE P&P AND UK DELIVERY
(Overseas and Ireland £3.50 per book)

The Way It Was *Stanley Matthews* £6.99
Sir Stanley Matthews, the most famous and revered England footballer ever, epitome of a generation of legendary players, tells his extraordinary life story in this poignant memoir completed just weeks before his death.

Psycho *Stuart Pearce* £6.99
One of the most popular and charismatic of football's hard men, famed for his total commitment to the game, tells his own story in a book as honest and straightforward as the man himself.

Vinnie *Vinnie Jones* £6.99
Football bad boy turned Hollywood superstar tells of his tough upbringing, the Crazy Gang years at Wimbledon and the time he nearly ended it all.

Gareth Edwards *Gareth Edwards* £7.99
The autobiography of a universally respected rugby superstar, offering fascinating anecdotes about the characters and events in the game and talking candidly about his glittering career.

TO ORDER SIMPLY CALL THIS NUMBER AND QUOTE REF *50 SPORTBIOG*

01235 400 414

or e-mail <u>orders@bookpoint.co.uk</u>

Prices and availability subject to change without notice